COSTUME JEWELRY

A PRACTICAL HANDBOOK
& VALUE GUIDE

FRED REZAZADEH

COLLECTOR BOOKS
A Division of Schroeder Publishing Co., Inc.

The current values in this book should be used only as a guide. They are not intended to set prices, which vary from one section of the country to another. Auction prices as well as dealer prices vary greatly and are affected by condition as well as demand. Neither the Author nor the Publisher assumes responsibility for any losses that might be incurred as a result of consulting this guide.

Searching for a Publisher?

We are always looking for knowledgeable people considered to be experts within their fields. If you feel that there is a real need for a book on your collectible subject and have a large comprehensive collection, contact Collector Books.

Cover design: Beth Summers
Book design: Michelle Dowling
Photos: Pitkin Studio

Printed in the U.S.A. by Image Graphics, Paducah, KY

Contents

Dedication

To my high school sweetheart and wife, Virginia, with whom I have shared the love and joys of collecting for a quarter of a century, and Gloria Rezazadeh, who taught me how to write.

Preface

I began collecting as a child. First, there were stamps and coins. Then, in 1965, as a teenager, I visited the attic of a turn of the century house my father had bought several years earlier. There, I found many old objects, including a trunk filled with vintage clothing, a few pieces of jewelry, and old books. Among the books were the memoirs of a teenage girl written in the 1890s and an 1848 edition of the history of Wisconsin, plus many nineteenth century first editions. I ignored the jewelry, but overnight, became an avid collector of rare books. While in college, I began buying Oriental rugs and later American Indian artifacts. Soon, I was stricken with the disease of collecting many different objects, most of which I could not display because of lack of space.

In 1984, my wife and I began our antiques business by renting a booth in a major antiques mall. Within a year we were operating from six malls in addition to attending weekend shows. Though I became more selective, my collecting hobby continued — swords, Islamic and Japanese arts, lamps, clocks, music boxes, and so on. My wife began collecting depression glass, dolls, and costume jewelry, and our teenage son began seriously collecting and repairing vintage radios.

At this time I began to look at collecting antiques not only as a business or hobby, but also as an investment for the future, a form of saving. What could I collect which was in abundant supply and could be purchased cheaply, but had a great potential for price increases within the next 10 or 20 years? Old toys of the 1950s and 1960s were one option, but costume jewelry seemed more appealing, especially since my wife was already collecting them and we had several years of buying experience and knowledge.

So began my collecting frenzy. I bought costume jewelry weekly at every flea market, show, estate or tag sale, and auction I attended. As this became known, dealers and individuals who had jewelry for sale contacted me. Some dealers would set aside their costume jewelry for me to inspect first, and auction houses and tag sales would make sure that I knew of their upcoming sales which included costume jewelry. At the time, when only a few were buying costume jewelry and just before the first books on the subject appeared, I must have provided a good business and hefty profits for many of these dealers. Soon, I began buying collections and jewelry throughout the Midwest and East Coast. I seemed to find costume jewelry at what I considered bargain prices everywhere — in Atlantic City or Chicago shows; large flea markets in Allentown, Pa., or Kane County, Ill.; antiques malls in the Washington D.C. area or Minneapolis; auctions in Des Moines or Milwaukee.

Today, my collection includes thousands of pieces covering the whole spectrum of costume jewelry production, from the common Coventry to the rare and early Hobe pieces. In putting together this collection, I have emphasized the breadth of the industry represented by different types of costume jewelry, defined broadly to include "fashion jewelry, both domestic and foreign." My objective in writing this book is to provide a comprehensive body of information on a broad range of jewelry, emphasizing the more common, rather than the unique and rare, types of jewelry which most collectors and dealers are likely to encounter in the market place. It is not intended to pique the interest of advanced collectors by showcasing many rare and hard-to-find pieces. Such a book is quite valuable, but realistically useful to a limited number of dealers and collectors. Rather, this book is intended as a useful tool for a large majority of dealers and collectors who seek information on a broad range of jewelry representative of the costume jewelry industry.

Chapter 1

An Introduction

Defining Costume Jewelry

Tracing the genesis of the term "costume jewelry" is an illusive task which even if successful, will not explain the creation of a large industry and world-wide markets for low priced and popular jewelry. According to one legend, Florence Ziegfeld was the first to use the term while ordering jewelry to match the costumes of his Ziegfeld Follies showgirls (see Chapter 3). Others credit Coco Chanel, for drawing a distinction between fine jewelry and that which is made of nonprecious material, and referring to the jewelry she selected to match her high fashion clothing as "costume jewelry."

The truth may actually lie elsewhere. Chances are that the term was first used by some now obscure Parisian "boutique" owner who referred to "custom" made jewelry matching fashion dresses (costumes) as costume jewelry. The first use of the term certainly precedes the 1920s date attributed to Coco Chanel and the opening of her shop at 31 rue Cambon and possibly, even predates her entrance on the scene with the opening of Chanel Modes. Pre-1920s advertisements in the United States were already referring to Parisian custom made jewelry to match fash-

ion dresses as costume jewelry. A 1917 advertisement by Ostby and Barton reprinted in Harrice Simons Miller's book, *Costume Jewelry*, claimed that the firm had been engaged, for at least a year, in providing costume jewelry to the public. In their advertisement, Ostby and Barton indicated that their jewelry used genuine precious and semiprecious stones set in 14K gold and encouraged the readers to ask for it by name — costume jewelry.

It is unlikely that Chanel's popularity and use of costume jewelry had reached the U.S. shores by 1916, impressing the eminent house of Ostby and Barton so much as to induce them to adopt the term for promoting their jewelry. But the fact that Chanel and her rival, Schiaparelli, as well as other haute couturiers are responsible for popularizing and legitimizing the use of costume jewelry to complement top fashion clothing cannot be disputed.

Regardless, costume jewelry became universally known as a type of jewelry that did not use precious metals and gemstones and was mass produced at a low cost. To many, it only meant cheap or cheaply made jewelry in contrast to expensive fine jewelry. The terms "fashion jewelry" used in the late 1950s and 1960s and "designer clothing and jewelry" used in the late 1970s and 1980s were coined to draw a distinction between the so called "cheap" jewelry and "better" jewelry which used silver and gold plated metals with semiprecious stones and were supposedly produced by superior designers. But, as we shall see, the distinctions are arbitrary and only marketing tools to revive the industry and liberate it from the stigma of "cheap jewelry."

The fact is that not all costume jewelry was inexpensive. The working class women and housewives did not frequent Hattie Carnegie's or Miriam Haskell's boutiques nor did they browse through specialty shops and jewelry departments at Macy's or Marshall Field's in search of an appropriate set of costume jewelry to match their high fashion Chanel dress. The rise of the costume jewelry industry was not linked to generating demand within the working class, but more so associated with the avant-garde, the rich and the famous. Mass consumption came later as the nation went through the experiences of the Great Depression and World War II.

Furthermore, the costume jewelry industry did not limit itself to the use of only rhinestones and pot metal. Gemstones such as sapphire and topaz; semiprecious stones such as garnet, amethyst, onyx, jade and turquoise; and materials such as ivory, coral, amber, and cultured pearls were used, though infrequently, in the production of costume jewelry. Gold, silver, and rhodium plated metals and even sterling silver, especially during WWII, were frequently used as choice metals by many costume jewelry manufacturers (see Boucher, Coro, Eisenberg, Hobe, Krementz, Monet, Napier, Trifari, Van Dell, and Vargas, Chapter 3).

Costume jewelry production is often presented as a strictly American phenomenon; this is only partially true. The bulk of production and demand for costume jewelry was in the U.S., but massive quantities were also produced in France,

Germany, Austria, and Czechoslovakia, not to mention the post WWII flood of costume jewelry made in Japan and Hong Kong. Unlike production, demand was always weak abroad. The pragmatic and unpretentious Americans readily accepted and wore costume jewelry as an alternative to fine jewelry. The European consumer, partly due to traditional class distinctions, always preferred the genuine over the "fake," even if the latter closely resembled the "real thing."

In the third world, although western high fashion clothing and accessories were enthusiastically adopted by the aristocracy and the elite, fine jewelry, especially high karat gold and gemstone jewelry, remained popular as the jewelry of choice. This is partly due to the fact that in the unstable and uncertain political environment of the third world, high karat gold and gemstones were always looked upon as near-liquid assets, easily convertible to cash when necessary.

Having eradicated the arbitrary distinctions between costume and fashion jewelry, we can broadly define costume jewelry as twentieth century popular and fashionable jewelry which was frequently mass produced and seldom employed karat gold and precious gemstones. In this author's opinion, the terms "fashion jewelry," "popular jewelry," and "costume jewelry" are interchangeable. The distinctions between these terms, if any, are minor and arbitrary, while meaningful similarities are broader and consistent.

Our stated definition of costume jewelry embraces the handset or "hand made" jewelry produced by Miriam Haskell, Hobe, and foreign producers, as well as jewelry with silver and semiprecious stones and material. Of course, the bulk of costume jewelry production did not include sterling silver and semiprecious stones or material, but these materials were used frequently enough to be included in our definition. Obviously, this definition also covers gold and silver plated jewelry.

Some readers and experts may dispute the author's definition of costume jewelry and find the terms "fashion" or "popular" jewelry more descriptive of the type of jewelry shown in this book. But, these terms do not resolve the confusion and ambiguities associated with the current restrictive definitions used in the literature which exclude a significant portion of the jewelry produced by the industry. A broader and clearer definition is certainly required to reflect the wide range of jewelry produced by both American and foreign manufacturers using a variety of materials and technologies.

Much of the jewelry shown in this book was produced from 1930 through the 1970s, the period of the rise and decline of the costume jewelry industry. Some of the pieces date as early as the turn of the century, with a few manufactured in the early 1980s; these pieces are included to show continuity in design or workmanship. As stated in the preface, the author's objective in writing this book is to provide information on a broad spectrum of jewelry produced during this period to make it useful as a reference tool for a large number of dealers and collectors. For this reason, I have intentionally avoided showing many rare and high priced pieces, emphasizing instead the more common type of costume jewelry ($10.00 – 400.00 price range) which most dealers and collectors are likely to encounter.

The Mystery of Supply and Demand, and Market Prices

Most price guides on antiques and collectibles, including books on costume jewelry, state that they should be used only as a guide and that prices are determined by supply and demand, and geographical location. But collectors and dealers are confounded by the substantial price variations and often, incorrectly, dismiss the price guide books as unrealistic and irrelevant. The confusion arises from the fact that the purpose and the meaning of price guides, and how they should be used, is often misunderstood by the readers, and none of the books, to the author's best knowledge, has provided sufficient information to resolve the problem. Following is an attempt to tackle the issue in-depth and hopefully lift the fog of confusion besetting all price guides.

Part of the problem is that listed prices are usually the "asked for," and not the "sold at," prices compiled by consulting several or more dealers whose jewelry is often displayed in the same books. Discounts of 10 – 20% are routinely given at flea markets, shows, and antiques malls. Discounting the book prices by 20% may provide us with a more accurate estimate of "sold at" prices, but it will not solve the puzzle of price variations.

Any dealer/collector knows that deeper discounts, perhaps as high as 50%, are possible at any show, antiques mall or flea market. This is because, unlike the markets for other commodities, inadequate information and knowledge permeates all levels of the antiques and collectibles market. Furthermore, unlike other markets where there is a relatively uniform average cost of production, there are substantial cost variations in the antiques market. Consider a commodity such as corn, the price of which is determined by the market forces of supply and demand in the Chicago Exchange, and known to all interested parties. A farmer will not sell his corn at $2.00 a bushel when the market price is $3.75 and all his neighbors are selling their corn at this price. Put simply, competition and interaction between supply and demand determine the market price and this price must reflect the cost of production per bushel which is uniform in the farm sector. Information or knowledge is an essential ingredient for the smooth operation of the markets. In general, when information is available, all transactions will be at the going market rate.

The antiques and collectibles market operates quite differently. While the supply of corn can be increased in case of higher corn prices, the supply of antiques cannot be increased and is relatively fixed. Any increase, if at all, can come only from undiscovered pieces which are limited. Given the fixed supply, the market price of antiques is determined by demand. The higher the demand, the higher the price.

Due to lack of information, antiques and collectibles do not have a uniform cost. A Miriam Haskell necklace with a book price of $165.00 can be purchased at various prices: $3.00 at a garage sale; $10.00 at a local flea market; $20.00 at a sparsely attended auction; or $100.00 at a well advertised costume jewelry auction. Only specialized dealers and collectors are well informed about costume jewelry market and prices. Most others, including some well experienced dealers who specialize in other lines of antiques, often have inadequate knowledge and information.

A person who sold the Miriam Haskell necklace for $3.00 at a garage sale probably did not even look for a mark and even if he did, how would he know anything about its maker, age, and value? His main objective is to get rid of the junk in the attic. A seller who may remember that it belonged to Grandma, may price it at $15.00 or $20.00 to see what happens in the first hours of the sale. Few will consult the library or professionals.

Many part-time flea marketers and dealers buy much of their merchandise at such garage sales. Since they handle a variety of merchandise with a quick turnover, they do not know about the market value of every piece they purchase, especially if the piece is not marked. Many of these pieces are priced according to cost and the dealer's estimate of its sale price. So a dealer who has bought the necklace for $3.00 may price it at $15.00 and sell it at $12.00 with a handsome profit. But even the more experienced dealers who know the necklace is a Miriam Haskell with a book price of $165.00 may sell it to you for much less. If the dealer has acquired it for only $3.00 at a garage sale or $20.00 at an auction, he may, after some bargaining, accept your offer of $100.00 and still make a hefty profit.

The author has bought Haskell necklaces for as low as $3.00 from experienced antiques dealers specializing in other lines, who had not even bothered to closely examine the costume jewelry they offered for sale from a box at $3.00 per piece. But, I have also paid as much as $125.00 for similar pieces. I have also received discounts of 50% or better from specialized dealers who sell only costume jewelry. The fact that I am a dealer, known to the seller, is at best, partially responsible for such discounts. Once, at a major Chicago area market, I purchased a Boucher pin and earrings set worth at least $150.00, priced at $125.00, for only $40.00. The dealer, who specialized in jewelry, later told me that he had bought the set for only $4.00 and preferred the turn-over in his money rather than waiting for the right costumer. For an active dealer, $40.00 turned over several times within a month can generate a far greater net revenue than the Boucher set would have realized selling at $125.00 after several months.

Lack of information and variations in costs are largely responsible for price variations. Geographical location is only partly responsible for price differentials, but price variations could be greater within the same region depending on the type of market attended, e.g., O'Hare show vs. a small Chicago area flea market or an antiques shop in Georgetown, Washington, D.C. vs. an antiques mall or market in Frederick, Maryland.

Given the nature of antiques markets described above, consulting books and price guides becomes imperative if the seller or buyer hopes to get a fair price. Any book or price guide on antiques will pay for itself many times over if it is consulted only once about a piece you wish to buy or sell, and about which you know little. Books are written to inform and price guides serve the purpose of providing the reader with an approximation of the estimated value of a piece of jewelry they own. Here, I have attempted to provide the reader with the best estimate of what a piece of jewelry can sell for in transactions involving both informed buyers and sellers. The same piece of jewelry may be purchased at higher or lower prices, but primarily because of market conditions described. The listed prices are based on a rather extensive survey of major shows, flea markets, and antiques malls, as well as the author's personal experience of purchasing several thousand pieces of costume jewelry each year, including every piece shown in this book.

If you have a piece of costume jewelry to sell to a dealer, expect no more than 25 – 50% of the prices listed in this book. It is often forgotten that a dealer has various costs in addition to the cost of purchasing your jewelry and cannot remain in business by paying near book prices.

Factors Influencing Market Prices

There are many factors that affect costume jewelry prices. Below, I have listed and explained five major determinants of value which may facilitate a more objective evaluation and appraisal of the jewelry you own and collect. Technically we could have simply stated that market prices are determined by supply and demand, but this would have disguised the importance of few variables that directly affect demand itself. I have further developed a value scale, classifying American costume jewelry according to value, for a quick general reference.

1. Rarity (Supply). The manufacturers of costume jewelry produced varying quantities of jewelry. Some major producers, like Coro, Coventry, and Trifari, produced a large volume of jewelry with thousands of pieces of the same design. Others like DeMario and McClelland Barclay produced a much smaller volume. Accordingly, it is more difficult to find a signed DeMario or Barclay vs. Coro or Trifari. Then, as a rule, other things being constant, a Barclay piece should command a higher price than a Coro due to rarity alone. However, some of the jewelry made by Coro or Trifari, such as jelly bellies and duettes, were also produced in limited quantities, and thus should be ranked higher in value based on rarity alone.

2. Consumer Demand. The market value of a piece of jewelry is directly related to demand for it. The higher the demand, the higher the price. But demand itself depends on collectors' incomes, tastes, and preferences. Sometimes collectors buy a certain piece, not because they necessarily like it, but because it is highly collectible with a good potential for price increases. For example, most collectors and dealers look for signed Miriam Haskell jewelry more than signed Sarah Coventry pieces because Haskell, though more expensive, is highly collectible. There are dealers who personally do not like Haskell jewelry, but constantly seek it because of high collectors' demand. There are also collectors who would never wear Miriam Haskell jewelry, but buy it for their collection because it is highly collectible. The higher the demand for a certain type of jewelry, the higher will be its value and rank in our value scale.

3. Design and Originality. Other things being constant, design and originality play an important role in determining prices. That is why advanced collectors will not frown at an unmarked piece which has original and quality design. After all, jewelry, especially handmade jewelry, is an esthetic piece of art and the design is an integral part of jewelry's appeal. All jewelry manufacturers produced some well designed pieces, but some of them consistently produced jewelry of superior designs, whether original or inspired by the jewelry of other periods such as

9

the Victorian, classic and renaissance jewelry. Among these, there are several producers whose jewelry is still unappreciated and underpriced — Hollycraft, Art, and Florenza. Others, well known for their designs and sometimes over estimated, will be discussed in the chapter on American costume jewelry.

Originality is another criterion for evaluating costume jewelry. Among several producers with original designs, Miriam Haskell would stand out. One may not like her jewelry, but one cannot deny her superior creativity and originality. Some pieces may show originality but not necessarily good designs (see Accessocraft and B.S.K., Chapter 3). Therefore, other things constant, original, well designed jewelry would be priced higher than that with average and common designs.

4. *Material and Workmanship.* If we were to judge costume jewelry only by the quality of the stones, Eisenberg, Hollycraft, Weiss, and Bogoff would win hands down. There were other American producers that used quality stones, but none consistently manufactured jewelry with such vibrance and glow which captures the collector's attention from a distance. Advanced collectors can identify an unmarked Eisenberg by just looking at the stones. The jewelry by the other three producers, Hollycraft, Weiss and Bogoff, is well underpriced and just beginning to be appreciated. The quality of the metal and workmanship is also of prime importance. The casting and stamping of the metal to show the design, the gold brush work and plating, the chains and other parts used, all combine to lend beauty and originality to a well designed piece. In this area, Eisenberg should be ranked high, but so does the jewelry of many others, including Trifari, Monet, Kramer, Danecraft, Symmetalic, Hobe, and some of Coro. Remember that costume jewelry was originally produced to emulate the real thing; the more a piece resembles fine jewelry, the higher it should be ranked on the value scale.

5. *Condition and Durability.* In the antiques market one always hears that condition is everything. The condition of a piece is very important but so is its durability since many collectors wear the jewelry they own. It is difficult to judge durability without a scientific test as those applied to other commodities. Short of that, the average condition in which we find the jewelry of a certain manufacturer attests to its durability. Any jewelry can be found in poor and damaged condition, but there is jewelry made by certain companies which consistently shows signs of damage and wear. Of course, lost stones and signs of wear are expected on any old jewelry, but seldom has the author found Star jewelry in excellent condition. Often, the chains have discolored or rusted, many stones are missing or dead, and the metal plating peeling, especially on the back of the jewelry. Down the list we should also include B.S.K., Leru, and lower quality Lisner, Kramer, and Coro. On the other hand, Monet, Boucher, Hobe, Carnegie, Eisenberg, Kermentz, and Weiss are generally found in good condition. For example, Krementz jewelry made 80 years ago or Monet pieces that were made in the 1940s and 1950s still shine as though they were made yesterday.

Value Scale*

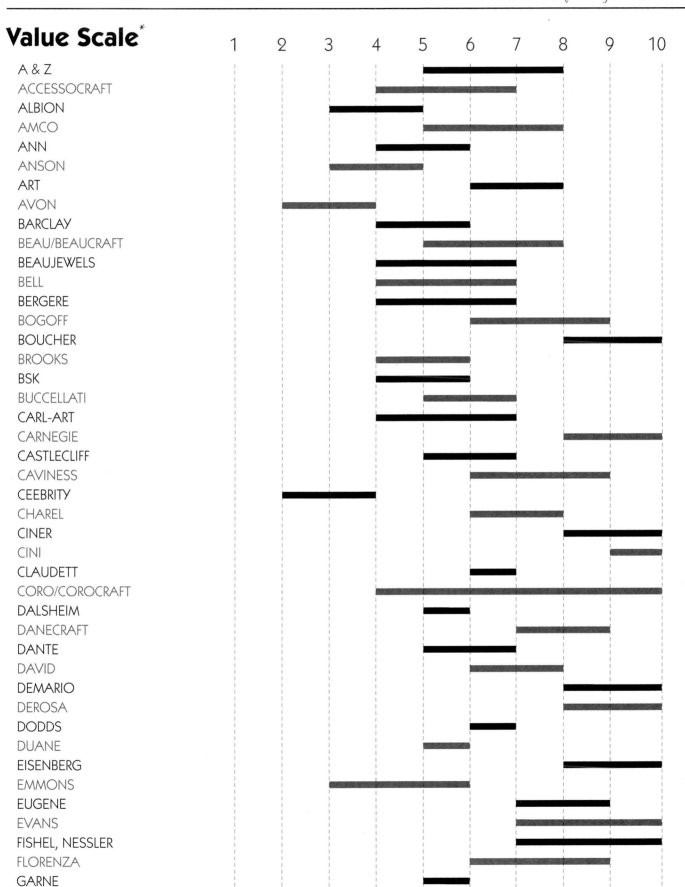

	1	2	3	4	5	6	7	8	9	10
A & Z					████████████████					
ACCESSOCRAFT				██████████████						
ALBION			████████							
AMCO					████████████████████					
ANN				██████████						
ANSON			███████							
ART						████████████				
AVON		██████████								
BARCLAY				██████████						
BEAU/BEAUCRAFT					███████████████████					
BEAUJEWELS				██████████████						
BELL				██████████████						
BERGERE				██████████████						
BOGOFF						██████████████████				
BOUCHER								██████████████		
BROOKS				████████████						
BSK				████████████						
BUCCELLATI					█████████					
CARL-ART				██████████████						
CARNEGIE								██████████████████		
CASTLECLIFF					████████████					
CAVINESS						██████████████				
CEEBRITY		██████████								
CHAREL						██████████				
CINER								██████████████		
CINI										██████
CLAUDETT						██████				
CORO/COROCRAFT				████████████████████████████						
DALSHEIM					██████					
DANECRAFT							██████████████			
DANTE					██████████					
DAVID						██████████████				
DEMARIO								██████████████		
DEROSA								██████████████		
DODDS						██████				
DUANE					██████					
EISENBERG								██████████████		
EMMONS			████████████████							
EUGENE							██████████████			
EVANS							██████████████████████			
FISHEL, NESSLER							██████████████████████			
FLORENZA						██████████████				
GARNE					██████					

Maker	1	2	3	4	5	6	7	8	9	10
GERRY'S			■	■	■	■				
GOLDETTE				■	■	■				
HAR								■	■	■
HICKOC			■	■	■					
HOBE							■	■	■	■
HOLLYCRAFT						■	■	■	■	
ISKIN					■	■	■	■		
JEANNE					■	■				
JJ				■	■	■				
JUDY LEE				■	■	■				
KAFIN				■	■	■				
KARU				■	■	■				
KORDA								■	■	■
KRAMER				■	■	■	■	■	■	
KREMENTZ						■	■	■	■	
LAGUNA				■	■	■				
LA REL					■	■	■			
LEWIS SEGAL			■	■	■					
LERU			■	■	■					
LISNER			■	■	■	■	■	■		
MARINO				■	■	■				
MARVELLA				■	■	■	■	■		
MATISSE					■	■	■	■		
MAZER/JOMAZ						■	■	■	■	■
McCLELLAND BARCLAY									■	■
MIRACLE					■	■				
MIRIAM HASKELL								■	■	■
MIZPAH							■	■		
MONET				■	■	■	■			
MYLU				■	■	■				
NAPIER					■	■	■	■	■	
NETTI ROSENSTEIN								■	■	■
NEWHOUSE					■	■	■			
ORA					■	■	■	■		
PAKULA					■	■	■			
PAM				■	■					
PANETTA						■	■	■	■	
PASTELI				■	■	■				
PELL					■	■	■			
PENNINO									■	■
POLCINI								■	■	■
REBAJES								■	■	■
REGENCY						■	■	■	■	
REINAD								■	■	■

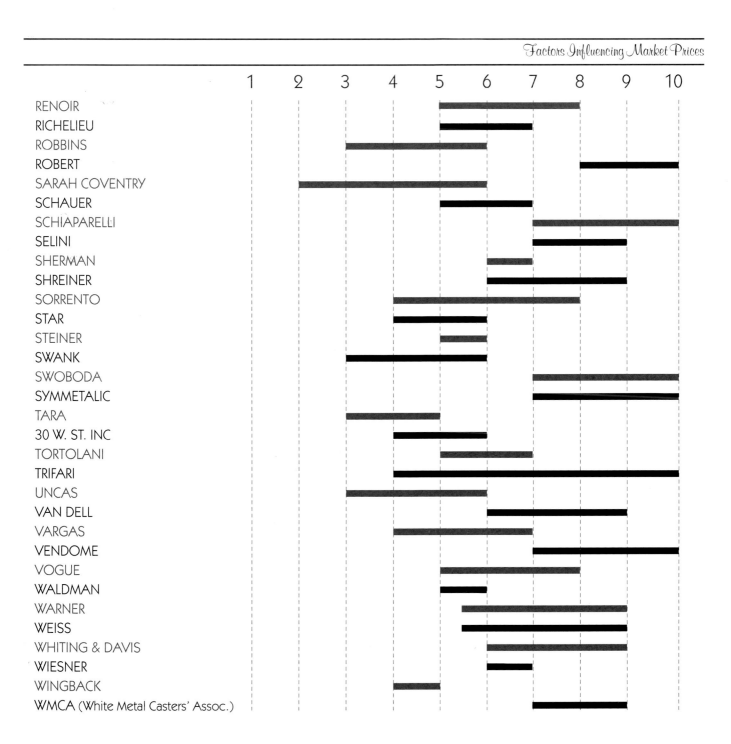

	1	2	3	4	5	6	7	8	9	10
RENOIR					▬▬▬▬▬▬					
RICHELIEU					▬▬▬▬					
ROBBINS			▬▬▬▬▬							
ROBERT								▬▬▬▬▬		
SARAH COVENTRY		▬▬▬▬▬▬▬								
SCHAUER					▬▬▬▬					
SCHIAPARELLI							▬▬▬▬▬▬			
SELINI							▬▬▬			
SHERMAN						▬▬				
SHREINER						▬▬▬▬▬				
SORRENTO				▬▬▬▬▬▬▬						
STAR				▬▬▬						
STEINER					▬					
SWANK			▬▬▬							
SWOBODA							▬▬▬▬▬▬			
SYMMETALIC							▬▬▬▬▬▬			
TARA			▬▬▬▬							
30 W. ST. INC				▬▬▬						
TORTOLANI					▬▬▬▬					
TRIFARI				▬▬▬▬▬▬▬▬▬▬▬▬▬						
UNCAS			▬▬▬▬▬							
VAN DELL						▬▬▬▬▬				
VARGAS				▬▬▬▬▬						
VENDOME							▬▬▬▬▬▬			
VOGUE					▬▬▬▬▬▬					
WALDMAN					▬▬▬					
WARNER					▬▬▬▬▬▬▬					
WEISS					▬▬▬▬▬▬					
WHITING & DAVIS						▬▬▬▬▬				
WIESNER						▬▬▬				
WINGBACK				▬▬						
WMCA (White Metal Casters' Assoc.)							▬▬▬▬▬			

* This list includes only American manufacturers except newer couture and designer jewelry. Schiaparelli is included because of her U.S. residency and business operations.

Costume Jewelry as an Investment

There is no index for costume jewelry or even antiques and collectibles to compare its performance against other major investment alternatives. Given the performance of the stock market in the past decade, it is difficult to identify many other investment alternatives that would have yielded a higher rate of return. But, in general, the appreciation of antiques and collectibles should be at least comparable to the performance of the bond and money markets.

It should be noted that there are major differences between investing in collectible costume jewelry and other investment alternatives such as stocks and bonds. First and foremost, costume jewelry is not a liquid or near liquid asset and cannot be readily converted to cash. Second, when costume jewelry is sold, whether through an auction house or to a dealer, its transaction cost is higher than stocks and bonds. Stocks sell at the market value less the transaction cost, while collectibles such as costume jewelry, when liquidated, almost always sell at below retail value, less the transaction cost.

But there are some advantages in investing in any line of antiques and collectibles, including costume jewelry. First, collectors derive satisfaction from owning and using their collection. This satisfaction, referred to as utility by economists, cannot be directly measured in monetary terms, but it has value which should be added to any monetary gains. For example, if you own and live in your house, you derive satisfaction from its use while it appreciates in value, but when the house is sold, the capital gain does not reflect its many years of use. Second, because of limited supply, antiques and collectibles seldom decline in value, while stock prices can fall as fast as they rise. In general, the risks involved in holding antiques as assets are lower than holding stocks. Third, stocks are bought at market prices, while antiques and collectibles, as discussed earlier, can be purchased at prices far below market value. This would provide the buyer with an opportunity for instant profit without speculation.

Of course, investing in costume jewelry is much more rewarding if you also enjoy collecting and even wearing them. But if your primary objective is investment and collecting is secondary, you cannot purchase the jewelry at retail prices. Remember, in general, you cannot sell the jewelry at above 40 – 50% of retail prices. Consequently, if you purchase the jewelry at retail prices, you must wait for at least several years before the appreciation of value will cover your initial investment. But because of wide price differentials explained in the previous section, you can always buy costume jewelry at a fraction of market prices. Generally, because of the pricing structure followed in this book, any displayed jewelry when bought at 20 – 30% of the average listed prices, will provide instant gains. You are still in safe territory with potential for future gains if you purchase the jewelry at 30 – 40% of average listed prices, but never pay more than 50% of the average listed price.

If the jewelry is purchased at below 50% of average listed prices, you are purchasing it at near or below wholesale prices and have maximized your chances of converting most of the future appreciation into profits. However, buying costume jewelry at these lower prices requires investment of time and time has value. If you highly value your time, then the following discussion will not be of much benefit to you. You can still invest in costume jewelry by buying it at occasional shows and antiques shops and malls, but in general, you will not be able to receive better than 20% discount. But if you do not place a high value on your time and/or enjoy hunting for old costume jewelry, then you can treat it as a recreational activity with a potential for substantial gains.

Costume jewelry at these lower prices can be generally purchased at garage sales, flea markets, and local auctions. Tag or estate sales are also good places to buy costume jewelry, particularly, on the second or third day of the sale, when unsold merchandise is offered at discounted prices or according to bids left with the proprietor. But in order to take advantage of these markets, you must first learn all you can about costume jewelry and market prices. Read as many books on costume jewelry as you can and attend major shows and flea markets. Browse through antiques malls and shops, look at and examine the jewelry offered for sale, and note the asking prices.

In order to be successful in your hunt, you need to be familiar with the environment of each of these markets. Garage sales are advertised in the classified section of your local paper. If you plan to go to a garage sale, attend early. Many garage sales open before the announced time and most of the bargain pieces are purchased within the first hour of the sale. There are in fact unethical and unprofessional dealers who contact the owners well in advance of the sale and use various lies and excuses about why they cannot attend on the day of the sale and after cajoling the unsuspecting owners, purchase most of the bargain pieces several days before the actual sale. Costume jewelry can be purchased at very low prices at garage sales, but the search is very time consuming and finding several good pieces may require attending many sales.

Actually, much of the jewelry purchased at garage sales will show up at local weekend flea markets or larger monthly regional markets. Here you can buy a large volume of jewelry within a few hours. Again, you will be more successful if you attend early, equipped with your magnifying glass. Many regional flea markets, for a higher fee, allow entry several hours before the opening time. Many professional dealers take advantage of this early entry and purchase many of the bargain pieces before the actual opening of the market. In fact, many major transactions at bargain prices are concluded among the dealers themselves or with professional dealers/collectors and pickers far in advance of the opening of the market. Each dealer, using his or her superior knowledge about a particular line of antiques, carefully examines the merchandise on each table

or in showcases in order to find a bargain, a great "find" or "sleeper" which can be purchased at a fraction of its market price, from another dealer who has not done his homework or specializes in another line of antiques. If you are knowledgeable about costume jewelry, you can always find bargains at such flea markets, even hours after its opening, but the earlier you attend, the greater will be your chances of finding many choice pieces at bargain prices.

Local auctions, not specialized major auctions, are another market for purchasing costume jewelry. These are also advertised in the classified section of your local newspaper. Most local auctions have a preview time for examining, sometimes a day, but often several hours before the auction time. Be sure you attend early and get a good look at the jewelry. Take a notebook and make notes on each piece that interests you. Always carry several costume jewelry price guides in your car and check the book prices for the same or comparable type of jewelry and write next to it your maximum bid for that piece of jewelry.

Since you are buying costume jewelry for investment, not just the fun of it, use only reliable price guides. One way to test the reliability of a price guide is to take several pieces of the jewelry displayed in the book to several reputable dealers and offer them for sale. If the offer prices are, at least, between 20 – 30% of the listed prices, you have a reliable price guide; otherwise, the listed prices reflect the author's fantasy world more than the realities of the marketplace. The same test should be applied to this or any book on antiques and collectibles, particularly, if investment is your primary objective.

Never exceed your written maximum bid. Some of the jewelry may sell at prices several times your maximum bid, but there will always be another day and another auction. Remember that it will take only two bidders to bid a piece of jewelry to or even beyond its retail price. This could be because two collectors are determined to buy a piece of jewelry at any price. Sometimes, dealers who already have a waiting customer may pay as much as 80% of the market value to purchase a piece of jewelry which they will sell within a week at a reasonable profit. But as an investor, you must think long term and minimize your initial cost so you can maximize your future gains.

Tag or estate sales are other places for purchasing costume jewelry for investment. These sales are usually held by an estate liquidating concern at the owner's premises. Tag sales are usually held for two to three days. Many tag sales use a numbering system on the first day; others are based on first come first served order. Where the number system is used, the numbers are given out several hours in advance of the sale, and at the time of the sale, entrance is allowed in accordance to numbers. Normally tag sales accept bids on any merchandise above a certain minimum price and many of them have a bid box. The collected bids are then examined at a predetermined time and if the merchandise has not sold at the regular tagged price, it will go to the highest bidder. At such sales, some of the merchandise, particularly, the choice pieces, sell on the first day, but many of the remaining items are sold at discounted prices, usually 50 percent, on the second day. Some sales allow formal or informal bargaining at the last few hours of the sale where the unsold pieces can be purchased at discounts up to 80 percent. If you go to tag sales with a considerable amount of jewelry for sale, you should attend both days of the sale and be preferably among the first group that is allowed entrance. A knowledgeable collector can always find bargains on the first day of the sale, but this would also allow you to carefully examine and evaluate the jewelry for purchase or bids on the second day. Normally you can buy all of the remaining jewelry that interests you at discounted prices on the second day, provided that you are among the first group allowed in the house.

Costume jewelry can also be purchased by placing an ad in the classified section of your local paper or through the Internet where you can reach thousands of sellers throughout the world. A popular site is the Collector's Supermall with thousands of classified ads which can be reached at http://www.csmoline.com. For America On Line members, enter the keyword Antiques and then follow the links on the menu, many of which have a special section on jewelry. There are also several specialized trade papers, such as *The Antique Trader*, where advertisements by many dealers and collectors offer jewelry for sale.

Major shows, specialized auctions, antiques shops, and malls are the other markets for purchasing costume jewelry. As you gain experience and knowledge about costume jewelry and prices, you will be able to find bargains at any and all of these outlets.

Following are two investment alternatives. Alternative 1 is designed for a modest budget of $1,000.00 – 2,000.00 per year for a relatively novice collector. Alternative 2 requires an investment capital of $2,000.00 – 5,000.00 per year for a relatively experienced and knowledgeable collector, but can also be used by investors and collectors who wish to spend more. Aside from differences in the initial capital, the two alternatives focus on two different categories of costume jewelry. The jewelry recommended for Alternative 1 is the more common and lower priced jewelry which of course has a lower potential for appreciation. But a novice collector is more likely to make mistakes and Alternative 1 minimizes the risks involved so that possible errors will not be costly mistakes. Alternative 2 recommends higher priced and relatively scarce jewelry with a greater potential for future appreciation, but requires a higher level of experience and knowledge. Actually, the system used for both alternatives is designed to trigger a buy order at prices which minimize potential losses and maximize potential gains in the future. Remember that you should buy any jewelry displayed in this book at 20 – 30% of average listed prices and such a price should trigger an automatic buy signal. Also remember that you should evaluate the jewelry based on the criteria discussed earlier in this chapter. Always make sure that the piece of jewelry you are purchasing is in good condition and of high quality; displays interesting and superior design and craftsmanship; and is, in general, appealing and attractive.

Once you have considered the above factors, follow the rules below.

INVESTMENT ALTERNATIVE I*
Discounted Prices Triggering Automatic Buy Order

Company	Necklace Under	Brooch Under	Bracelet Under	Earrings Under
ART	$12.00	$8.00	$10.00	$4.00
BSK	$8.00	$5.00	$6.00	$3.00
BERGERE	$9.00	$5.00	$6.00	$3.00
BOGOFF	$14.00	$9.00	$10.00	$5.00
BOUCHER	$20.00	$14.00	$16.00	$8.00
CARNEGIE	$14.00	$10.00	$11.00	$5.00
CINI	$25.00	$14.00	$20.00	$10.00
CINER	$18.00	$12.00	$14.00	$7.00
CORO				
Rhinestone	$9.00	$5.00	$6.00	$3.00
Metal	$7.00	$4.00	$4.00	$3.00
Plastic	$8.00	$4.00	$5.00	$3.00
DANECRAFT (Sterling)	$14.00	$8.00	$10.00	$5.00
DEMARIO	$30.00	$16.00	$20.00	$10.00
EISENBERG	$25.00	$16.00	$20.00	$9.00
EMMONS	$7.00	$4.00	$4.00	$3.00
FLORENZA	$13.00	$8.00	$10.00	$5.00
HAR	$18.00	$11.00	$14.00	$8.00
HASKELL	$24.00	$16.00	$17.00	$7.00
HOLLYCRAFT	$14.00	$9.00	$10.00	$5.00
HOBE (except Plastic)	$18.00	$12.00	$14.00	$6.00
JUDY LEE	$11.00	$7.00	$8.00	$4.00
KRAMER	$13.00	$7.00	$10.00	$4.00
LISNER	$10.00	$8.00	$8.00	$3.00
NAPIER	$12.00	$6.00	$8.00	$4.00
ORA (Rhinestone)	$14.00	$7.00	$10.00	$4.00
PENNINO	$30.00	$13.00	$18.00	$10.00
REGENCY	$13.00	$9.00	$11.00	$5.00
RENOIR	$12.00	$5.00	$8.00	$3.00
S. COVENTRY	$6.00	$3.00	$4.00	$2.00
TRIFARI	$12.00	$6.00	$8.00	$3.00
WEISS	$15.00	$9.00	$10.00	$5.00

* discounted listed prices are for typical average jewelry made by each company.

INVESTMENT ALTERNATIVE II
Buy the jewelry of following companies at 20 to 30 percent of average listed prices:

ART	Especially pavé set pieces and those with multicolor stones or unusual designs.
BOGOFF	Especially those with color rhinestones. Pins are less common.
BOUCHER	Especially early enamel pieces and those with early MB mark.
CARNEGIE	Especially early pieces, interesting figurals, and tremblers.
CINI	Especially sculpture-like early sterling pieces.
CORO	Only jelly bellies, Duettes, sterling pieces, Corocraft and Vendome.
DEMARIO	Any marked piece.
DE ROSA	Any marked piece.
EISENBERG	Especially early figural pieces, sterling silver, early Eisenberg Ice pieces, and any set.
FLORENZA	Especially pieces with sculptured and unusual stones and any set.
HASKELL	Especially early pieces, elaborate necklaces and pins with elaborate floral clusters, and any set.
HOLLYCRAFT	Especially bracelets and necklaces.
HOBE	Especially early pieces, sterling silver, and all figurals.
KORDA	Any marked piece.
KRAMER	Especially elaborate rhinestone pieces.
LISNER	Especially atomic & Art Moderne designs, baguette rhinestones or with rhinestones of unusual shapes.
MATISSE	Especially attractive enameled sets.
MC. BARCLAY	Any marked piece.
MAZER/JOMAZ	Especially sets.
ORA	Especially pavé set multi-color rhinestone pieces.
NAPIER	Only elaborate rhinestone sets and early sterling silver sets.
PENNINO	Any marked piece.
REBAJES	Any marked piece.
REINAD	Any marked piece.
ROBERT	Especially sets.
SWOBODA	Any necklace or bracelet and all sets.
SYMMETALIC	Any marked piece, but especially necklaces and bracelets.
TRIFARI	Especially jelly bellies, figurals pieces, early TKF pieces, enameled jewelry with foil-less or sculptured stones, and sterling silver pieces.
WEISS	Especially attractive sets.

Displaying and Storing Your Jewelry

If you frequently wear your jewelry, the best place to store it is in a jewelry box, cabinet or chest. If you have pieces to display, the best method is to use jewelry display boxes. These are glass top cardboard boxes of various sizes with a cotton or foam filling. They can be ordered individually or in quantity from suppliers who advertise in antique journals. A 16" x 12" x 2" box can be purchased for $5.00 – 6.00. If you have pieces which are thicker than ⅔", such as bangles and bracelets, a 2" deep box is necessary. Make sure your jewelry does not press against the glass because it can break while handling and stacking the boxes.

There are various ways you can organize your jewelry for display. You can organize pieces according to type of jewelry, such as sets, necklaces, bracelets, and earrings, creating as many categories as you like. You can separate signed necklaces from unmarked pieces, or display only necklaces made by a certain company. The author's jewelry is organized according to this book's contents. Make sure you label each box both on the glass and on the side of the box using small adhesive label tags. If you wish, you can further identify each piece displayed in the box using a 6" x 4" card. This card can be placed under the foam in the box or in an envelope securely taped on the bottom of the box. Another option is to use a separate notebook listing your jewelry in each box with the purchase price and estimated book price. Store your jewelry display boxes in hard plastic storage boxes which can be purchased at most department stores or ordered from suppliers that advertise in antiques journals. If you wish to invest a little more money, there are storage boxes made especially for these display boxes which can be ordered from the same suppliers.

Some collectors prefer to display their jewelry in a show case or curio cabinet. This may be suitable for small collections, but will not work for extensive collections of several thousand pieces. Furthermore, the use of display boxes allows for portability of your collection. They can easily be taken in and out of a safe in your house or a safety deposit box in a bank. The boxes also enable you to organize your jewelry according to your taste and show all or part of it to your friends and collectors just as you would a photo album.

If you have an extensive collection, it is necessary to insure it since most home insurance policies have a limit of a few thousand dollars covering jewelry. The easiest way to insure your costume jewelry is to get a lump sum coverage of a certain amount rather than having each piece appraised. Talk to your insurance agent about the options available. If necessary, you can provide them with a photograph of each box with an estimated average price as well as the price range for the jewelry in each box. Regardless, photographing and keeping an inventory of your jewelry is a wise measure substantiating your claim in case of theft or fire. Keep these photographs and documents in a separate place, such as a locked office desk at work or a bank safety deposit box.

Cleaning Your Jewelry

My wife, who has an extensive collection of costume jewelry and frequently wears the pieces, has her own method of cleaning them. She would not wear a piece unless it is thoroughly cleaned, and for her this requires the following process. She drops her jewelry into a bucket of lukewarm water mixed with dishwashing soap and scrubs them with a soft toothbrush, using mainly the suds. She then rinses each piece and lays it face down on a thick, soft towel, using another towel to wipe and dry them individually. She uses the hair dryer after wiping the jewelry.

Over the years she has cleaned approximately two thousand pieces of jewelry using this method and though she has lost some stones, her jewelry is sparkling clean with no sign of rust or discoloration. I do not know if her success can be attributed to good luck or her quick drying method, but for her, the satisfaction of wearing thoroughly clean jewelry outweighs the agony of damaging some pieces.

I would not dare use the same method cleaning my jewelry and would recommend against it. When cleaning your jewelry, never submerse or wash them under running water. If you do, you run the risk of loose and lost stones, rust, and discoloration. Water is the enemy of costume jewelry, especially pieces that use foil-back stones. At best, washing in water will cause dislodged stones, often loosening their backing, which will have a darker and duller color when glued back in place. Over the years I have bought the inventory and remnants of several bankrupt jewelry stores and have noticed discoloration in the brand new rhinestone jewelry of the 1960s and 1970s in their original boxes. When the discolored stones are removed, one can see the foil is intact, but with rust and patina on the edges. Since these pieces were never sold or used, I can only attribute the discoloration to humidity. Of course, more damage would occur if you submerse your jewelry in water.

My method of cleaning is quite safe and simple, using ordinary tools that can be found in any home. These are a tweezer, a set of needles of various sizes, a soft baby toothbrush, Q-tips, two towels, and a dental pick which can be purchased at any drugstore. First, using the sharp edge of the needle or dental pick, carefully loosen and remove all the foreign particles such as food, wax, lipstick, etc., from the piece you are cleaning. You can use the tweezer to remove hair and loosened particles lodged in the crevasses. If there is minor rust on the metal, carefully remove it with a pencil eraser. You may have to carefully loosen the surface rust with a needle before removing it.

Prepare a solution of approximately a cup of water per teaspoon of dishwashing detergent. Using a Q-tip, dampen the tip mostly with suds and carefully rub and clean each piece held upside down. You can then use the other end of the Q-tip and remove excess liquid. Or if necessary, dampen a Q-tip in clear water and go over the piece again. The same method can be followed using a baby toothbrush, especially if the piece of jewelry has sharp and pointed edges or lots of dirt on it. Finally, dry the piece face down between two towels, blotting lightly. If you use a Q-tip, you may have to use the tweezer to remove any cotton caught by the sharp edges of a piece.

You can use alcohol instead of water and soap to clean your jewelry following the same process. Alcohol does a good job as a disinfectant, but it will not work as well removing lumps of dirt and reviving the glitter of the stone. In cases of extremely dirty pieces of jewelry, you may have to repeat the above steps several times.

Do not get discouraged; be patient and the result will be a sparkling piece of jewelry which will please you for many years to come.

Repairing Your Jewelry

For the serious collectors, major repairs such as re-enameling, adding or deleting certain parts, and replating the metal are not acceptable. However, minor repairs, such as replacing lost stones, are permissible. Here, simple repairs that can be undertaken by any novice collector are discussed.

Rhinestones of various sizes and colors can be bought at specialty bead shops or ordered from suppliers which advertise in antiques journals.

If you have a large collection and wish to repair your jewelry yourself, an investment of $100.00 – 300.00 purchasing damaged and odd pieces of jewelry with various rhinestone colors will certainly pay off. You can buy these at flea markets or at most antiques shops and malls. Some dealers sell damaged and odd pieces in a bag.

Remove all the stones and findings and organize them according to color and size in small plastic boxes or you could organize the jewelry itself according to stone colors and remove the stones from each piece as you need them.

For tools, you need a set of needles, two pairs of needlenose pliers, a small folding knife with a fine blade, several small screwdrivers of various widths, and some type of glue such as Epoxy 330 or Crazy Glue. Epoxy 330 is better, but takes time to prepare; Crazy Glue is quick but more difficult to use. Crazy Glue should not be used on glass stones without foil backing.

To replace a discolored or dead stone, first you must find another stone matching in size and color. This could be a formidable task if you are repairing certain types of jewelry. For example, Florenza, Art, Hollycraft, Schiaparelli, and Regency costume jewelry often have unique stones of certain colors and shapes which are quite different from stones used on other jewelry. For these, a satisfactory and professional repair usually requires using their own damaged and odd jewelry for replacement stones. Others, such as Eisenberg, Weiss, and Bogoff have such glowing and superior stones that replacement with other stones will not be satisfactory. However, the stones from these three companies are often interchangeable. Ora stones can also be used as substitutes. The color stones from old Czechoslovakian, Austrian, and some French jewelry have a different shade and glow and should be replaced with the same type of stones from damaged pieces. For most other rhinestone jewelry, a satisfactory replacement stone can usually be found. Since there was an abundance of mass-produced Coro, Coventry, Lisner, and Trifari, finding damaged pieces with replacement stones is not difficult. However, Trifari clear stones have a different shade and often lose their foil backing when they are removed.

To remove a replacement stone from damaged and odd pieces, begin carefully with your smallest needle and change to a larger size as required. Too much force may chip the edges of the rhinestone or remove it without its back foil.

The task must be approached patiently, with slow attempts rather than a strong jerk. For handset stones, use the sharp edge of the knife to push back the prongs. Make sure you do not apply too much force and break them. Also make sure you do not scratch the stone.

Once you have the replacement rhinestone, remove the discolored stone and clean the socket of all excess glue and debris. Try the replacement stone for size and color. It should look the same as the neighboring stones and not stand out in size or color. Finally, put a very small amount of glue in the socket and using a tweezer or your fingers, set the replacement stone in place. If using your fingers, put the stone face down on the tip of your finger, and holding the piece of jewelry face down in your other hand, align the hole with the stone and press the piece on it. You can then use the end of the tweezer to push the stone so it fits correctly. If you use instant glue, make sure it is not gel glue. The liquid glue is a very difficult glue to handle, but will give immediate results. You must use a very small amount of it and make sure that it does not touch the top of the stone and dull it. To make sure you do not use too much glue, put a dab of glue on a piece of paper; use another piece of paper rolled to a small point to apply the glue to the socket. After some practice, you can apply the glue directly and remove any excess glue from the socket by using the same type of rolled paper which will absorb most of the glue. You can follow the same procedure using epoxy 330 glue, but use a toothpick to apply the glue and the other end of it to remove excess glue.

The same method can be used for replacing faux pearls, beads, and other stones mounted on costume jewelry. But missing beads which are held by brass or copper wire on jewelry made mostly by Miriam Haskell, Roberts, and

DeMario are difficult to replace and should be left to professionals. Often, most of the wires have oxidized and attempting to replace one may damage and break the rest of the wires. Restringing a broken faux pearl or beads necklace is an easy but time consuming task. For this, the author recommends purchasing a how-to-do book (usually under $20.00) from a hobby or specialty beads shop where you can also buy the strings, findings and other supplies. In fact, any serious collector should have a basic knowledge of how different types of jewelry are made and consulting a book in the public library would be very useful. You can also take a course in jewelry making at a local community college or private lessons from a local artisan who normally hold classes in their shop or home.

Left: *Necklace and bracelet made of genuine garnet beads. $300.00 – 450.00.*

Opposite page: *Left: Small onyx pin mounted on silver. $40.00 – 60.00. Right: Small mother-of-pearl pin on gilded brass mounting. $35.00 – 50.00. Center: Edwardian necklace and matching bracelet in silver, onyx, and faceted brilliants. $200.00 – 250.00.*

Chapter 2

The Early 1900s

The costume jewelry shown in this chapter was manufactured in the early 1900s and generally dates no later than the early 1930s. Specialized Art Nouveau, Art Deco, and Arts and Crafts types of jewelry which were produced during the same period, but do not adhere to our definition of costume jewelry in Chapter 1, are not included. Most of the jewelry shown is unmarked jewelry, though some may have been produced by major manufacturers of costume jewelry which often did not mark their pre WWII jewelry. Some signed early jewelry by specific American manufacturers is displayed in Chapter 3 and others in the chapter on gold filled and silver jewelry. Early marked and unmarked jewelry are also shown in chapters 4, 5 and 9.

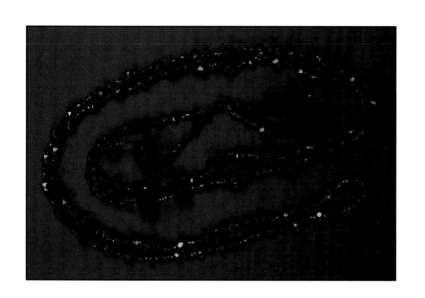

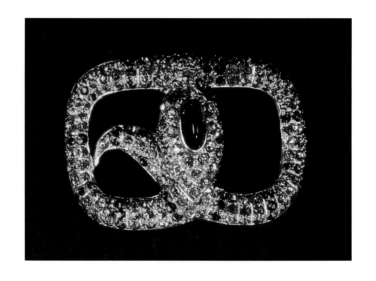

Opposite page, top left: *Long strand of faceted Bohemian glass beads (flapper beads). $60.00 – 85.00.*

Opposite page, top right: *Left: Festoon necklace in gilded brass with simulated pearl and faceted stones. $75.00 – 85.00. Right: Necklace in gold filled chain with tourmaline drops. $75.00 – 100.00.*

Opposite page, bottom left: *Center: Pendant in clear faceted and sculptured stones on velvet string. Marked WMCA, the trademark of White Metal Casters' Association, Inc. Early 1930s. $50.00 – 80.00. Left and right: Two Bohemian glass necklaces made of faceted glass beads. $65.00 – 95.00.*

Opposite page, bottom right: *Belt buckle in clear, green, and red stones, depicting a serpent. Marked F.N.CO., the trademark of Fishel, Nessler & Co., New York City. The firm was in business from mid the 1860s to mid 1930s. $150.00 – 200.00.*

Top right: *Shoe buckles with paste stones. The top pair is marked EVERGRIP, PAT APPL'D FOR, F.B.N.CO. The middle pair is marked HOLFAST. $45.00 – 60.00 pair. The bottom pair is unmarked. $30.00 – 45.00.*

Bottom right: *Top left: Brooch with multicolored paste stones. $40.00 – 65.00. Top right: Snake bracelet with woven gilded brass body. These were usually made during the pre-Civil War era of gold with gemstone eyes. $80.00 – 125.00. Center: Sash pin made in brass with simulated hasp. $50.00 – 85.00. Lower left: Portrait of a couple, hand-painted on porcelain and mounted on gilded brass. $45.00 – 65.00. Lower right: Pin with large amethyst glass stone on antiqued brass mounting. $45.00 – 65.00.*

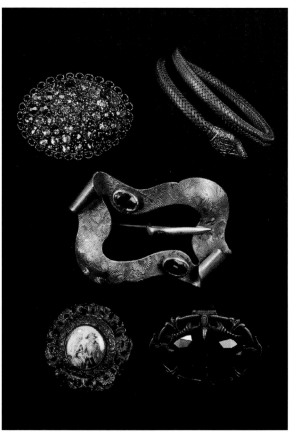

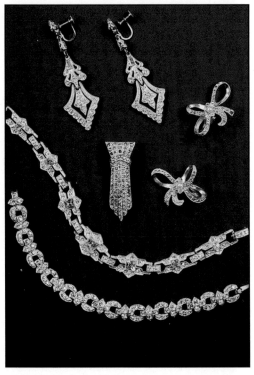

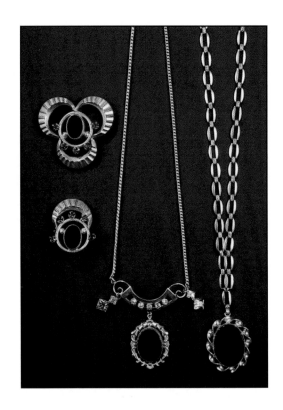

Opposite page, top left: *Two 1930s brooches. Top: $60.00 – 85.00. Bottom: $40.00 – 60.00.*

Opposite page, top right: *Intaglio jewelry in glass simulating jade, carnelian, and black onyx. These were fashionable during the Victorian era and were also manufactured in the 1930s during the Victorian Revival period. Top left: Earrings with sterling silver mountings. $30.00 – 45.00. Top right: Pendant on brass mounting. $75.00 – 100.00. Bottom: Bracelet on brass mounting. $75.00 – 100.00.*

Opposite page, bottom left: *Top: Edwardian screw back earrings. $25.00 – 40.00. Center: Hair ornament. Marked F.N.CO., trademark of Fishel, Nessler & Co., $40.00 – 60.00.*
Top right: Clip bow earrings, Pat. # 1,967,965, and unique Marino clips. Ca. 1934. $20.00 – 30.00. (See Marino, Chapter 3.) Bottom: Two white metal bracelets with clear stones. $35.00 – 50.00 each.

Opposite page, bottom right: *Gold top or gold filled jewelry. Center: Pendant with onyx and clear stones. Marked with letter M superimposed over letter C, trademark of I. Michelson Co., founded in Philadelphia early 1860s and out of business by 1916. $50.00 – 75.00. Upper left: Brooch with polished onyx in the center, marked with initials CM in similar formulation as the center necklace and 1/20 12kt Gold Filled. $35.00 – 55.00. Lower left: Unmarked gold filled pin, possibly made by the same manufacturer. $20.00 – 35.00.*
Right: Unmarked pendant with polished onyx stone. $35.00 – 55.00.

Top: *Unmarked bracelet with multicolored marquise stones mounted on gilded brass with filigree metal work. $65.00 – 95.00.*

Middle: *Six unmarked brooches with diverse motifs. The lower center piece is marked sterling on an applied plaque and features a large faceted genuine amethyst stone. $150.00 – 250.00.*
Others, $45.00 – 75.00.

Bottom: *Two slender bracelets with interesting clasps. The top piece is in gilded, pressed, and stamped goldtone metal with clear faceted paste stones. The clasp is marked FISCHER'S PAT SNAP. $40.00 – 60.00. The lower piece with identical clasp features carved coral central stone, plastic coral, and glass beads with marcasite accent. The clasp only is marked PAT SNAP. $65.00 – 95.00.*

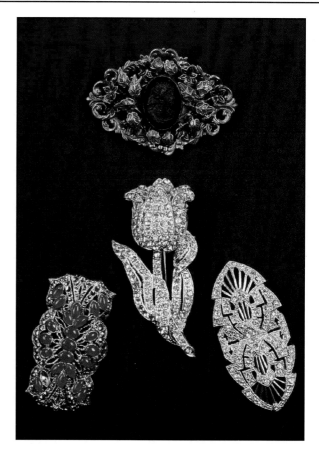

Top left: *Left: Locket with a lady's portrait in a glass bead frame. Fancy chain. $75.00 – 100.00. Center: Locket with black glass cameo with early 1930s photograph inside. $50.00 – 75.00. Right: Gold filled locket on a book chain. $125.00 – 150.00.*

Top right: *Top: Brooch with glass cameo imitating lapis lazuli mounted on enameled metal work in floral design. $65.00 – 95.00. Center: Very large tulip brooch with rhinestones on white metal. $60.00 – 85.00. Lower left: Brooch highlighted by imitation carnelian stones. $50.00 – 70.00. Right: Large white metal brooch with rhinestones. $45.00 – 65.00.*

Left: *Left: Pendant in gilded brass and faceted Bohemian glass beads. $75.00 – 100.00. Right: Festoon type necklace featuring moonstones. $125.00 – 150.00.*

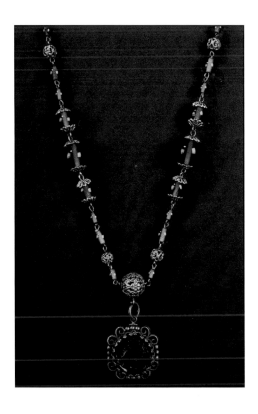

Top left: *Bohemian glass and filigree bead necklace with a framed black glass cameo. $65.00 – 95.00.*

Top right: *Left, top center and right: Diverse group of beauty and bar pins made of gold top, gold filled silver, polished, enameled, embossed, and engraved. These were especially popular at the turn of century. The tiny piece at lower left is a gold filled negligee clasp, and the three matching pieces at the upper right are marked Pat. June 21, 1910. $10.00 – 45.00 each. Center: Two hat ornaments, slender hair ornament, and a small unmarked pin with sculptured clear glass stones, possibly made by White Metal Casters' Association. $25.00 – 45.00 each.*

Right: *Top left and right: Champleve belt buckle highlighted by emerald green cabochon glass stone. $30.00 – 50.00. Top center: Dome-shaped pin with handset cobalt blue faceted stones. $45.00 – 65.00. Center: Two interesting pieces. The upper piece is a sterling silver butterfly fur clip/pin with hinged wings decorated with rhinestones. Marked JB inside a bottle or bell-shaped symbol. $95.00 – 150.00. The lower piece is a sunburst brooch made of brass with dangerously sharp and pointed ends decorated with geometric colored stones which certainly would have failed today's safety standards. $35.00 – 50.00. Lower left: Link bracelet of brass set with simulated pearl and rhinestones. $40.00 – 65.00. Center right: Gold top pin. $15.00 – 25.00.*

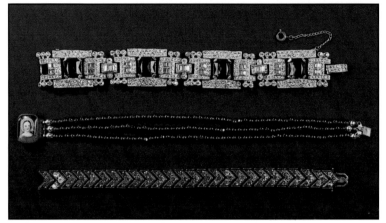

Top left: *Two flexible bracelets, one in the original box, marked Carmen, the trademark of Briggs Co., Attleboro, MA. Ca. 1910. $35.00 – 65.00. Add 20 percent for original box. Deduct 30 percent for bracelets with initials and monograms.*

Top right: *Upper left and right: Pair of rhinestone dress clips with Pat. # 1,801,126. Ca. 1932. $50.00 – 65.00. Center: Belt buckle. Gilded brass. Marked PF with an inverted cross between the two letters. $30.00 – 45.00. Center left and right: Pair of dress clips with a bird over flowers. $45.00 – 65.00. Remainder: Three dress clips. $30.00 – 60.00 each.*

Bottom right: *Top: Art Deco rhinestone bracelet featuring emerald stones. $65.00 – 95.00. Center: Bracelet with three strands of genuine garnet beads and hand-painted miniature portrait clasp. Every collector who also repairs jewelry will inevitably become tempted with the idea of rescuing some damaged jewelry. This bracelet is the author's attempt of combining garnet beads from a damaged 1900s necklace and a clasp from a 19th century portrait bracelet. No price. Bottom: Sterling silver and clear stones bracelet marked L & M on two leaves. Trademark of Leach & Miller Co., Attleboro, MA, in business from the early 1900s to early 1930s. The clasp is also marked patented July 7, 1925. $90.00 – 145.00.*

Chapter 3

American Costume Jewelry

This chapter covers 111 American manufacturers of costume jewelry, providing information on company history and marks and in most cases a few examples of their jewelry. Over 30 additional American manufacturers are identified in other chapters. In case of major manufacturers, several examples of their jewelry had to be shown in order to cover the broad range of jewelry they produced at different price levels. To the author's best knowledge, this is the most comprehensive attempt at providing background information on many known manufacturers of costume jewelry and a representative display of their jewelry. It is certainly not the first attempt, nor should be the last, because there are major gaps in our knowledge about the manufacturers of costume jewelry and their products. Interested readers should refer to the bibliography for a list of other efforts which have enhanced and deepened our understanding and appreciation of costume jewelry and its manufacturers. There are also several books that focus on or devote a section to designer jewelry.

Information on manufacturers of costume jewelry is scarce and fragmented, but the interest in collecting costume jewelry has encouraged many writers to research the subject and several books have already gone beyond the mere pictorial display of the jewelry to provide the readers with background information on the manufacturers. In compiling the background information on manufacturers, the author found the *Jewelers' Circular Keystone* an indispensable source, relying upon various editions for information on trademarks and locations. Some of the information on circa dates and personalities was also extrapolated from the same source. But several additional books were also relied upon for background information and are identified in the bibliography with an asterisk before the name of the author(s). The author also contacted many current manufacturers seeking information on company history and trademarks.

The description of the "typical" or different types of jewelry produced by many manufacturers is based on the author's knowledge of and familiarity with the collectible jewelry available in the market and would inevitably reflect the author's deficiencies and biases. Furthermore, given the nature of fragmented information, some contradictory and speculative, mistakes concerning personalities, location, and dates are quite possible and unavoidable. For this reason, the author welcomes readers' corrections, comments, and criticism.

There were many more manufacturers of costume jewelry, perhaps more than several hundred, about which we know little, but whose unmarked jewelry is encountered daily in the collectible market. There is a need for extensive and in-depth research to uncover such companies and gather information on their history and the type of jewelry they manufactured. Provided the readers will welcome this author's effort, future efforts will hopefully focus on systematic study of unmarked costume jewelry and its many unknown manufacturers in order to achieve a better and more comprehensive understanding and appreciation of the costume jewelry industry and its beautiful creations that shall continue to bedazzle our children and grandchildren well into the next century.

As a final note, the author uses the terms "marked" and "signed" interchangeably when identifying the manufacturers of the jewelry displayed, but prefers as correct, usage of "marked." Such a preference should not be surprising to those who are knowledgeable about other lines of antiques and collectibles, where marked mass-produced products are not usually referred to as signed, even in case of mass-produced art pottery, much of which reflects a more direct involvement of the individual producer. To refer to a mass-produced Coro pin as "signed" Coro is equivalent to referring to a depression glass saucer as "signed" Heisey, an old phonograph as "signed" Edison, a tea leaf ironstone teapot as "signed" Meakin, and a Model T car as "signed" Ford. The term "signed" should be reserved for works of art and products which reflect the labor and talents of their creator and their direct involvement in all or several phases of its production. Most costume jewelry would not fall into this category. Of course, using the correct term in no way reduces the beauty and value of costume jewelry, nor does it deny the talents and creativity of its many producers. As readers know, identifying products by their trademarks has not detracted interest from Meissen porcelain, Northwood glass, Rolex watches, and Parker pens, to mention a few. The demand for collectible costume jewelry shall continue to rise on an international scale; already some American-made pieces are commanding much higher prices in Europe and Japan than on the U.S. market.

Accessocraft

Two Monocraft (forerunner of Monet) salesmen, Edgar Rodelheimer and Theodore Steinman, founded Accessocraft in New York City, about 1930. The firm is still in business under the leadership of Theodore Steinman's son, Paul Steinman. Accessocraft manufactured a variety of jewelry and accessories with bold, innovative designs. Not every woman would necessarily find Accessocraft jewelry appealing, but it was admired by a particular class of consumers who appreciated the originality and uniqueness of its designs. Accessories produced included buckles, opera glasses, magnifying glass necklaces, and cobra and chain belts. Accessocraft also collaborated with well-known personalities in the fashion industry, such as Pauline Trigere and Anne Kline, introducing specialized lines of jewelry under their names. Accessocraft jewelry is usually marked with the company name on the back of the jewelry or on a metal tag attached to the chain. In relative prices, Accessocraft jewelry is not very expensive in the collectible market, nor was it when it was originally sold. In 1951, a pair of earrings could be purchased for $3.00 – 6.00, while pins sold for $6.00 – 10.00.

Left: *Accessocraft bracelet with alternating pottery and metal rings. $35.00 – 50.00.*

Right: *Lower left: Accessocraft hinged bracelet covered with snake leather inserts. $30.00 – 50.00. Center: Accessocraft locket with a large, forest green central stone. $40.00 – 55.00. Top: Pair of Accessocraft earrings made of seed beads. $15.00 – 25.00.*

Albion

No information regarding dates, location, and manufacturer of the jewelry marked Albion was available as of this writing. To the best of the author's knowledge, only one piece of Albion jewelry has ever been displayed in books on costume jewelry. Albion jewelry is very scarce on the collectible market which suggests that the manufacturer either did not mark much of the jewelry or was not in business for a very long time. The limited number of pieces seen by the author suggests that the jewelry was possibly manufactured between the mid 1950s to the early 1960s. When marked, the jewelry is marked either A or Albion.

Top: Pair of marked Albion earrings with gold washed metal leaves and simulated pearls. $10.00 – 15.00. Bottom: Necklace and matching earrings with pink opaque glass stones. $35.00 – 50.00.

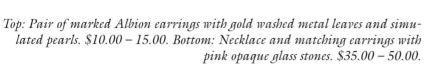

Amco

Amco is the trademark used by A. Micallef and Co., Inc., founded in 1919 in Providence, R.I. The company manufactured gold, gold filled, and silver jewelry including rings, cameo brooches, pendants, bracelets, and earrings. Amco jewelry has elegant and classic designs somewhat comparable to Van Dell jewelry. Much of the jewelry found in the collectible market is gold filled jewelry. The firm was still in business in the late 1970s, located at 100 South Street, Providence, R.I., but it may now be out of business since the author was unable to locate them at the above address.

Top: Gold filled pendant with matching earrings marked AMCO, 1/20 12 kt G.F. $35.00 – 50.00. Bottom: Attractive AMCO necklace and matching earrings with gold filled leaves and handset foil-less faceted blue stones. $100.00 – 140.00.

Ann

The author could not find any definite and reliable information on the manufacturer of the jewelry marked Ann. The Ann jewelry seen by the author employs quality rhinestones mounted on white or rhodium plated metal. The jewelry is of average to above average quality and not very common in the market. This may be the first exposure of Ann jewelry in a book on costume jewelry.

Top: Large brooch possibly depicting a sea creature. Marked ANN. $50.00 – 85.00. Lower left: Ann floral pin. $30.00 – 50.00. Lower right: Small rhinestone pin. $12.00 – 18.00.

Anson

Olof Anderson, an emigrant from Tansdorp, Sweden, was the founder of Anderson Tool & Die Co. which produced tools and dies for the jewelry industry. After WWII, the firm entered the jewelry business manufacturing men's collar holders, cuff links, and tie chains. In 1948, the current name Anson Incorporated, was adopted and the company began offering a complete line of men's jewelry. In 1967, women's jewelry was introduced. Anson, Inc., is located in Providence, R.I., and as of 1994 was still in business.

Various marked Anson pieces, 1930s – 1970. Only the lower center pin is for women. Tie tacks. $10.00 – 25.00. Cuff links. $15.00 – 30.00. Lady's rhinestone pin. $15.00 – 30.00.

Art

The background information on jewelry marked Art is very sketchy and little is known about its operations. The Art trademark was used by several companies but the Art jewelry shown here was probably produced by Art Mode Jewelry Creations Inc. The company was founded in the late 1940s and based on the designs and material used, must have continued its operation into at least the late 1960s. Art jewelry can be found in a broad range of designs and quality, and like Florenza and Hollycraft jewelry, is well under priced and not fully appreciated.

Some of the Art jewelry is similar to Florenza jewelry, resembling Victorian and Renaissance Revival jewelry. These pieces employ quality, uniquely colored rhinestones combined with fine filigree or stamped metalwork. These and figural pins, some of which are pavé set in a multitude of colors, are becoming very collectible and shall continue to rise in prices. Other pieces are of lower quality and resemble the average jewelry made by other major producers, such as Coro, Lisner, and Trifari.

Art brooch with marbleized glass.
$35.00 – 60.00.

Top left: *Outstanding Art creation using multicolored stones with special effect combined with faceted marquise and pastel stones. Rare find as a set. $350.00 – 450.00+.*

Top right: *Top: Art earrings with floral design made of painted metal. $20.00 – 30.00. Center left: Art earrings with pastel stones and pearl accented by green enamel leaf. $20.00 – 30.00. Center: Art brooch with pastel guilloche enamel insert surrounded by pearls on fine metalwork. $60.00 – 75.00. Center right: Art earrings with cabochon stones mounted on antiqued metal base. $20.00 – 30.00. Bottom: Art earrings with faux pearls and turquoise combined with antiqued metalwork. $30.00 – 40.00.*

Bottom left: *Top: Art earrings. $20.00 – 28.00. Center: Art butterfly brooch and matching earrings set with stones of various colors complemented by green enamel leaves. These were purchased as a set, but it appears that the earrings shown in the previous photograph also match this brooch. $65.00 – 90.00. Bottom: Art necklace with cabochon stones complemented by pastel rhinestones. $65.00 – 95.00.*

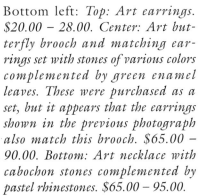

Bottom right: *Top: Art pin and matching earrings in shape of a crown with imitation rubies, pearls, and turquoise demonstrating the quality and workmanship which characterize most of Art jewelry, not yet fully appreciated on the collectible market. $100.00 – 135.00. Bottom left: Art dragonfly pin with open metalwork and enameled flowers. $50.00 – 75.00. Bottom right: Art brooch with mother-of-pearl and antiqued metalwork accented with simulated turquoise, pearls, and rhinestones. $45.00 – 65.00.*

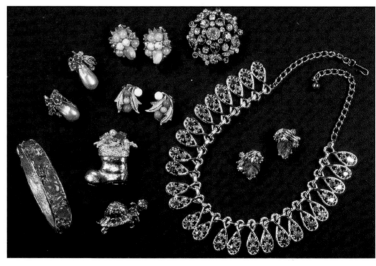

Top left: *Left: Art pendant of silvertone metal and red opaque stones. $45.00 – 65.00. Center: Art necklace showing interesting open metal-work enhanced by coin drops. $45.00 – 65.00. Right: Art brooch and earrings displaying silver on gold in an open work filigree design. $50.00 – 75.00.*

Top right: *Art necklace and matching earrings with high quality textured metal surface set with topaz rhinestones. $70.00 – 100.00.*

Bottom left: *An exceptional design with Oriental motif inspired by antique Chinese jewelry which normally combined jade with high carat gold. $200.00 – 250.00.*

Bottom right: *Left: Art hinged bracelet set with amber nuggets. $50.00 – 65.00. Pearl earrings with enameled leaves. $30.00 – 40.00. Top: Two pairs of Art earrings. $25.00 – 35.00. Art brooch. $35.00 – 45.00. Center: Art turtle pin. $25.00 – 40.00. Art golden boot pin. $30.00 – 45.00. Right: Art silvertone necklace set with aurora borealis rhinestones. $45.00 – 65.00. Art earrings. $25.00 – 35.00.*

Left: *Left: Red cabochons and clear rhinestones are combined with white enameled leaves to create this Art floral fruit pin. $35.00 – 50.00. Right: A large red central cabochon stone is used to decorate this figural bird pin marked Art. $70.00 – 95.00.*

Above: *Art trembler depicting a butterfly landing on a flower. $35.00 – 60.00.*

Avon

Jewelry marked AVON is distributed by the Avon Products, Inc., famous for its cosmetic products. The firm was founded in 1886 by D. H. McConnell, Sr. as California Perfume Company. The Avon line was introduced in the late 1920s; the company changed its name to Avon Products, Inc., in 1939. The company was exceptionally successful, largely due to its direct marketing approach, selling its products through local Avon representatives. Later, Avon added jewelry, giftware, and lingerie to its long list of cosmetic products. Avon jewelry varies in quality from cheaply made jewelry to interesting pieces that are comparable to better Sarah Coventry and average Coro jewelry. The jewelry is not yet widely collected, but is sought by collectors of Avon products.

Very large Avon necklace set with imitation stones. This is a better than average Avon piece that came in a cushioned box inserted inside another box. Despite fancy packaging, a glance would clearly indicate that imitating fine jewelry or the "real thing" was not the manufacturer's intention. $25.00 – 40.00. Avon earrings. $10.00 – 15.00. Avon acorn with faux pearl inserts. $15.00 – 20.00.

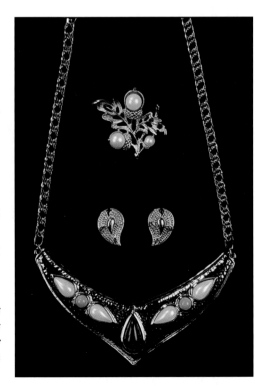

Top left: *Left: Avon pendant and matching earrings with simulated pearls. $15.00 – 20.00. Center: Avon cameo pin. $8.00 – 12.00. Right: Avon pendant and matching earrings with higher quality rhinestones in a pleasant arrangement. $25.00 – 40.00.*

Top right: *Left: Two pairs of Avon earrings. $5.00 – 10.00 each. Avon mouse figural pin. $12.50– 20.00. Center: Avon pendant. $10.00 – 15.00. Right: Avon plastic bracelet imitating carved Oriental ivory. Marked Made in Hong Kong. $10.00 – 15.00. Avon owl figural pin. $15.00 – 20.00. Avon imitation coral pin. $10.00 – 15.00. Bottom: Bracelet. $10.00 – 15.00.*

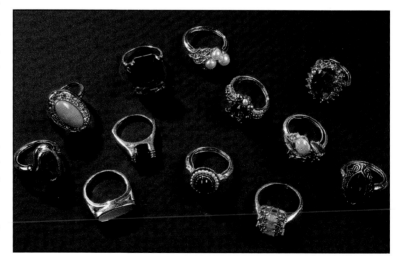

Right: *A group of higher quality Avon rings. $10.00 – 25.00.*

Barclay

The author could not find any information on Barclay's history. According to several individuals who actually sold the jewelry in the 1950s, the firm was a prolific manufacturer of costume jewelry in the 1940s and 1950s, selling its jewelry through better department stores, including Marshall Field's in Chicago.

Much of Barclay's jewelry is of average quality with clear and multicolored rhinestones in designs somewhat similar to average Coro or Lisner jewelry. The firm also manufactured metal and enameled tin jewelry. Marked pieces are not very common and this may be the first exposure of the firm's jewelry in a book on costume jewelry. Signed pieces are marked Barclay on clips or clasps, but the author strongly suspects that not all of the jewelry was marked. The Barclay trademark should not be confused with McClelland Barclay whose jewelry is also displayed in this chapter.

Top: Hand-painted tin flowers with black cabochon central stones make up these Barclay earrings. $20.00 – 30.00. Center: Barclay necklace in silvertone metal decorated with rhinestones. $40.00 – 60.00.

Beau/Beaucraft

Beau and Beaucraft are registered trademarks of Beaucraft, Inc., founded in 1947 in Providence, R. I. Both marks are found on sterling silver jewelry manufactured by the company. Several other trademarks which combine the letter B with "Ster" or "sterling" were also used by the company. Beaucraft also manufactured fine jewelry made of 14k gold. These are always marked Beau, 14k, and cannot be confused with the silver jewelry. The company is still in business, located in Providence, R.I. and has a Fifth Avenue showroom in New York City.

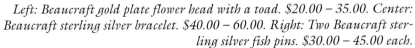

Left: Beaucraft gold plate flower head with a toad. $20.00 – 35.00. Center: Beaucraft sterling silver bracelet. $40.00 – 60.00. Right: Two Beaucraft sterling silver fish pins. $30.00 – 45.00 each.

Sterling silver musical note jewelry by Beaucraft. Top left and right: Two small, identical pins. $15.00 – 20.00 each. Center: Large pin with matching screw back earrings. $50.00 – 70.00. Bottom: Round pin. $30.00 – 45.00.

Beaujewels

Many dealers and several books on costume jewelry attribute the trademark Beaujewels to Beaucraft, Inc. According to the rumors, the company used Beaucraft on sterling silver jewelry and Beaujewels on its rhinestone and bead jewelry. But Beaucraft advertisements in the trade journals always list the company's trademarks and it has never claimed Beaujewels as one of its registered marks. Inquiries placed with the company confirmed this fact and sent the author in search of the real manufacturer of Beaujewels jewelry. Further inquiries produced no definite and reliable results.

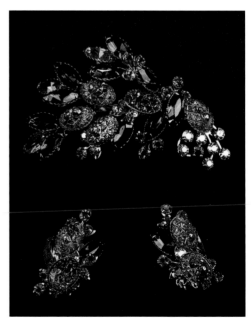

The jewelry marked Beaujewels was possibly manufactured by Bowman Foster, Inc., during 1950s – 1960s period. The firm went out of business in the 1970s. The 1984 *Jewelers' Circular* lists the trademark Beaujewels inside an oval frame as that used by Bowman and Foster with no current address which normally indicates "out of business" status.

Beaujewels jewelry is attractive and of above-average quality. Most of the jewelry found on the collectible market is either rhinestone or bead jewelry. The pieces shown here are typical examples of Beaujewels jewelry.

Large brooch and matching earrings with marquise and sculptured stones. Marked Beaujewels. $60.00 – 85.00.

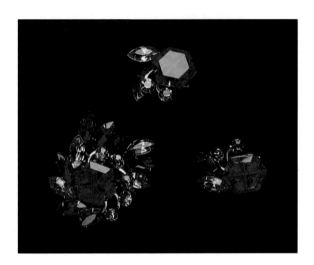

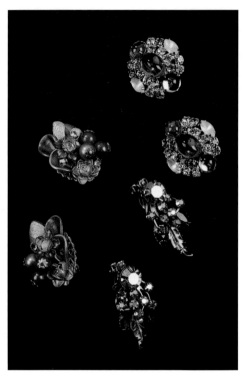

Above: *Pin and matching earrings in red faceted stones of various shapes. $40.00 – 65.00.*

Right: *Three pairs of Beaujewels earrings. $20.00 – 30.00 each.*

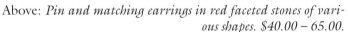

Bergere

Bergere is the trademark used by Herbert & Pohs, Inc., founded in New York City around 1947. The company discontinued production sometime in the mid 1960s. Bergere jewelry, which exhibits fine workmanship and quality designs, is just beginning to be noticed and demanded by collectors. Although the firm sold its jewelry nationally through fine department stores, such as New York's Lord & Taylor and Marshall Field's in Chicago, it must have manufactured limited quantities of each line, since its jewelry is not very common in the market today. Most of the jewelry seen by the author appears to have

been made in the late 1950s and 1960s. This suggests that earlier postwar pieces will be extremely rare and difficult to find.

Compared to other contemporary costume jewelry, Bergere jewelry was not very expensive. In 1951, a single-strand bead necklace could be purchased for $5.00 and drop or button earrings for $2.00. In the mid 1950s, Bergere introduced a line of Art Moderne meshed or stamped metal jewelry which it advertised as having "the look of real jewelry." These pieces are somewhat similar to metal jewelry manufactured by other major companies, such as Monet and Trifari. At the time, the prices ranged from $4.00 for small cuff bracelets to $11.00 for very wide giant mesh bracelets.

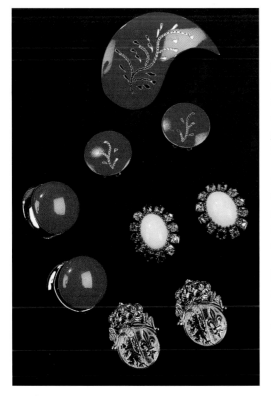

Left: *Top: Pin and matching earrings with enameled surface and engraved stylized tree. $35.00 – 50.00. Center: Two pairs of marked Bergere earrings. Left, with domed plastic "stone," and right, with opaque white glass framed by blue rhinestones. $15.00 – 25.00 each. Bottom: Bergere metal earrings with heraldic design. $25.00 – 40.00.*

Right: *Top: Bergere metal necklace. $20.00 – 35.00. Bottom: Bergere flexible metal bracelet. $25.00 – 35.00.*

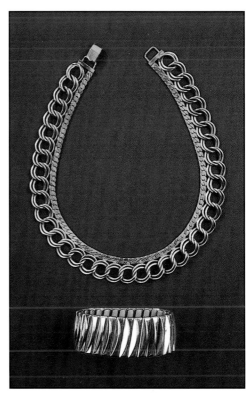

Bogoff

Bogoff was founded in Chicago in 1946. The *Jewelers' Circular* lists the trademark belonging to Spear Novelty Co., of Chicago. Bogoff jewelry displays elegant and graceful designs employing top quality rhinestones with tremendous glitter and reflections. The stones are usually set on rhodium plated or silvertone metal, demonstrating fine workmanship. In many ways Bogoff jewelry resembles Eisenberg jewelry, but it is not as high in quality or prices. The jewelry must have been manufactured in relatively limited quantities since it is not very common in the collectible market. It is not clear when Bogoff went out of business, but based on the designs of the jewelry seen by the author, it must have not lasted beyond the late 1960s. The jewelry is usually marked Bogoff or Jewels by Bogoff. Because of its good quality and attractive designs, Bogoff jewelry will continue to rise in prices. Currently, an average rhinestone necklace can be purchased for about $45.00, though the asking price may be quite higher, particularly in East Coast shows and antique malls.

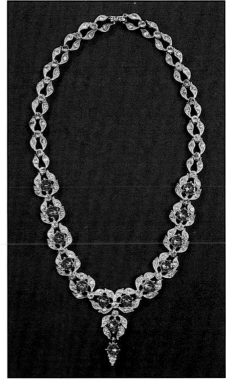

Elegant Bogoff necklace combining blue and clear rhinestones in classic Bogoff design that instantly identifies its maker. $175.00 – 250.00.

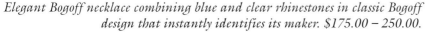

Top left: *Bogoff necklace and earrings reflecting the company's graceful designs. $150.00 – 200.00.*

Top right: *Bogoff necklace and matching earrings. $150.00 – 200.00.*

Bottom left: *Left: Bogoff earrings in a superb arrangement of pearls and rhinestones. $50.00 – 70.00. Bogoff semicircle rhinestone earrings. $35.00 – 50.00. Center: Bogoff necklace with crescents embracing brilliant rhinestones. $125.00 – 175.00. Right: Two pairs of Bogoff earrings. Top: Rhinestone hearts and pearl earrings. $45.00 – 60.00. Clear rhinestone earrings. $35.00 – 50.00. Hearts, crescents, and lacy designs were Bogoff hallmark.*

Bottom right: *Left: Small Bogoff pin with imitation ruby stones. $40.00 – 65.00. Bogoff bracelet. $50.00 – 75.00. Top center: Large Bogoff brooch. $75.00 – 100.00. Bottom right: Pair of Bogoff earrings. $40.00 – 50.00. Top right: Two pairs of Bogoff earrings. $30.00 – 45.00 each.*

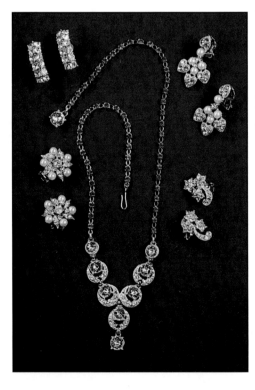

Boucher

Marcel Boucher, possibly the greatest designer and producer of costume jewelry in America, was born in France and trained as an apprentice to Cartier. He emigrated to the United States in the early 1920s and during the early 1930s designed jewelry for the Mazer Brothers in New York. In 1937, he established the Marcel Boucher and Cie Company in New York. Boucher produced the most exquisite costume jewelry, unsurpassed by any other, until it became a subsidiary of the Dovorn Industries, a watch manufacturing company, around 1972.

Boucher's jewelry reflected the classical tradition with highly creative and imaginative designs utilizing excellent rhinestones resembling gemstones. Technically superb with excellent metalwork, his costume jewelry can easily be mistaken for the "real thing." Sapphire, emerald, and ruby colored stones, especially in baguette and cabochon form, sometimes combined with turquoise and pearls and accented with

quality enamel work, are the hallmarks of his jewelry.

Marcel Boucher died in 1965, but his wife, Sandra Boucher, led the company until 1972. An able and creative designer in her own right, Sandra Boucher joined Marcel Boucher in 1949 as Sandra (Raymonde) Semensohn and worked as his assistant and designer until 1958. She then worked for Tiffany, but returned in 1961 and married Marcel in 1964. After the firm was sold, she worked as a designer for Ciner Manufacturing Company.

Marcel Boucher's talent and creativity, placing him among the very best of costume jewelry designers and producers, are just beginning to be appreciated. Accordingly, all of his jewelry is collectible with expected rise in prices. Most Boucher jewelry is signed and carries an inventory number. Earlier marks are Marboux or MB in a cartouche. Somewhat later marks are Marcel Boucher and Boucher. Based on the author's experience, it appears that Marboux was used on lower quality jewelry.

Above left: *Pair of Boucher earrings set with baguette rhinestones. $40.00 – 65.00. Boucher brooch, marked M. $150.00 – 200.00.*

Above right: *Large tree brooch set with faux turquoise. Marked Boucher with inventory #1594P. $250.00 – 300.00.*

Top left: *Circle pin set with clear and baguette simulated sapphire stones, marked Boucher with inventory #5580. $125.00 – 150.00. Two pairs of marked Boucher earrings, with inventory #6568 on the upper pair and 8222E on the lower pair. $50.00 – 75.00 each.*

Bottom left: *Boucher bracelet with simulated coral stones. $90.00 – 125.00. Two pairs of marked Boucher earrings with inventory #9753E on the left pair and 289 on the right pair. $60.00 – 85.00 each.*

Bottom right: *Interesting and unusual Boucher necklace and matching earrings in gold metal showing twisted fabric texture and buttons. Marked BORDOUX with inventory #1057. $200.00 – 300.00.*

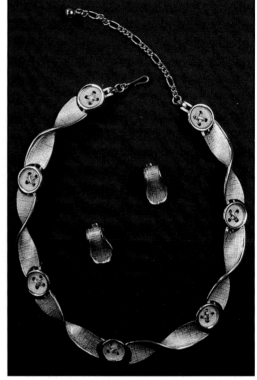

Above: *Bottom left: Boucher metal flower clip earrings. $50.00 – 80.00. Center: Boucher necklace. $200.00 – 250.00. Top: Boucher metal leaf pin. $45.00 – 65.00. Boucher earrings set with clear and baguette blue sapphire stones. Boucher manufactured different variations of this type of jewelry set with multicolored stones. $65.00 – 95.00. Top right: Boucher metal leaf pin and matching earrings with inventory #6829. $100.00 – 140.00.*

Bottom left: *Outstanding Boucher pin and earrings combining turquoise and rhinestones set on knotted gold metal. Marked Boucher with inventory #8467P. $300.00 – 400.00.*

Bottom right: *Exquisite brooch and matching earrings set with typical Boucher combination of turquoise and rhinestones. Unmarked. Pat. #136,452, but this could possibly be design patent number which would date the piece in the 1940s. As a rule, only marked jewelry is shown in this chapter, but this is one of three unmarked sets displayed in this chapter hoping that the readers could assist in identifying the jewelry. Two other manufacturers produced a similar type of jewelry. $600.00 – 850.00.*

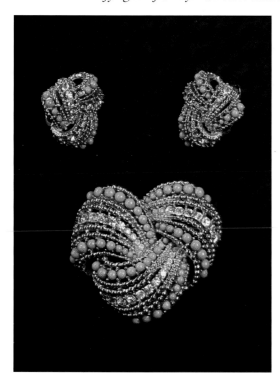 

Left: *Pendant and matching earrings with large faceted emerald stone and clear rhinestone accent. The green glass stone shows internal cloud and imperfections to better simulate emerald. The pendant can also be worn as a pin and has a clasp for removing the chain. Marked Boucher with inventory number 7937PN. $450.00 – 600.00.*

Opposite page, top: *Early Boucher pin decorated with round ruby red and clear rhinestones. MB mark. $250.00 – 400.00.*

Opposite page, bottom left: *Outstanding Boucher bird brooch reflecting Boucher's superior artistic design and highly skilled craftsmanship. $400.00 – 600.00.*

Opposite page, bottom right: *Boucher peacock pin in gold plated metal with cabochon and faceted rhinestones and enamel body. Marked Boucher with inventory number 3098. $350.00 – 500.00. Bracelet and matching earrings with satin plastic inserts. Marked MAR-BOUX with inventory number 792. $100.00 – 150.00.*

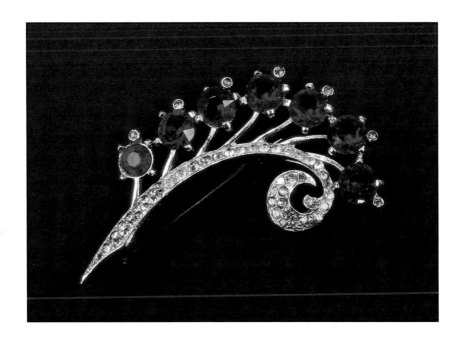

Brooks

No definite information regarding dates and manufacturer of jewelry marked Brooks could be gathered by the time of this publication. Based on the material and designs of the jewelry available in the collectible market, it must have been manufactured in the 1960s and 1970s. Most of Brooks jewelry is made of goldtone light metal enhanced by rhinestones and sometimes gold thread wire work. It is usually marked Brooks with a copyright symbol on a raised rectangular portion on the back of each piece.

Top: Brooks guitar pin. $35.00 – 45.00. Center: Brooks Christmas tree pin. $25.00 – 40.00. Bottom: Brooks Christmas tree earrings. $35.00 – 50.00.

BSK

As of this date, there is no information available on the name, location, and history of the firm that manufactured the jewelry marked BSK. Based on the designs of the jewelry available in the market, it appears that it was produced approximately between 1950 and the early 1970s. Most of the pieces are small, some with rhinestones which appear to be of Austrian origin. Both metal jewelry without stones as well as rhinestone studded jewelry were manufactured. Enamelwork was also used on some of the jewelry. BSK jewelry is of average quality, some with interesting and original designs, but not necessarily desirable as wearable jewelry by too many women or exciting to collectors. Among their intriguing work are metal pieces decorated with animal skins, such as zebra or tiger.

Top: Genuine cheetah skin decorates this marked BSK pin and earrings. $65.00 – 95.00. Bottom: BSK cat pin exhibiting quality craftsmanship. $45.00 – 65.00. Two BSK leaf brooches. $35.00 – 50.00.

BSK jewelry is not rare, but neither is there an abundance of it on the market. It normally sells at low to middle range prices. Any information on BSK history and jewelry provided by the readers is appreciated by the author.

Right: *Top left: BSK jewelry often reflects motifs derived from nature, such as this pin and matching earrings made of gold plated leaves. $40.00 – 60.00. Top right: BSK pin with a basketful of flowers. $35.00 – 45.00. Bottom: BSK pin with a plastic flower accompanied by gold plated leaves. $20.00 – 30.00. Gold plated BSK circle pin. $18.00 – 25.00. Right: BSK shell pin decorated with clear rhinestones. $20.00 – 30.00.*

Bottom left: *Left: Attractive BSK necklace and matching earrings with pastel plastic inserts. $50.00 – 85.00. Right: BSK necklace with multicolored pastel plastic inserts. $35.00 – 50.00. A pair of similar BSK screw back earrings in lavender color. $25.00 – 35.00.*

Bottom right: *Top: BSK goldtone necklace in floral design enhanced by pink rhinestones. $30.00 – 45.00. Center right: Two small BSK pins. $10.00 – 15.00 each. Left: Three pairs of BSK earrings. $15.00 – 25.00 each. Bottom: BSK bracelet with sculptured blue stones. $25.00 – 35.00.*

Buccellati

This trademark belongs to Buccellati Inc. which was the manufacturer of primarily antiqued silvertone jewelry in both traditional and modern designs. The firm went out of business sometime in the 1970s, but the author is not aware of the exact dates of operation. The firm's jewelry is in thick and chunky metal, giving the impression of aged silver. It is usually marked Mario Buccellati or just Buccellati in script signature form.

Top: Hinged bracelet and matching earrings. Marked Buccellati. $75.00 – 100.00.
Bottom: Buccellati earrings. $30.00 – 50.00.

Carl-Art

Carl-Art Inc., was founded around 1937 in Providence, R.I. The firm manufactured sterling silver and gold filled jewelry and accessories. The trademark used by the company consists of an arrow going through the letters CA. Most of the Carl-Art jewelry is small sterling silver pieces and novelty items. The firm also manufactured 14k gold chains and charms. Carl-Art ceased operations sometime in the late 1980s. The last listing of the company name with a current address is in the 1984 *Jewelers' Circular.*

Sterling silver horseshoe and head pin. CA with an arrow mark.
$35.00 – 45.00. Sterling silver earrings with hematite stones. CA
with an arrow mark. $35.00 – 45.00.

Carnegie

Hattie Carnegie was born in Vienna in 1886 as Henrietta Kanengeiser. While in her teens, the family emigrated to the U.S. and adopted the name Carnegie. In the early 1900s she ventured into retail apparel business by opening several dress and hat shops in New York City. Her success led in 1918 to the founding of the Hattie Carnegie, Inc., which consisted of a chain of chic Parisian-style boutiques that retailed Carnegie-designed clothing. She also began manufacturing jewelry to accent and complement her dresses which was initially sold at the same outlets. Her early jewelry, though not abundant, covers a broad range, including lavalieres, shoe buckles, hair and scarf ornaments. By the mid 1920s, her success and national popularity led to the mass production of her clothing and accessories which were wholesaled to other shops and department stores.

Almost from the beginning, Carnegie's boutiques were frequented by the rich and famous. Among her clientele were many prominent socialites and artists, including Joan Crawford. In relative prices, her jewelry was always expensive. All Carnegie jewelry is highly collectible, though somewhat overrated since the quality and designs of her jewelry do not always compare favorably with the jewelry of other major manufacturers such as Boucher, Haskell, Mazer, Hobe, Ciner, DeMario, DeRosa, Trifari, and Eisenberg.

Carnegie jewelry is frequently marked Hattie Carnegie or Carnegie. A third mark, not found as frequently and apparently unregistered, is HC within a diamond framed by a semi-oval. Carnegie jeweled hair ornaments and cases may be marked POOPED PUSSY CAT or POOPED POODLE.

Top right: *Silver necklace set with simulated turquoise makes up this Carnegie creation inspired by early nomadic Asian jewelry. HC mark. Rare among Carnegie jewelry. $150.00 – 250.00.*

Right: *Carnegie bug pins. Both marked Hattie Carnegie on an applied oval plaque. The silver bug on the right is a trembler with wings on springs. $95.00 – 135.00. Book and asking prices for this pin vary from $90.00 to 200.00. Gold pin. $70.00 – 100.00.*

Top left: *Carnegie floral pin and matching earrings with enamel leaves and framed glass petals. $85.00 – 135.00.*

Top right: *A Carnegie fish pin decorated with simulated turquoise and pearl. $75.00 – 100.00*

Bottom left: *A Carnegie cat with minute rhinestones and black enamel combination. This pin is seldom found in good condition; usually some of the stones are missing. $65.00 – 95.00.*

Bottom right: *Carnegie bracelet in blue rhinestones featuring a large cloudy blue cabochon central stone. $75.00 – 100.00.*

Castlecliff

Castlecliff, Inc., was founded by Clifford Furst in New York City around 1945. Operating from its Fifth Avenue, headquarters, Castlecliff acquired a reputation for manufacturing quality costume jewelry. Some of its jewelry was in plain gold plated metal, sometimes enameled, while others were set with rhinestones, beads, and pearls. The firm aggressively marketed its jewelry advertisements in all of the major "fashion" magazines such as *Harper's Bazaar* and *Vogue,* presenting its products as the "talked about jewelry." Although marketed through fine department stores such as Bloomingdale, Castlecliff jewelry was not very expensive. In the mid 1950s, earrings sold at an average price of $6.00 and necklaces could be purchased for $12.00 – 15.00. The jewelry is usually marked with the company name. According to various sources, Castlecliff stopped production around 1970, but the 1977 *Jewelers' Circular* lists Castlecliff Jewelry, Inc.

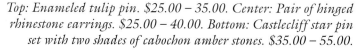

Top: Enameled tulip pin. $25.00 – 35.00. Center: Pair of hinged rhinestone earrings. $25.00 – 40.00. Bottom: Castlecliff star pin set with two shades of cabochon amber stones. $35.00 – 55.00.

Caviness

Capitalizing on her success in the garment industry, Alice Caviness began production of costume jewelry after WWII. The jewelry exhibits bold designs and is not very common in the collectible market. Disregarding the name and evaluating the jewelry based strictly on designs, originality, and workmanship, one must concede that Caviness jewelry is highly overrated and overpriced in the collectible market. Although Caviness died in 1983, production continued under the leadership of her partner, Lois Stevens. The firm is still in business, located in Malverne, Long Island, N.Y.

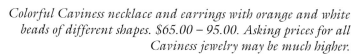

Colorful Caviness necklace and earrings with orange and white beads of different shapes. $65.00 – 95.00. Asking prices for all Caviness jewelry may be much higher.

Left: *Top: Sterling silver Caviness wheel pin with cultured pearl. $35.00 – 50.00. Bottom: Two pairs of Caviness earrings. $35.00 – 45.00 each.*

Right: *Bracelet and matching earrings made of iridescent beads. Marked Alice Caviness. $60.00 – 95.00.*

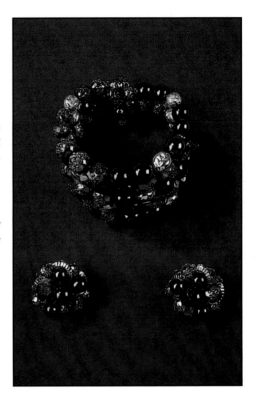

Celebrity

Jewelry marked Celebrity was apparently marketed through home party plans similar to Emmons and Sarah Coventry by a New York based company with a possible name of Celebrity Jewelry Co. Actually, the trademark Celebrity is the officially registered trademark of Norman Kivitz Co., also listed as Celebrity Jewelry Co., located in Philadelphia. According to a phone conversation with Mark Kivitz, an executive of the Norman Kivitz Company, the firm manufactures only fine jewelry made of precious metals and gemstones, and is in no way related to the New York outfit that distributed the costume jewelry shown here.

Celebrity jewelry is of variable quality. Some of the jewelry is in silver or goldtone metal in modern designs lacking ornamental imitation stones. Others employ faux pearls and rhinestones. The rhinestone jewelry is usually of higher quality and commands higher prices on the collectible market. Three types of trademarks were used. Celebrity; Celebrity, N.Y. on an oval plaque; and Celebrity with copyright symbol. Only one piece in a set may be marked.

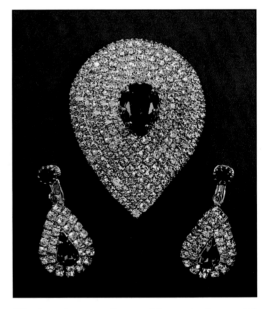

Pin/pendant and matching earrings with green central stone in a field of clear rhinestones. Marked CELEBRITY. This is one of the better Celebrity pieces. $40.00 – 75.00.

Left: *Top: Low quality Celebrity brooch and matching earrings. Pierced gold wash metal with a large pearl-like central "stone." $20.00 – 30.00. Lower left: Pair of clip earrings with metal rose mounted on black glass. $12.00 – 18.00. Lower right: Celebrity metal ram pendant. $10.00 – 18.00.*

Right: *Two antiqued silvertone metal pieces marked CELEBRITY. Pendant. $15.00 – 20.00. Bracelet. $20.00 – 25.00.*

Charel

Charel is the trademark used by Charel Jewelry Co., Inc., established in Brooklyn, N.Y., about 1945. The firm manufactured a complete line of costume jewelry, some showing Art Moderne influence. Some of the jewelry employs light and pastel colored plastic inserts set on plated metal in subdued modern designs. Charel jewelry is not very common and has received little exposure in books on costume jewelry.

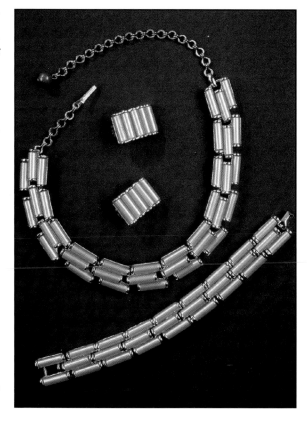

Necklace, bracelet, and earrings with pastel plastic inserts, marked Charel. $125.00 – 165.00.

Charel necklace. $60.00 – 90.00. Two pairs of marked Charel earrings. $30.00 – 40.00 each.

Ciner

Ciner Manufacturing Company, a family owned enterprise, was founded by Emanuel Ciner in 1892, producing expensive fine jewelry. Ciner began making costume jewelry in 1931 and is still in business. The company produced a broad range of pieces resembling fine jewelry and marketed them through select high priced stores. Ciner jewelry is characterized by beautiful designs, superbly executed by employing high quality small stones in a variety of colors, turquoise, and pearls, combined with superior gold plate metalwork. To identify a Ciner in a showcase, look for many tiny stones of different colors arranged adjacent to each other, sometimes combined with tiny turquoise and pearls in floral patterns. Post WWII Ciner costume jewelry is always signed Ciner, a registered trademark used since 1892; it is not clear whether all of the jewelry was marked.

Exquisite bracelet and earrings by Ciner in a delicate and timeless arrangement of faceted rhinestones simulating ruby and diamond. $150.00 – 200.00.

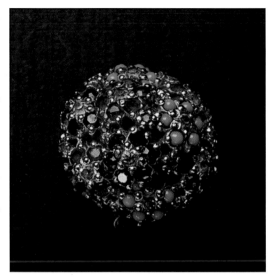

Left: *Ciner owl pin. $70.00 – 100.00. Ciner pin decorated with simulated turquoise. Like Boucher, Ciner frequently employed turquoise in many masterful creations. $100.00 – 145.00. Ciner earrings with pearl drops. $40.00 – 65.00.*

Right: *Ciner ring using a variety of stones simulating gemstones and exhibiting fine craftsmanship for which Ciner is famous. Rings were not common among Ciner jewelry. $200.00 – 250.00.*

Cini

Cini was founded in Boston, Mass., by Guglielmo Cini in 1922. The firm is the manufacturer of sterling silver and gold jewelry. Guglielmo arrived in the U.S. from Italy at the age of 17, already familiar with the art of jewelry making. Soon his talents as a great designer and craftsman were recognized, building a large clientele, including movie and theatrical stars. Cini sterling silver jewelry reflects the skill and talents of a master jeweler, creating exquisite sculpture-like jewelry avidly sought by collectors today. Some of the jewelry is reproductions of antique jewelry, but many pieces are Cini's original creations with the look of classical and 19th century designs.

Sterling repoussé, filigree, or solid three dimensional jewelry, sometimes hand wrought, were his hallmark. Even many cast pieces were hand-finished. Some of the jewelry employed foil-less colored stones in tasteful and elegant designs. Cini jewelry is easy to identify; look for antique style three-dimensional sterling silver jewelry with classical motifs. Cini jewelry is usually, but not always, signed Cini. The company ceased production around 1970, but it resumed operations in 1993.

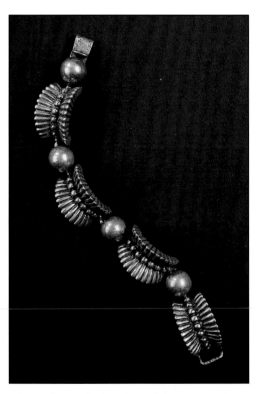

This sculptured silver bracelet is a typical creation of the master jeweler Guglielmo Cini. $200.00 – 350.00.

Top left: *Poison ring opened, showing the inner compartment.*

Top right: *Sterling silver Cini crown pin and earrings. $125.00 – 175.00.*

Bottom left: *Cini sterling silver poison ring with cameo-like face reminiscent of antique European jewelry. Rings were not common Cini jewelry. $250.00 – 350.00.*

Claudette

Claudette is the trademark belonging to Premier Jewelry Co., Inc., first used in 1945. It is not clear for how long the jewelry was manufactured, but it is the author's opinion that the trademark was not used for an extended period, perhaps, not beyond the mid 1950s. Marked Claudette, jewelry is extremely rare and those pieces seen by the author employ quality rhinestones in a multitude of colors and shapes demonstrating fine workmanship. The jewelry has received little attention; this may be its first exposure in a book on costume jewelry.

Marked Claudette clip earrings with speckled cabochon stone surrounded by iridescent rhinestones. $30.00 – 45.00.

Coro

If a curious collector or admirer of costume jewelry decides to explore Grandma's jewelry box, he or she will probably find at least one piece signed Coro. The company was a prolific producer of costume jewelry in thousands of diverse designs at affordable prices. The history of Coro dates back to 1901 when Emanuel Cohn and Gerald Rosenberg opened a small shop in New York selling jewelry and personal accessories later becoming known as Coro. The mark incorporates the first two letters of each partner's name.

The company expanded rapidly, partly due to the work of a prolific designer, Adolph Katz, who created many designs which were loved and bought by people of all ages, and a dynamic master salesman, Royal Marcher, who successfully directed the sales and marketing. By the mid 1920s, Coro was the largest manufacturer of costume jewelry with a workforce of over 2,000 and at the depth of the Great Depression when many plants were shutting down or operating below capacity, Coro built a new modern plant in Providence. The company continued to grow, with manufacturing operations extended internationally to England, Canada, and Mexico. Coro ceased production in 1979 after the retirement of Rosenberg, but Coro, Inc., in Canada was still in operation as of 1990.

The broad range of designs and immense volume of jewelry produced by Coro at all price levels — as low as fifty cent pins sold in five-and-dime stores to as high as hundred dollar pieces offered for sale in specialty shops — defies description in a brief essay. Suffice to say that some rhinestone studded Coro jewelry can compare with the very best produced by the industry.

Coro used many different marks, among which Coro (in use since 1919) is the most common, found on low as well as high quality jewelry. Coro Craft (in use since 1937) was initially used on higher quality pieces of jewelry as well as personal accessories, while Corocraft (one word) was used after WWII. Marks that incorporate a box and a Pegasus (winged horse) were used primarily after the war. Other trademarks which include the name Coro are Coro Elegant and Coro Supreme used on pearl jewelry; Corograms used on jewelry initials; Corolite used on jewelry as well as personal accessories; Coro Radiance, Corochrome, Coro-Klad, Coro Magic, and Coro Originals.

Over 70 additional trademarks lacking the company's name were also used. Among these are Aristocrat and Valiant (on pearls); Quick-Trik and Round the Clock (earrings only); Dream-boat (lockets); Andree (accessories); and Cellini, Jewelcraft, Colorama, Debutante, Duette, Maharani, Paragon, Raven, Splendor, and Vendome.

Early Coros, Duettes, figurals with a clear lucite central stone known as a jelly belly, Mexican sterling pieces, some Corocrafts, most Vendomes, and well designed sets of the 1930 – 1950s are highly collectible.

Above left: *Top: Coro Duette. $130.00 – 160.00. Rhodium plated Coro brooch combining clear and blue rhinestones in a floral design. $60.00 – 85.00. Center: Coro necklace. $40.00 – 60.00. Right: Coro Pin and matching earrings. $35.00 – 50.00.*

Above right: *Top left: Large Coro Duette. $140.00 – 175.00. Top right: Pavé set Corocraft pin. $50.00 – 75.00. Center: Coro brooch and matching earrings in floral motif set with clear rhinestones. $50.00 – 65.00. Bottom: This Coro brooch combines rhinestones of various colors and shapes in an attractive floral design. $50.00 – 75.00. Coro link bracelet. $30.00 – 45.00.*

Opposite page, top left: *Coro necklaces. $40.00 – 65.00 each. Coro bracelet. $35.00 – 45.00.*

Opposite page, top right: *Corocraft goldtone necklace set with clear baguette rhinestones. $85.00 – 135.00.*

Opposite page, bottom left: *Left: Two pairs of Coro earrings, one set with plastic and the other with simulated pearls. $12.00 – 18.00 each. Top: Coro flexible bracelet with a large topaz stone surrounded by pearls. $50.00 – 70.00. Center: Large Coro-craft brooch combining simulated pearls and rhinestones in a floral motif. $50.00 – 85.00. Bottom: Coro pin and matching earrings. $50.00 – 75.00. Right: Coro coral glass cameo mounted on sterling vermeil. $50.00 – 75.00.*

Opposite page, bottom right: *Top: Coro earrings. $20.00 – 25.00. Center: Large circle brooch with iridescent rhinestones of unusual color seen only on Coro and jewelry made by two other companies. $45.00 – 65.00. Coro necklace. $35.00 – 50.00. Bottom: Coro necklace. $50.00 – 65.00.*

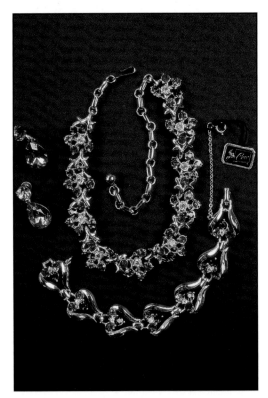

Opposite page, top left: *Parure consisting of necklace, bracelet, and earrings set with large faux turquoise nuggets accented by blue rhinestones. $95.00 – 135.00.*

Opposite page, top right: *Top left: Coro necklace with rhinestones of different shapes in typical Coro floral motif. $45.00 – 65.00. Top right: Coro floral spray pin. $35.00 – 50.00. Bottom: Coro bracelet and matching pin with plastic and topaz stones set on antiqued gold-tone metal base. The author has seen this bracelet with a slightly different shape and clasp. It is possible that one of them has been altered. $60.00 – 75.00.*

Opposite page, bottom left: *Top: Coro earrings with large yellow plastic stones and enameled flowers. $20.00 – 30.00. Pair of screw back earrings with large ruby stones. $15.00 – 25.00. Center: Large Coro coin brooch. $60.00 – 90.00. Bottom: Coro necklace. $45.00 – 65.00.*

Opposite page, bottom right: *Left: Pair of Coro earrings with large aquamarine stones. $20.00 – 30.00. Top: Coro necklace with multicolored stones. $50.00 – 75.00. Bottom: Higher quality Coro bracelet with multicolored stones. $50.00 – 85.00.*

Top right: *Very large hand-painted Coro brooch. $60.00 – 90.00.*

Below: *Coro jewelry with plastic inserts. Necklace. $35.00 – 50.00. Bracelet & matching earrings. $40.00 – 50.00. Bracelet. $25.00 – 35.00.*

Below, right: *Matching necklace, bracelet, and earrings in floral pattern. Marked Coro. $90.00 – 135.00.*

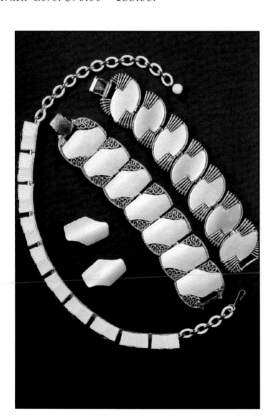

Top left: *Top right: Coro pin. $30.00 – 45.00. Right: Two pairs of Coro earrings with aurora borealis stones. $20.00 – 30.00 each. Center: Coro necklace. $45.00 – 65.00.*

Top right: *Top: Three Coro figural bird pins with large central stones. $40.00 – 60.00 each. Left: Small Coro floral pin with clear rhinestones. $35.00 – 45.00. Butterfly pin with multicolored stones. $35.00 – 45.00. Center: Coro dancing girl pin with pink baguette stones. $40.00 – 60.00. Right: Pair of Coro textured metal earrings. $20.00 – 25.00. Small metal apple pin. $15.00 – 20.00.*

Bottom left: *Left: Coro horseshoe pin and matching earrings with mother-of-pearl inserts. $35.00 – 50.00. Center: Coro necklace with red plastic inserts and beads. $35.00 – 50.00. Right: Coro necklace with beige and brown plastic inserts. $40.00 – 65.00. Similar Coro earrings. $20.00 – 27.50.*

Bottom right: *Top left: Coro leaf pin and matching earrings. $40.00 – 60.00. Right: Coro necklace. $40.00 – 65.00. Bottom: Coro necklace. $50.00 – 70.00.*

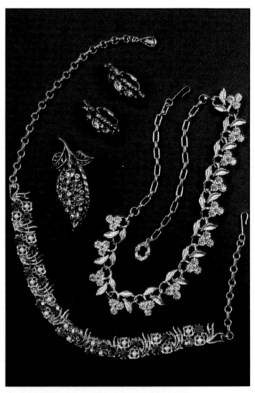

Top left: *Exquisite higher quality Coro necklace and earrings with metal leaves and various faceted stones of different colors and shapes. $95.00 – 140.00.*

Top right: *Coro three strand pearl necklace with fancy sterling clasp. Coro pearl jewelry in good condition is relatively rare. $150.00 – 200.00.*

Bottom left: *Coro enamel necklace and matching bracelet. $50.00 – 75.00. Pair of Coro enamel earrings. $12.50 – 17.50.*

Bottom right: *Left: Matching necklace, bracelet and earrings in floral design. $80.00 – 125.00. Right: Matching necklace and pin with textured metal leaves and rhinestones. $65.00 – 95.00.*

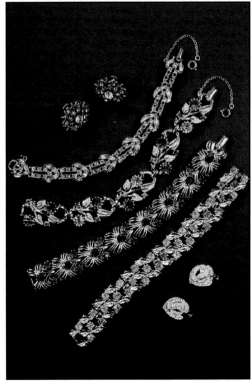

Top left: *Two Coro necklaces with cabochon stones. $40.00 – 65.00. Bracelet with dome-shaped plastic stones. $25.00 – 45.00 each.*

Top right: *Four Coro bracelets with diverse designs. $30.00 – 50.00 each. Two Coro screw back earrings. $20.00 – 30.00.*

Bottom left: *Top: Two Coro necklaces. $40.00 – 65.00 each. Two pairs of Coro earrings. $20.00 – 30.00 each. Bottom: Coro bracelet with sculptured flower stones. $35.00 – 55.00.*

Bottom right: *Top center: Coro-craft brooch in sterling vermeil depicting two birds and flowers. $85.00 – 135.00. Center left and right: Pair of Coro screw back earrings. $20.00 – 35.00. Bottom: Large Coro brooch with plastic "stones" and green rhinestone accent. $40.00 – 65.00. Also, three Coro novelty pins. $20.00 – 35.00 each.*

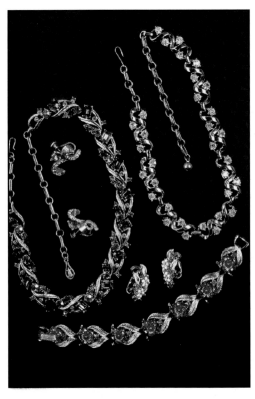

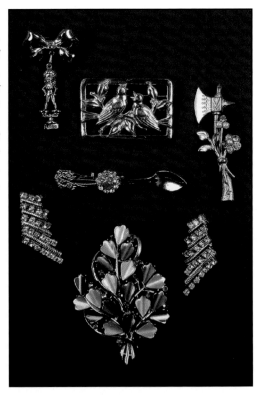

Dalsheim

Dalsheim was founded in New York City by Maurice J. Dalsheim in the late 1930s. The 1943 *Jewelers' Circular* lists the company as Dalsheim Accessories, Inc. Most of the jewelry was not signed and carried a tag identifying the company. Consequently, unless a piece is marked or still has the label attached, attribution is not possible. Some of the marked jewelry is made exclusively of seed pearls, glass or plastic beads. An April 1951 Dalsheim advertisement in *Vogue* magazine offers a line of jewelry made of "genuine bone." The necklace is priced at $2.00 while the earrings and bracelet could be purchased for $1.00 each. Other jewelry manufactured by the company includes small goldtone novelty pins resembling classically inspired Victorian designs, sometimes accented with enamel work. The jewelry may be marked White Jet or Dalsheim.

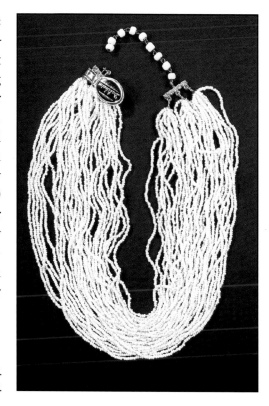

Impressive multistrand seed beads necklace with Dalsheim tag.
$40.00 – 65.00.

Danecraft

Victor and Thomas Primavera learned the jewelry trade from their father and in the 1930s owned the Primavera Brothers Jewelry Company, manufacturing costume jewelry. After his brother's death, Victor founded Danecraft, Inc., in 1939, in Providence R.I. During WWII, the company changed its name to Felch and Co., with Victor Primavera as president. After his death in 1977, the company changed its name again to Felch-Wehr Company. The firm is still in business manufacturing silver and vermeil jewelry which is marketed under the name Danecraft in better department stores.

Danecraft is known for quality silver jewelry with designs similar to the Scandinavian silver jewelry, occasionally set with stones and pearls. The firm aggressively promoted its jewelry, particularly its Wingback earrings, in the 1950s by advertising in major journals. The Wingback fastener was a unique design used by Danecraft as a substitute for clip and screw fasteners. The 1950s ads promoted this technology as "a totally new way to wear earrings." In the mid 1950s, a typical Danecraft sterling set sold for $25.00 – 35.00, while a pair of earrings had an average price of $6.00 – 10.00. (See also Wingback.)

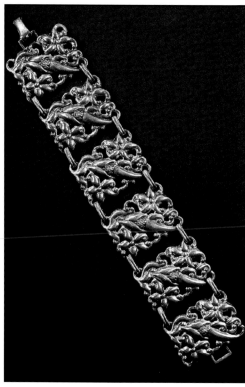

Sterling silver bracelet marked Danecraft. Typical earlier Danecraft jewelry similar to Scandinavian silver jewelry. $90.00 – 140.00.

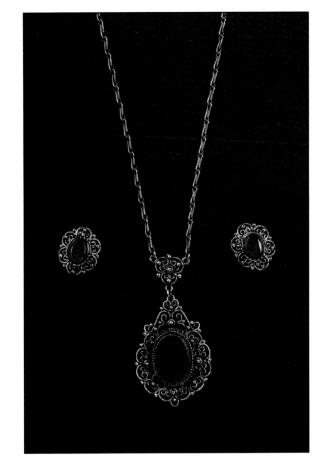

Top left: *Delicate Danecraft pin and matching earrings in sterling vermeil and cultured pearls depicting a bunch of grapes.* $100.00 – 150.00.

Top right: *Pendant and matching earrings with carnelian stone on filigree sterling vermeil metalwork. Marked sterling, Danecraft.* $75.00 – 100.00.

Bottom left: *Left: Three pairs of Danecraft sterling silver earrings.* $30.00 – 45.00 each. *Center: Sterling silver Danecraft bracelet.* $60.00 – 90.00. *Upper right: Danecraft sterling silver cat pin.* $35.00 – 50.00.

Dante

Dante is the registered trademark of Dante Inc., manufacturer primarily of men's jewelry and accessories found on the collectible market today. The company ceased operations in the 1970s. Dante jewelry is of exceptionally high quality. Some display linear Art Deco influences; others employ high quality and large imitation stones which immediately attract attention, especially on men's jewelry. Some of the jewelry was not marked and came in fancy marked boxes. If you find an unboxed set, look for the mark on the tie pin or tack.

Cuff links and tie pin with iridescent dome-shaped stones called "volcanic" by Dante. Tie pin and box marked Dante. $35.00 – 50.00.

B. David

B. David is the trademark of B. David Co. The firm is still in business, located in Cincinnati, Ohio. According to company spokesperson Vicki Petersman, the company was founded in 1945 and has a steady workforce of approximately 20 people. Currently the firm also manufactures fine jewelry made of precious metals and gemstones.

David Jewelry is usually enhanced by rhinestones in elegant and somewhat traditional designs. It is usually of above average material and quality. Several trademarks were used by the company. The most common marks are B. David inside an oval frame or b. David arranged inside a divided square. The third trademark used by the firm consists of letters bd arranged diagonally. B. David jewelry should not be confused with Ben David Jewelry, operating in Utah, which uses BDJ as its trademark.

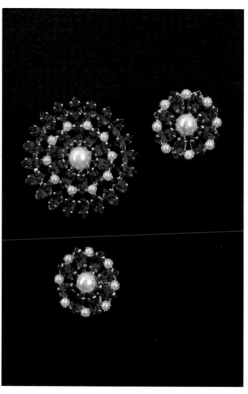

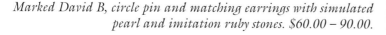

Marked David B, circle pin and matching earrings with simulated pearl and imitation ruby stones. $60.00 – 90.00.

DeMario

DeMario was founded in New York City by Robert DeMario in 1945. The company ceased production in 1960, not from lack of interest or demand, but because of DeMario's decision to quit the business and retire to Florida. DeMario jewelry is characterized by beautiful designs which often incorporate faceted beads, pearls, and rhinestones arranged in an array of harmonious colors. DeMario jewelry is often mistaken for Haskell jewelry because of similarity of designs and materials. The jewelry is relatively rare and enjoys high prices in the collectible market. Rarity alone is not responsible for high prices; recognized for superior craftsmanship and wonderful designs, the jewelry is treasured by collectors who are unwilling to part with their DeMario jewelry even at book prices. DeMario jewelry is usually marked with the company name.

Pin and matching earrings marked DeMario. Excellent design and craftsmanship which characterize all DeMario jewelry. $175.00 – 225.00.

DeRosa

DeRosa was founded by Ralph DeRosa in New York City, about 1935. The company was among the early manufacturers of very high quality costume jewelry. The major period of production was from 1935 to the mid 1950s, though the company lingered until late 1960s.

DeRosa Jewelry exhibits unique designs and superb craftsmanship. Unusual stones and outstanding metalwork are combined in masterful creations unsurpassed by any other manufacturer of costume jewelry. Some of the jewelry combines faux pearls and rhinestones mounted on sterling vermeil. Much of DeRosa jewelry was not marked and finding a signed piece is truly a collector's delight. Accordingly, signed pieces command exceptionally high asking prices and because of insufficient numbers traded, are difficult to price accurately.

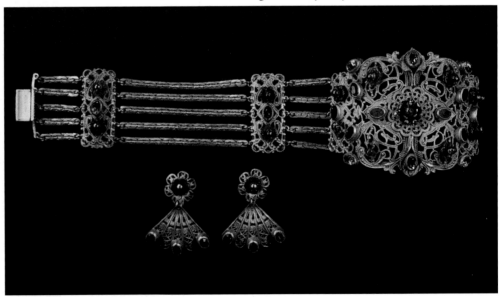

Ornate bracelet and matching earrings displaying elaborate metalwork combined with unusual rhinestones. Marked DeRosa. Top quality and craftsmanship by a family of master jewelers and designers. Unfortunately, insufficient numbers of this type of DeRosa jewelry are traded to give an accurate price estimate.

Attractive trembler pin in sterling vermeil and faux pearl surrounded by clear rhinestones and matching earrings. Both marked sterling, DeRosa. Pin. $250.00 – 300.00. Earrings. $100.00 – 150.00.

Dodds

Little is known about the manufacturer of the jewelry marked Dodds. Based on the designs and material used by the manufacturer, the jewelry was possibly produced 1950s – 1960s. Dodds jewelry is of higher quality, employing top quality multicolored and iridescent cabochon and faceted stones mounted on gold plated metal base. The jewelry is relatively scarce and has received little exposure in books on costume jewelry. When signed, the jewelry is marked Dodds after a copyright symbol on a raised portion on the back of one or more pieces. The mark is not always legible.

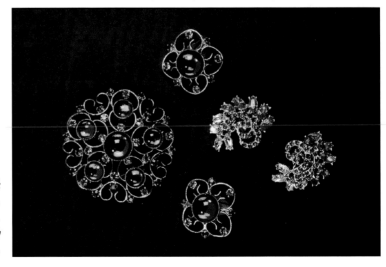

Pin and matching earrings with open work mounted by amber cabochon and faceted stones. Nearly illegible Dodds mark. $55.00 – 70.00. Pair of marked Dodds earrings decorated with clear and topaz rhinestones. $25.00 – 40.00.

Duane

Background information on the manufacturer of jewelry marked Duane is scarce and what the author was able to gather was based on hearsay and quite speculative. The manufacturer must have been in business for only a short period or failed to mark most of its jewelry. For this reason, the jewelry is extremely rare and this may be its first exposure in a book on costume jewelry. Duane jewelry was possibly manufactured no later than the early 1950s and is often found in less than satisfactory condition. Although rare, Duane jewelry is of average quality and all of the pieces seen by the author are in clear rhinestones with simple traditional designs. Signed pieces are marked DUANE on the clasp or clip.

Necklace in clear baguette and round rhinestones. Marked Duane on an applied oval plaque. $50.00 – 75.00.

Eisenberg

Founded in Chicago in 1914 by Jonas Eisenberg who emigrated to the U.S. around 1880, the company initially produced high quality ready-to-wear clothing complemented by glittering accessories produced by other firms, including Agnini & Singer, under special contract with Eisenberg. The jeweled accessories, employing the best of Austrian rhinestones provided by the Swarowski Company, created a complete and distinctive high fashion look for Eisenberg clothing.

Soon, it became apparent that not only the clothing, but also the sparkle of embellished accessories, bedazzled the costumers. Thus began the production and marketing of Eisenberg jewelry about 1930. In 1958, the company abandoned the production of clothing in order to focus exclusively on jewelry production. In 1977, it became a division of Berns-Friedman and as of early 90's continued production under the leadership of Karl Eisenberg, the founder's grandson.

Eisenberg jewelry has not only beautiful and elegant designs, but also quality materials, superior workmanship, and the best shimmering stones in the industry. It has its own distinctive look which can be recognized from a distance and seldom mistaken with another jewelry, unless the mistaken piece itself happens to be an unmarked Eisenberg. The jewelry was never sold at low prices and the 1950s advertisements carry prices of $10.00 to $30.00 per piece.

Early Eisenbergs were not marked, but around 1935, the company used the mark Eisenberg Original. This mark was used from 1935 to 1945. During WWII, because of government restrictions, the company used sterling silver (1941–1945). Another mark, script letter E, was also used during war years. The mark Eisenberg in script was used as early as 1935, but registered in 1981. Eisenberg Ice in block letters was used during 1945–1958 period. The jewelry manufactured during 1958–1970 period was not generally marked. The company began using Eisenberg Ice in script letters in 1970, but many pieces were not marked and carried only a tag.

All Eisenberg is collectible and should rise in value, but collectors prefer sterling pieces, Eisenberg Ice, and especially artistic figural pieces, many of which were created by Ruth M. Kamke, the Eisenberg designer from 1940 to 1972.

Top left: *Necklace and matching earrings marked Eisenberg. $250.00 – 300.00. The asking price may be much higher.*

Top right: *Brilliant topaz and clear rhinestones are combined in this typical Eisenberg Ice brooch and matching earrings. $150.00 – 190.00. The asking price may be as high as $250.00.*

Bottom left: *Top: Pair of Eisenberg clip earrings with typical Eisenberg lacy pattern. $50.00 – 85.00. Right: Eisenberg necklace and matching earrings. $175.00 – 235.00. Lower center: Eisenberg bracelet. $85.00 – 135.00. Lower left: Pair of earrings in champagne pink. Marked Eisenberg Ice. $50.00 – 85.00.*

Bottom right: *Left: Pair of Eisenberg earrings. Script E mark. $40.00 – 60.00. Center: Eisenberg bracelet with brilliant marquise stones in the center. $90.00 – 140.00. Right: Pair of earrings in shades of lavender. Marked Eisenberg Ice. $60.00 – 90.00.*

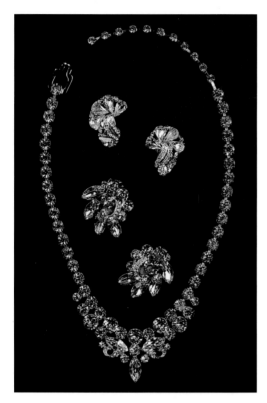

Top left: *Top: Two pairs of Eisenberg earrings. $50.00 – 85.00. Bottom: Impressive Eisenberg necklace to complement any formal evening dress. $200.00 – 250.00.*

Top right: *Pair of vermeil king and queen fur clips. Early script Eisenberg Original mark. Not sufficient number traded to give an accurate price estimate.*

Bottom left: *Delicate and charming Eisenberg Ice pin and matching earrings. $165.00 – 225.00.*

Bottom right: *Eisenberg pieces with delicate lacy pattern. Left: Earrings. $50.00 – 85.00. Center: Bracelet. $120.00 – 160.00. Upper right: Pair of earrings. $50.00 – 85.00. Lower right: Necklace. $150.00 – 200.00.*

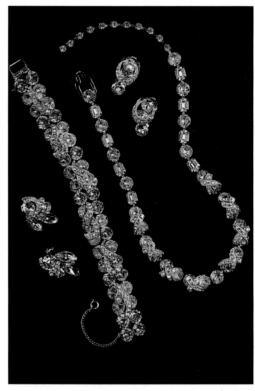

Top left: *Eisenberg Ice ring with yellow topaz stone. This ring came in several colors. $80.00 – 140.00.*

Top right: *Mexican silver and Aztec face carved in green jade with Eisenberg Original script mark. The author, who never passes on an Eisenberg piece, had to reflect on this piece for a day before purchasing it. It is so atypical of Eisenberg jewelry that one must immediately assume that it is a fake. But the signature appears to be original. Insufficient number traded to provide an accurate price estimate.*

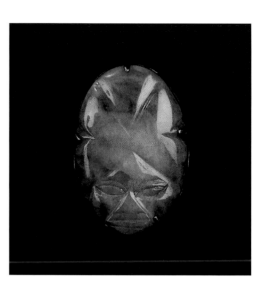

Bottom left: *Top right: Eisenberg bracelet. $80.00 – 120.00. Top left: Pair of Eisenberg earrings of a more recent manufacture. $30.00 – 50.00. Bottom: Two Eisenberg necklaces. Left: $85.00 – 135.00. Right: $95.00 – 145.00. The author has seen these pieces priced as high as $200.00 each.*

Bottom right: *Top: Eisenberg enamel earrings. $30.00 – 50.00. Upper right: Eisenberg pin with multicolored stones. $60.00 – 95.00. Lower left: Early Eisenberg pin with Eisenberg Original script mark. $85.00 – 130.00. Center: Eisenberg owl pin. $90.00 – 140.00. Top left and lower right: Two Eisenberg Christmas tree pins. Apparently the early pieces were not marked and came with the tag. $50.00 – 90.00.*

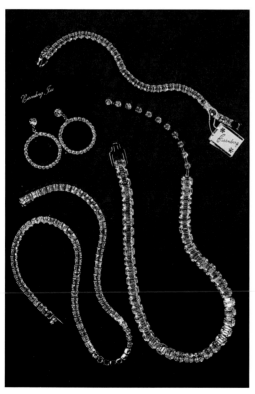

Emmons

Emmons Jewelers, Inc. was founded by Charles H. Stuart in 1949 utilizing the marketing concept popular in the 1950s through the 1970s, distribution through home parties and shows. The company, anchored in Newark, N.Y., was primarily a distributor of costume jewelry designed and manufactured by others under contract with Emmons.

The concept of selling jewelry through home parties was exceptionally successful and it elevated, within a short period, Emmons and its sister company, Sarah Coventry, to the status of a major company in the costume jewelry industry. The new marketing approach provided the 1950s housewives with part-time work opportunities and a chance to socialize with friends and acquaintances. Thousands of women acting as hostesses sold Emmons and Sarah Coventry jewelry to millions of guests who attended the home fashion shows. The company went out of business in the early 1980s.

Emmons marketed a broad range of jewelry with varied quality and designs. Some of it can be compared with the jewelry of other major producers, but most of it, though of durable quality, lacks imaginative and artistic designs or the embellishments found on other jewelry.

There is an abundance of Emmons on the market, though it is not as common as Sarah Coventry and jewelry made by other major manufacturers, such as Coro and Trifari. The common pieces can be purchased for under $20.00 and a majority of the better pieces for under $50.00. However, with the rising prices of costume jewelry in general, and as some collectors are forced to shift their interest to more affordable jewelry, Emmons' prices are expected to rise.

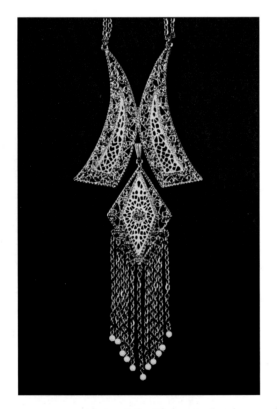

Above, left: *Elaborate, but low quality Emmons metal necklace. $35.00 – 50.00.*

Above, right: *Top left: Emmons circle pin. $15.00 – 25.00. Top right: Large Emmons brooch. $25.00 – 40.00. Center: Emmons pendant and earrings. $35.00 – 60.00.*

Top left: *Emmons ring with simulated pearls and turquoise. $30.00 – 45.00.*

Top right: *Emmons woven mesh metal bracelet. $15.00 – 25.00. Emmons multi-strand chain necklace. $15.00 – 25.00. Emmons brooch with multicolored rhinestones. $25.00 – 40.00. Emmons silvertone horse figural pin. $25.00 – 35.00.*

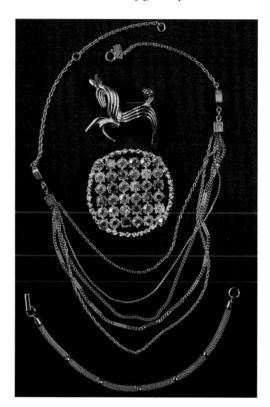

Bottom left: *Top left: Three pairs of Emmons earrings. $15.00 – 25.00 each. Center: Emmons bracelet with black opaque glass stones. $20.00 – 30.00. Right: Emmons chain necklace with black plastic bead drops. $15.00 – 20.00. Bottom: Emmons pin and matching earrings with large black stone mounted on round silvertone metal base. $45.00 – 60.00.*

Bottom right: *Two Emmons rings. $15.00 – 25.00 each.*

Eugene

Eugene worked as a designer for Miriam Haskell before manufacturing jewelry under his own name around 1950. Eugene jewelry is stylistically similar to Haskell, DeMario, and Robert jewelry with even more emphasis on pearls and beads and lesser use of rhinestones. The jewelry must have been produced in limited quantities since it is relatively rare today. The firm stopped production around 1960. The jewelry is usually marked Eugene, an apparently unregistered trademark.

Two pairs of marked Eugene earrings. Right: Gold leaf and pearl combination similar to Haskell, DeMario, and Robert jewelry. $45.00 – 70.00. Left: Gold leaf and emerald green rhinestones. $45.00 – 70.00.

Evans

Evans Case Company founded in the early 1920s and famous for its compacts, cigarette cases, and lighters, also produced costume jewelry. Beginning in the 1920s, Evans manufactured beautiful enamel jewelry which is scarce in the collectible market today. The late 1920s enamel jewelry shows Art Deco influences which were becoming popular at that time and somewhat resemble the Czech and other contemporary jewelry, except it employs enamel work rather than imitation stones to highlight the designs. In the 1950s, Evans manufactured a line of enamel jewelry, applying the same technology they used on their guilloche enamel compacts and cases. This type of jewelry, some showing Art Moderne influence, is exceptionally beautiful and rare. Most of the jewelry is in pastel colors with translucent satin-like shimmering enamel work combined with gold plated metal. In the late 1950s, a necklace and earrings set could be purchased for about $15.00 to 20.00 and bracelets for $10.00 to 15.00. Lucky is the collector who finds any of these pieces at reasonable prices today. The jewelry is usually marked Evans, often on a small metal tag attached to the necklaces.

Parure consisting of necklace, bracelet, and earrings in pastel guilloche enamel. Marked Evans. $200.00 – 250.00.

Florenza

Florenza is the trademark used by Dan Kasoff Inc., founded in New York City, around 1955. It appears that Kasoff was not directly involved in jewelry production and instead sold well-developed designs to jobbers who undertook the production and distribution of the jewelry. The company ceased operations sometime in the mid 1960s. Florenza jewelry has distinctive designs inspired by Renaissance Revival jewelry which was so favored during the Victorian era. The jewelry exhibits excellent metalwork, frequently in antiqued gold-tone, ornamented by distinct and superior rhinestones of pastel, frosted, and aurora colors. Some of the jewelry uses cameo or intaglio as the central stone, complemented by colored rhinestones which mounted on delicate filigree and antiqued metalwork resemble the older Victorian jewelry. Put simply, Florenza jewelry is characterized with quality workmanship, quality material, and quality designs.

Florenza jewelry is a true sleeper in the collectible costume jewelry market and is just beginning to be noticed as one of the best and well designed jewelry of the post WWII period. In a sense, the collectible market has treated Florenza jewelry as it did Boucher jewelry 20 years ago, not granting it the recognition and accolade it well deserves, While many collectors and trend followers, impressed by the exaggerated book prices, are preoccupied with Schiaparelli and Caviness jewelry, Florenza jewelry can be purchased at bargain prices and because of this, is among the best investment costume jewelry. Someday Florenza jewelry will find its rightful place among the top echelon of costume jewelry manufacturers in post WWII America, even though it never was the jewelry of the rich and the famous. The author never passes up Florenza jewelry, not even the lower quality pieces.

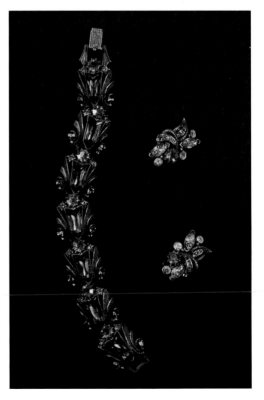

Above left: *Florenza necklace. Hand-painted porcelain in enameled frame. $60.00 – 95.00.*

Above right: *Exquisite Florenza bracelet with unusual iridescent stones. $85.00 – 125.00. Earrings. $35.00 – 50.00.*

Top left: *Florenza bracelet and earrings in floral design made of pastel pink plastic beads and rhinestone accent. $65.00 – 90.00.*

Top right: *Florenza pendant and matching earrings reminiscent of antique jewelry. $80.00 – 120.00.*

Bottom left: *Masterful creation by Florenza with antiqued metalwork and famous Florenza stones of various shapes. $85.00 – 125.00.*

Bottom right: *Top: Florenza earrings with iridescent stones. $40.00 – 60.00. Center: Victorian inspired brooch with opaque glass stones complemented by pearls and rhinestones. $60.00 – 85.00. Bottom: Florenza earrings displaying antique openwork accented by rhinestones. $35.00 – 50.00.*

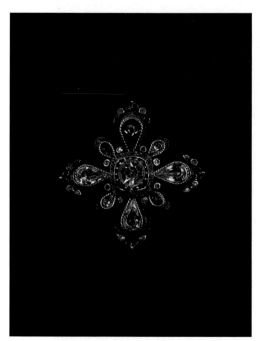

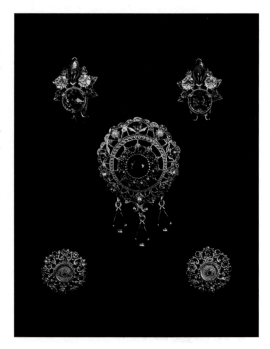

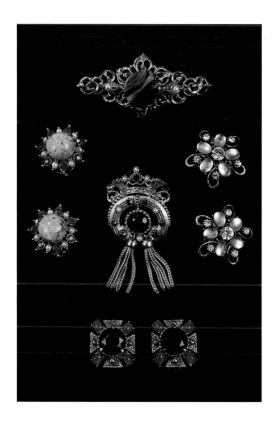

Top left: *Top: Large Florenza filigree brooch highlighted by an imitation jade stone. $50.00 – 75.00. Center left: Imitation turquoise, pearls, and rhinestones are combined to create this pleasant pair of Florenza earrings. $35.00 – 50.00. Center: Victorian style brooch with antiqued metalwork. $65.00 – 95.00. Center right: Florenza earrings with frosted cabochon stones mounted on antiqued silver base. $30.00 – 45.00. Matching necklace not shown. $65.00 – 90.00. Bottom: Florenza earrings with opaque glass and red cabochon stones. $40.00 – 60.00.*

Top right: *Bracelet and earrings with enameled metal complemented by faux pearls. Marked Florenza. $60.00 – 85.00.*

Bottom left: *Exquisite Florenza brooch with frosted and aurora stones. For somewhat similar design, see Kramer. $85.00 – 130.00. Matching earrings not shown. $45.00 – 65.00. Pair of Florenza earrings. $40.00 – 60.00.*

Left: *Top: Florenza earrings with opaque cabochon stones simulating dark carnelian stones. $30.00 – 45.00. Bottom: Necklace with mesh metal and central cameo replicating classic Victorian stone cameo jewelry. Marked Florenza. $65.00 – 95.00.*

Bottom left: *Florenza necklace and matching earrings in satin white aurora borealis stones. $75.00 – 100.00.*

Bottom right: *Top: Florenza hat ornament and matching earrings. $95.00 – 140.00. Bottom: Pair of Florenza earrings. $40.00 – 55.00.*

Garne

The Garne trademark was used by Garne Jewelry which was in business from the 1940s possibly until the 1960s. Most of the marked Garne jewelry seen by the author is in popular 1940s and 1950s styles, employing clear rhinestones. The jewelry is of average quality often with traditional designs. It is not clear whether all of the jewelry was marked, but signed pieces are marked Garne Jewelry on the back or clasp of each piece. The jewelry is not very common.

Top: Clear rhinestone necklace in traditional classic design. Marked Garne. $30.00 – 50.00. Bottom: Frosted and pink stones are combined to create this attractive pin and matching earrings, marked Garne.

Gerry's

No definite and reliable information regarding dates, location, and manufacturer of the jewelry marked Gerry's could be obtained by the date of this publication. The trademark was used by several manufacturers including Gerry's Creations Inc., which until recently was located in Folcroft, Penn. Although listed in the phone directory, the firm must have ceased operations sometime in 1996 and the author was unable to contact them at their last current address or listed number.

Gerry's jewelry found in the collectible market consists primarily of figural pins decorated with a variety of material, particularly simulated pearls, rhinestones, and plastic. The jewelry is relatively common and of average to below average quality. Signed pieces are usually marked Gerry's with a copyright symbol on a raised portion on the back of each piece.

Several examples of Gerry's figural pins. $10.00 – 35.00 each.

Goldette

Goldette is the trademark for Ben Gartner/Circle Jewelry Products founded in New York City around 1958. The firm manufactured costume jewelry with designs showing Victorian and Oriental influences. Much of the firm's production emphasized metalwork, sometimes highlighted with enamel work or a large central stone. Other pieces include combining colored rhinestones with turquoise, pearls, and other imitation stones in traditional designs mounted on goldtone or plated metal. Typical Goldette jewelry is of average quality with average prices. The jewelry is usually marked Goldette on an applied oval plaque.

Top right: *Goldette pendant with amethyst stone and bead drops. $40.00 – 60.00.*

Above, center: *Goldette pendant and matching earrings with a small flower on black enamel field. $35.00 – 50.00.*

Bottom right: *Goldette locket covered with guilloche enamel front depicting a pair of roses. Good quality material. $35.00 – 50.00. Goldette pin with simulated turquoise and rubies. $25.00 – 40.00.*

Har

As of this date, no information concerning the manufacturer, location, and dates of production of jewelry marked Har was available. The designs suggest that the firm must have operated during the 1950s to mid 1960s period. Har jewelry has interesting designs, some showing Oriental influence. Some of the jewelry is pavé set in floral designs, while others combine pearls and rhinestones of different colors and shapes set on a gold plated metal base, sometimes accented with enamel work. The company also manufactured cast figural pieces with Eastern and Oriental motifs, and other figural pieces which emphasize the metalwork, accented with rhinestones and sometimes exquisitely enameled.

All of Har jewelry reflects quality workmanship and fine metalwork. It is relatively scarce with above average price range. The jewelry showing Oriental motifs or extensive enamel work is rare and commands higher prices, usually above $200.00 per piece.

Turtle pin decorated with imitation pearl, turquoise, and ruby stones. Quality material and workmanship. $80.00 – 120.00.

Hickok

Hickok Manufacturing Company, Inc., in Rochester, N.Y., has been in operation since at least the early 1900s. The firm has always been a major manufacturer of men's jewelry and accessories, beginning with collar buttons, cuff links, and cravat ornaments. Hickok's jewelry is sought only by collectors of cuff links and men's jewelry along with the jewelry of other major manufacturers of men's jewelry such as Swank and Anson. The jewelry is usually marked with a company name, often in minute letters and in hard-to-see places. The company also used over a dozen other trademarks, including HMCO, Savoy, and KRISTOL.

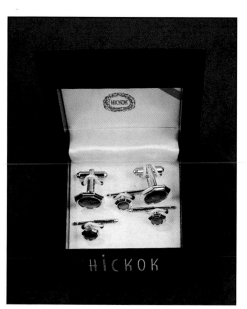

Left: *Set of Hickok men's jewelry. $20.00 – 35.00.*

Right: *Hickok men's cuff links and tie tack for fishing enthusiasts. $25.00 – 35.00.*

Hobe

The history of Hobe jewelry can be traced back several generations to mid 19th century Paris and Jacques Hobe, a reputed master goldsmith recognized throughout Western Europe as a producer of fine jewelry. Jacques Hobe had three sons who continued the tradition of making superior fine jewelry. One of them, also named Jacques, was impressed by the use of machinery and automation brought about by the Industrial Revolution and saw a great potential in adapting the new technologies to mass produce fine jewelry. His son, William Hobe, went a step farther and made the name Hobe famous for its mass-produced and elegant costume jewelry. Today, William's grandson, Bruce Hobe, continues that tradition.

According to the legend, William Hobe, working as a representative of a German company selling theatrical costumes, comes to New York and approaches Florence Ziegfeld to purchase Hobe's costumes for the famed Ziegfeld Follies. Florence places a large order for the costumes, but also asks William to create inexpensive but real looking jewelry to complement the showgirls' costumes. Thus begins William Hobe's venture in America and the founding of a firm to produce costume jewelry. According to the same legend perpetuated by the Hobe family, the term "costume jewelry" was first used by Florence Ziegfeld whenever he referred to the jewelry purchased from William for his showgirls.

Hobe jewelry demonstrates excellent and elegant designs with high quality stones embellishing superior silver or gold plated metalwork. The workmanship is excellent especially on its reproductions of antique jewelry, such as the replicas of the jewelry of the European courts which employed semiprecious stones such as turquoise, lapis, jade, and agate, all handset and accented with multicolored enamelwork. During the 1950s, Hobe was the jewelry of choice in Hollywood, favored by many producers and movie stars and used to complement the costumes of actresses in movies and fashion models in advertising promotions. Hobe advertisements claimed that the jewelry was handmade in their entirety, in platinum, gold or sterling. Without a doubt, Hobe is among the very best of costume jewelry manufacturers in America.

Post WWII Hobe jewelry is usually signed Hobe, a trademark registered in 1948 and in use since January, 1926. There are several other marks used, but apparently not registered, which show Hobe inside a geometric frame such as an oval (1958 – 83) or triangle (1933 – 57). The company literature also shows two trademarks, Hobe in a crown, and Hobe under crossed swords, which are pre 1900s and must predate the founding of the company in the U.S.

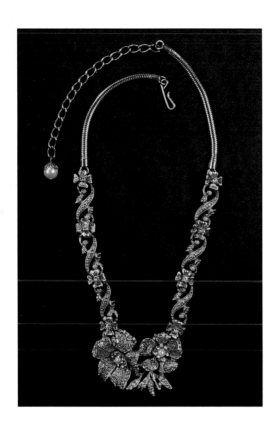

Opposite page: *Top: Two pairs of marked Hobe earrings. Left: $25.00 – 35.00. Right: $40.00 – 60.00. Bottom: Hobe multi-strand necklace and matching earrings made of plastic beads. $40.00 – 65.00.*

Top left: *Marked Hobe, necklace with floral design in textured gold metal, set with rhinestones and simulated pearls. Excellent design and workmanship which are Hobe trademark. $150.00 – 250.00.*

Top right: *Silver Hobe hair ornament with three handset stones. Marked Made in France. Hobe. $150.00 – 250.00.*

Right: *Hobe hair ornament displaying intricate filigree metalwork highlighted by two large stones with canary yellow rhinestone accent. Marked Hobe on applied plaque. $250.00 – 350.00.*

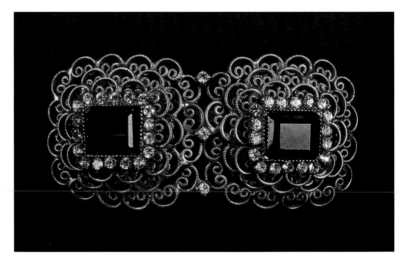

Top left: *Hobe brooch in form of a tree made of goldtone wires terminating in suspended imitation pearls. Marked Hobe. $125.00 – 175.00. Pair of marked Hobe earrings of similar material and construction. $40.00 – 60.00.*

Top right: *Left: Hobe cross with antiqued gold filigree metalwork decorated with garnets. Hobe plaque mark. $175.00 – 225.00. Right: Round Hobe hair ornament in antiqued gold filigree metalwork complemented by multicolored faceted stones. Hobe Plaque mark. $200.00 – 250.00.*

Opposite page, top left: *Top left: Pin with a polished jade glass stone mounted on 12kt gold plated base. Hobe plaque mark. $45.00 – 70.00. Left: Figural brooch of a flamenco dancer in black and red faceted stones. $100.00 – 175.00. Center: Pendant in polished agate (?) with gold plate metal insert depicting an Oriental scene. Marked Hobe on the chain clasp. $85.00 – 125.00. Right: Figural pin depicting a flute-playing musician. $125.00 – 165.00.*

Opposite page, top right: *Top: Hobe bracelet with textured metal whirls set with baguette rhinestones. Hobe plaque mark. $85.00 – 125.00. Center right: Pair of Hobe earrings set with simulated pearls and rhinestones. $30.00 – 50.00. Sterling silver floral brooch. Marked sterling, Hobe on an applied triangular plaque. $100.00 – 150.00. Lower right: Bracelet made of silver chains held together with blue baguette rhinestone knots. Marked Hobe on the clasp. $45.00 – 70.00. Bottom: Hinged bracelet made of textured goldtone metal set with small cabochon black stones. Hobe plaque mark. $65.00 – 95.00.*

Opposite page, bottom left: *Three pairs of marked Hobe clip earrings featuring pearls. $25.00 – 45.00 each.*

Opposite page, bottom right: *Center left: Delicate pin and matching earrings with small and slender clear rhinestones. Hobe plaque mark on the pin. $65.00 – 95.00. Also pictured: Six pairs of marked Hobe earrings with diverse designs and materials. $25.00 – 45.00 each.*

Hollycraft

Hollycraft, apparently an unregistered trademark, was used by Hollycraft Corporation founded in the mid 1940s by an Armenian emigrant (Ottoman subject), Joseph Chorbajian, in New York City. The firm continued operations until at least the late 1960s. It should be pointed out that there is contradictory information regarding the company name, dates, and whether the firm itself actually manufactured the jewelry.

Hollycraft jewelry exhibits beautiful designs, well executed, employing a rainbow of excellent and distinctive rhinestones, sometimes accented with enamel work. Rhinestones used on Hollycraft jewelry are similar to those found on Florenza and some Regency jewelry. These are usually of pastel colors with brilliant glow emanating from the depth of the stones, and extremely difficult to replace. Fortunately, Hollycraft jewelry is not only marked, but also dated. It is very enchanting and collectible jewelry and, like Florenza, yet to be fully appreciated.

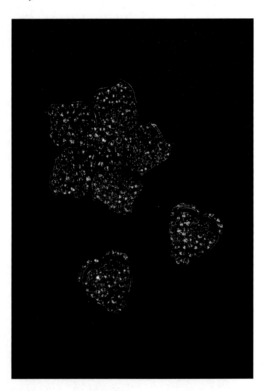
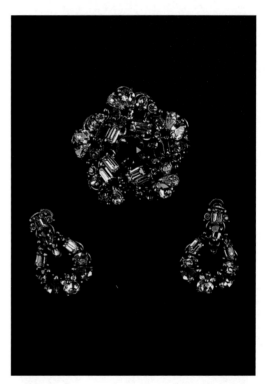

Above left: Leaf-shaped pin and matching earrings with pavé set rhinestones on japanned metal base. Marked Hollycraft. $75.00 – 100.00.

Above right: Pin and earrings marked Hollycraft. These are typical Hollycraft jewelry with beautiful pastel stones which can be identified from a distance. Pin marked Hollycraft Corp., 1953. $60.00 – 95.00. Earrings marked Hollycraft Corp., 1953. $40.00 – 60.00.

Opposite page, top left: More Hollycraft gems. Top left: Pin in floral design. Signed Hollycraft Corp., 1950. $40.00 – 55.00. Top right: Pair of rectangular clip earrings. $45.00 – 65.00. Lower left: Screw back earrings. $35.00 – 50.00. Lower right: Rhinestone studded earrings with multicolored stones surrounding a large, faceted brilliant amethyst stone. Signed Hollycraft Corp., 1950. $60.00 – 85.00.

Opposite page, top right: Top and center: Two pairs of Hollycraft earrings demonstrating creative skill and craftsmanship that characterize Hollycraft jewelry. $45.00 – 65.00. Top center: Hollycraft Christmas pin. $45.00 – 65.00. Bottom: Atypical Hollycraft leaf pin with dark gray and white satin stones. $40.00 – 65.00.

Jeanne

As of this date, no information on manufacturer, location, and date of production of Jeanne jewelry was available. The mark is found on whimsical and figural jewelry originally sold at specialty stores. Most of the jewelry emphasizes metalwork complemented by imitation stones. The quality and workmanship are above average relative to other costume jewelry in the collectible market. Jeanne jewelry is not very common and commands slightly above average prices. Most figural pins can be purchased for under $60.00, though the asking price may be much higher.

Large rooster brooch, marked Jeanne. $50.00 – 70.00.

J.J.

J.J. is the registered trademark of Jonette Jewelry Co. located in East Providence, R.I. The company was founded about 1935 by Abraham Lisker as Providence Jewelry Co. and later changed names to Lisker & Lisker Inc. when Abraham's brother Nathan joined the company. The firm discontinued operations during WWII due to metal shortages brought about as the result of government restrictions. After the war Abraham Lisker had to start the company again and combined the names of his parents John and Etta, in naming the firm Johnette Jewelry Co. Abraham Lisker is now retired and lives in Florida. His son, Gordon Lisker, has been leading the company sine the 1970s. According to him, the company has a workforce of approximately 80 employees which is supplemented by a similar number before Christmas. Today, the firm manufactures a larger volume than in the past, despite the fact that certain jobs are farmed out to other companies.

J.J. Jewelry consists primarily of figural and novelty pins. According to Abraham Lisker, the company moved in this direction during the early years because of its success in selling ballerina and mother-of-pearl figural pins. These were usually priced at $1.00 apiece. Christmas pins were another J.J. specialty. J.J. Jewelry is of average to better than average quality, marked J.J. with a copyright symbol before or after the name.

Above left: *Group of figural pins by J.J. Banjo player with moving limbs. $50.00 – 75.00. Pelican. $25.00 – 40.00. Owls. $20.00 – 25.00. Stylized wings. $20.00 – 30.00.*

Above right: *More J.J. figural pins. $15.00 – 40.00.*

Judy Lee

Judy Lee is the trademark belonging to Blanch-Ette Company, founded in the late 1950s. The company employed marketing and distribution methods similar to Emmons and Coventry. The jewelry is of average quality and not very common in the market. Some of the pieces have interesting traditional designs set with top quality rhinestones. Although collectible, Judy Lee jewelry has not yet captured the interest of many collectors. Some dealers put a high asking price on their Judy Lee jewelry, but most of it can be purchased at average prices. As rising prices of very collectible costume jewelry make purchase of top brands prohibitive for most budgets, demand for signed jewelry such as Judy Lee, Coventry, Emmons, and Lisner will increase and so will the prices. Judy Lee jewelry is usually marked Judy-Lee (in use since 1958), but another mark, Judy-Lee Jewels, may also be found.

Top right: *Rhinestone necklace and matching earrings featuring large simulated pearls. Marked Judy-Lee. $60.00 – 90.00.*

Bottom left: *Large Judy-Lee brooch decorated with quality green and citrine rhinestones. $45.00 – 65.00.*

Bottom right: *Judy-Lee ring with green marquise central stone surrounded by small green rhinestones. $20.00 – 35.00.*

Above left: *Four pairs of earrings, all marked Judy-Lee. $20.00 – 40.00.*

Above right: *Top left: Judy Lee pin with plastic flower. $12.50 – 20.00.*
Center: Judy Lee bracelet in floral motif, set with imitation pearl and rhinestones. $25.00 – 40.00.
Bottom: Pair of Judy Lee rhinestone earrings. $20.00 – 35.00.

Kafin

Background information on the manufacturer of Kafin jewelry is scarce and sketchy though the firm's jewelry has been displayed in several books on costume jewelry. Kafin was a New York based company operating from the 1950s to the 1960s. The firm's jewelry is of average to above average quality and not very common in the collectible market. The firm produced both rhinestone and metal jewelry. When signed, the jewelry is marked Kafin of New York or Kafin in script signature form.

Metal link bracelet. Marked Kafin. $25.00 – 40.00. Two attractive pairs of earrings with glass cabochon stones. Both marked Kafin. $20.00 – 35.00 each.

Karu

It is not clear whether the jewelry marked Karu, Karu Fifth Ave., and Karu Arke Inc., was manufactured by the same company. The jewelry found in the market appears to have been manufactured from the 1950s to at least the 1970s. Much of the Karu jewelry employs iridescent crystal beads and aurora borealis rhinestones set on goldtone metal.

Karu cameo pendant. White on black plastic. $25.00 – 35.00. Two pairs of Karu earrings. $15.00 – 20.00.

Korda

Jewelry marked Korda appears to be associated with the 1940 release of the movie, "Thief of Baghdad," produced by Alexander Korda, directed by Ludwig Berger et al. With the exception of few pieces, all the pieces seen by the author are also marked "Thief of Baghdad." According to the rumor among collectors, these pieces were presented by Korda to the cast and crew of the movie. But such a tale seems as imaginary as the subject of the film itself. The author has seen about a dozen different pieces marked "Thief of Baghdad," and if each piece was manufactured in a limited quantity of only 1,000, the total number would exceed the number of cast and crew engaged in the making of the movie. At least many, if not all, manu-

factured pieces must have been offered to the public for promotion and/or sale. But if the story is true, it would render each piece of Korda among the rarest of costume jewelry ever manufactured in the U.S., and for this reason, even much more desirable and collectible.

It appears that some of the pins reflect the fantasy theme of the movie and others may be copies of the ornamental jewelry worn by the cast in the movie. But this is mere speculation and the puzzle can only be solved with more research. Korda jewelry is not only enchanting and of high quality, but it is also extremely rare. Even more limited is the number of collector/dealers who are willing to part with their pieces. When a Korda piece presents itself, do not hesitate. The prices are expected to continue to climb in the future.

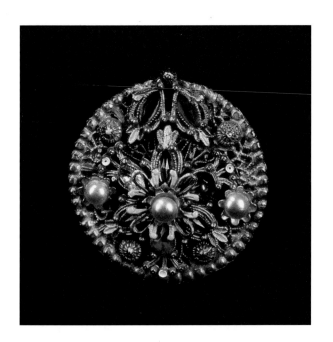

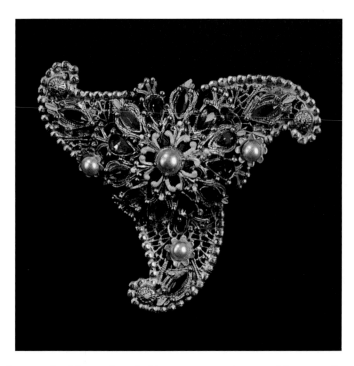

Above left: *Circle pin with intricate and elaborate metalwork decorated with pearl and rhinestones complemented by enamel work. Marked Korda, Thief of Baghdad. $150.00 – 200.00.*

Above right: *Delicate Korda brooch with similar construction as the above piece. $200.00 – 275.00.*

Kramer

Kramer Jewelry Creations was founded in New York in 1943 by Louis Kramer. The company was in business until about 1980 and manufactured some of the most luxurious and artistic costume jewelry. Much of the jewelry in the 1940s and 1950s was designed by Louis Kramer himself.

Like Coro, the company produced a broad range of jewelry at different price levels. In general, the higher priced jewelry was usually marked while lower quality pieces carried only a tag. Some of the beautiful jewelry created by Kramer is from its "Real Look" collection produced in the 1950s. These were usually signed and carried a tag marked "Golden Look" or "Diamond Look." A 1955 Kramer advertisement in *Vogue* offers this type of jewelry at $2.00 to $20.00 per piece which was relatively cheap compared to the jewelry of other contemporary manufacturers. The company also produced jewelry for Christian Dior marked Kramer for Christian Dior. In the 1950s to early 1960s, Kramer produced many designs with plastic inserts combined with pearls and rhinestones. These are creative designs employing plastic instead of rhinestones which became scarce during WWII, and are yet to be appreciated by collectors of plastic jewelry.

Most of the marked Kramer jewelry is signed either Kramer of New York or just Kramer. The former was used on earlier jewelry. The Trademarks Diamond Look and Golden Look were first used in 1948 and 1950, respectively.

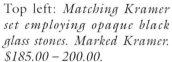

Top left: *Matching Kramer set employing opaque black glass stones. Marked Kramer. $185.00 – 200.00.*

Top right: *Left: Two pairs of Kramer earrings. $30.00 – 40.00. Kramer pin. $50.00 – 65.00. Center: Kramer necklace. $75.00 – 100.00. Right: Pavé set floral brooch. Marked Kramer of N.Y. for Christian Dior. $250.00 – 300.00. Small Kramer grape pin. $25.00 – 30.00.*

Bottom left: *Kramer crescent brooch and matching earrings set with amethyst rhinestones. $100.00 – 150.00.*

Bottom right: *Kramer parure consisting of necklace, bracelet, and earrings, combining opaque black glass and clear rhinestones in a classic Kramer design. Marked Kramer of New York. $225.00 – 300.00.*

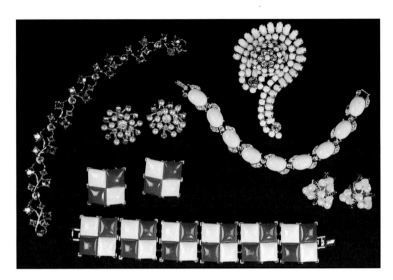

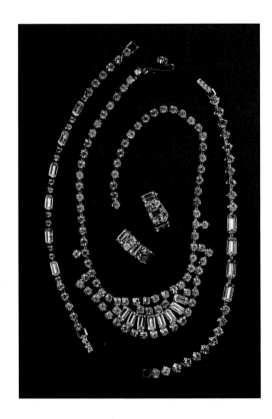

Above left: *Top left: Kramer bracelet. $35.00 – 50.00. Center: Pair of Kramer pearl earrings. $30.00 – 45.00. Top right: Large brooch with white opaque glass and clear rhinestones. An early Kramer piece. $75.00 – 95.00. Kramer link bracelet with white plastic inserts complemented by rhinestones. $30.00 – 45.00. Bottom: Matching Kramer bracelet and earrings of white and brown plastic in quilt-like motif. $65.00 – 95.00. Pair of Kramer pearl earrings. $30.00 – 40.00.*

Above right: *Top, left to right: Exquisite Kramer flower head brooch with canary yellow and amber marquise stones surrounding a large, round amber rhinestone. $120.00 – 150.00. Pair of round Kramer earrings set with green rhinestones. $25.00 – 35.00. Blue Kramer clip earrings. $30.00 – 40.00. Pink Kramer earrings. $35.00 – 45.00. Center: Bracelet with frosted light green stones and rhinestone accent. $65.00 – 95.00. Bottom: Kramer earrings. $35.00 – 45.00.*

Left: *Left: Kramer bracelet. $35.00 – 50.00. Center: Matching Kramer necklace and earrings. $100.00 – 150.00. Right: Kramer bracelet. $35.00 – 50.00. All of these pieces were purchased together and may be parts of the same set.*

Opposite page, top left: *Assorted Kramer earrings. Pearl earrings are set with genuine cultured pearls. $40.00 – 55.00 each. Others. $20.00 – 35.00.*

Opposite page, top right: *Parure consisting of necklace, bracelet, pin, and earrings with yellow plastic inserts and rhinestone accent. Marked Kramer. $95.00 – 145.00.*

Krementz

Krementz and Co. was first established by a group of investors with the objective of producing fine jewelry. But, the company became a leading manufacturer of collar buttons and cuff links produced in their Newark, N.J. plant. Krementz also produced other types of jewelry such as 10k and 14k gold jewelry set with pearls and precious stones in late Victorian and Art Nouveau styles, as well as scarf pins and jewelry findings using gold plated metal. The plated metal was actually rolled gold plate using a method similar to the making of Sheffield silver, whereby the base metal is sandwiched between two layers of gold and fused under intense pressure and heat. This produced an exceptionally durable gold plating which has lasted nearly a century despite the jewelry's frequent use by the owners over many years. The company advertisements indicated that their 14k gold overlay was thirty times as thick as the gold in ordinary costume jewelry. As the demand for collar buttons declined by the 1930s, the company expanded into the area of women's jewelry and by 1950 nearly half of the revenues was generated from the sale of this jewelry. The firm is still in business today.

Krementz jewelry was never cheap. In the mid 1950s, necklaces sold for $20.00 – 30.00 and a pair of earrings for $12.00 – 20.00. Krementz jewelry has classically traditional designs, beauty, and elegance. The company rightfully claimed that its jewelry was in the "tradition of precious jewelry." One of the designs for which the company is famous is their golden rose earrings and pins. Krementz jewelry was produced using the best of material, technology, and workmanship. Most pieces found in the market are small pieces of jewelry such as pins with cultured pearls and rhinestones set on quality gold plated metal.

Not all Krementz jewelry is signed and the mark is sometimes in awkward places, such as on the pin stem. Most signed pieces are marked Krementz. Another mark used since 1930 is a set of armor with the word "Heraldic" diagonally arranged inside a shield. Other marks are Ju-Kay (since 1907); Snap-Bar, used on cuff links (since 1940); and picture of a snap with bent ends (since 1896).

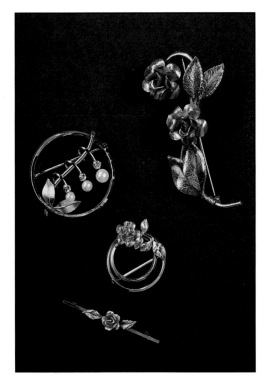

Left: *Top left: White gold pin with three cultured pearls. Marked Krementz on pin stem. $50.00 – 70.00. Top right: Krementz pin with gold leaves and two famous Krementz roses. $45.00 – 65.00. Center: Krementz gold wreath pin. $25.00 – 40.00. Bottom: Delicate Krementz bar pin with Krementz rose and two leaves in the center. $25.00 – 35.00.*

Bottom left: *Three floral Krementz pins. Top: With cultured pearls. $65.00 – 95.00. Left: With three roses. $45.00 – 70.00. Bottom: With a Krementz rose and two large leaves. $45.00 – 70.00.*

Bottom right: *Krementz floral pin in 14kt gold overlay with cultured pearls and enameled leaves. $50.00 – 70.00. Krementz pin and matching screw back earrings with love knot motif in two shades of gold. Marked Krementz, 1/20 12kt gold filled. $75.00 – 100.00.*

Laguna

Laguna is the registered trademark of Royal Craftsmen Inc., founded in New York City in 1944. The mark is often found on simulated pearl jewelry. The company also manufactured beaded jewelry, using plastic, colored glass, and faceted crystal beads. This type of jewelry, also marked Laguna, somewhat resembles the post WWII German beaded jewelry (see section on German jewelry). Laguna jewelry is of average to below average quality with prices comparable to lower quality Coro or Lisner jewelry. Most earrings can be purchased for under $15.00 in the collectible market.

Top and center: Two pairs of Laguna earrings made of red glass beads. $25.00 – 30.00. Top: Round pair of earrings with white satin finish, marked Laguna. $10.00 – 15.00. Bottom: Cut crystal beads were used to create these Laguna earrings. $25.00 – 30.00 each.

La Rel

La Rel is the trademark for La Rel Originals founded in New York City around 1953. The firm manufactured an assortment of chic rhinestone jewelry, including rings and lockets, in subdued traditional designs. Both clear and colored rhinestones were used, sometimes combined with quality opaque colored glass stones. If rhinestone jewelry was ever manufactured with the objective of complementing an evening dress, particularly dresses with classic designs, La Rel has fulfilled the task skillfully. The jewelry is of average to above average quality and can be purchased at average prices. But La Rel jewelry is not very common and should command higher prices in the collectible market, and this may well happen as the jewelry receives more attention and exposure in future costume jewelry books. The jewelry is usually marked La Rel or La Rel Originals. The mark on early pieces may also include "rhinestone magic."

Necklace in elegant traditional design. Marked La Rel. $45.00 – 65.00. Two pairs of La Rel earrings. $30.00 – 40.00 each.

Leru

Leru seems to have specialized in the production of summer jewelry. The term refers to the type of jewelry worn to complement summer attire in the 1950s and 1960s. The jewelry usually is in white or light and pastel colors. The bulk of Leru jewelry found in the collectible market is of this type, with light and pastel color stones mounted on white plastic and metal base in floral patterns. Sometimes opaque glass beads run the length of the piece, complementing the metalwork. Other major manufacturers, such as Coro, Lisner, and Kramer, also produced similar jewelry for summer wear. This type of Leru jewelry is of average to below average quality and is often found in worn and below average condition. Perhaps summer perspiration is partly responsible for the condition in which the jewelry is found. Leru also produced other jewelry which combines metal and plastic in Art Moderne designs. Both types of jewelry can be purchased at average to below average prices with a good potential for deep discounts. The inflated book prices (asking prices) for this type of Leru jewelry can be realized for mint condition pieces, in box.

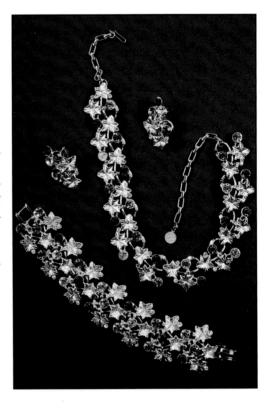

Top right: *Top: Leru necklace and matching earrings with pastel rhinestones mounted on plastic flowers. $45.00 – 65.00. Book and asking prices may be much higher. Center: Leru bracelet with three rows of alternating satin finish plastic and rhinestones. $30.00 – 45.00. Bottom: Pair of Leru earrings with plastic flowers. Similar to the top piece. These are typical Leru "summer" jewelry. $15.00 – 20.00.*

Left: *Art Moderne Leru necklace and earrings with plastic inserts. $40.00 – 65.00.*

Right: *Leru necklace, bracelet, and earrings in floral motif. $50.00 – 75.00.*

Lewis Segal

The author could not find definite and reliable information on the manufacturer of the jewelry marked Lewis Segal. There were several now defunct firms with the name Segal, but it is not clear which, if any, of them manufactured the jewelry shown here. Segal jewelry is of about average quality. Signed pieces are marked Lewis Segal or Lewis Segal California on the earring clips.

A sample of common Segal jewelry. Top two pieces are made of convex iridescent glass disks. $30.00 – 40.00 each. Center column: Two pairs of Segal earrings made of black glass. The top pair is in faceted glass. $15.00 – 20.00. The bottom pair is in textured glass. $25.00 – 35.00. Remaining earrings. $10.00 – 15.00 each.

Lisner

D. Lisner and Company was founded in New York City in the early 1900s. The *Jewelers' Circular* of various years lists the company as manufacturer and sometimes wholesaler of jewelry and novelties. The mark Lisner in block letters, most frequently found on the firm's jewelry, was first used in 1959. Much of Lisner's jewelry is similar to average Coro jewelry and the two companies competed in the average to lower priced costume jewelry market. Some Lisner jewelry is of much higher quality, employing superior aurora borealis and other rhinestones in "atomic" and other modern designs. These command higher prices in the collectible market and for some reason are popular in Europe. According to several dealers returning from Paris and London markets, this type of Lisner jewelry was normally priced much higher than in the U.S. collectible market. The 1997 edition of *Miller's International Antiques Price Guide* shows a pair of Lisner earrings at about $100.00 which can ordinarily be purchased at much lower prices in the U.S. market. Some of the Lisner jewelry employs colorful plastic inserts, sometimes accented with rhinestones, showing Art Deco influence which is underpriced in the market at this time. In the late 1970s, the firm was listed as Lisner-Richelieu Corporation, but the current listed name of Richelieu Corporation does not include Lisner.

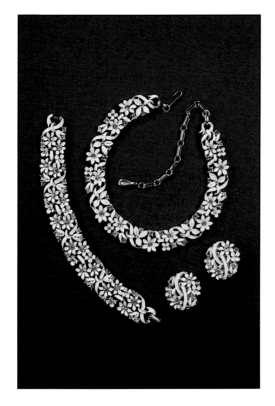

Top left: *Necklace, bracelet, and earrings in floral design with white enamel and multicolored rhinestones. $70.00 – 100.00.*

Top right: *Marked Lisner necklace, bracelet, and earrings combining simulated pearls and rhinestones. $75.00 – 100.00.*

Bottom left: *Top: Two pairs of Lisner earrings with sculptured plastic "stones" and rhinestone accent. $35.00 – 50.00. Bottom: Lisner necklace combining rhinestones and plastic inserts in a floral motif. $35.00 – 55.00.*

Bottom right: *Four pairs of Lisner earrings. $15.00 – 25.00 each. Lisner necklace. $45.00 – 65.00.*

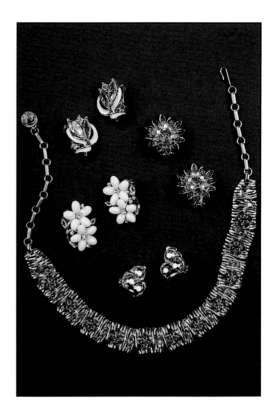

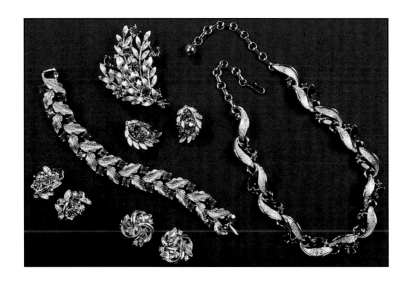

Top left: *Top left: Lisner pin with sculptured plastic "stones." $35.00 – 45.00. Top right: Lisner earrings with sculptured plastic "stones." $30.00 – 40.00. Center: Lisner bracelet with sculptured plastic "stones" in two shades of blue. $40.00 – 65.00. Bottom: Lisner necklace and matching earrings with plastic inserts and rhinestone accent. $50.00 – 75.00.*

Top right: *Right: Lisner necklace with textured metal leaves and green marquise rhinestones. $35.00 – 50.00. Top center: Floral brooch and matching earrings marked Lisner. $30.00 – 50.00. Center left: Bracelet combining textured metal leaves with red rhinestones. $30.00 – 45.00. Lower left: Two pairs of Lisner earrings. $15.00 – 25.00 each.*

Bottom right: *Top: Matching pin and screw back earrings. Marked Lisner. $35.00 – 50.00. Center: Pair of Lisner earrings. $25.00 – 35.00. Bottom: Lisner necklace in floral design using multicolored rhinestones. $45.00 – 65.00.*

Left: *Lisner necklace with simulated pearl and rhinestones. $35.00 – 50.00. Five pairs of earrings marked Lisner. $15.00 – 30.00 each.*

Right: *Top left: Pair of leaf-shaped Lisner rhinestone earrings. $15.00 – 25.00. Lower right: Necklace marked Lisner. $45.00 – 70.00. All others: Five Lisner pins with diverse designs. $25.00 – 40.00 each.*

Marino

As of this date, no definite information regarding the location and dates for the company that used the Marino trademark was available. The older jewelry found on the collectible market is of much higher quality. Most of the jewelry emphasizes metalwork and lacks decorative imitation stones. Not all of the jewelry is marked, but the firm used a unique earring clip which is stamped with a triangular floral design on both sides and Pat. #1,967,965 (ca. 1934). Only marked pieces are shown in this chapter. For possibly unmarked Marino jewelry, see Chapters 2 and 7.

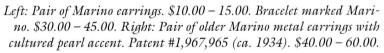
Left: *Pair of Marino earrings. $10.00 – 15.00. Bracelet marked Marino. $30.00 – 45.00. Right: Pair of older Marino metal earrings with cultured pearl accent. Patent #1,967,965 (ca. 1934). $40.00 – 60.00.*

Marvella

Marvella is the trademark initially used by Weinrich Bros. Co. (also H. Weinrich Company, Inc.), founded about 1911 in Philadelphia. The 1915 *Jewelers' Circular* lists the firm with an address at 1200 Arch St., in Philadelphia, but it appears that it also operated, perhaps at a much later date, from New York City. The 1943 *Jewelers' Circular* gives a New York address for the firm with the 1950 entry listing it as H. Weinrich Co. It appears that the Weinrich Brothers were jobbers specializing in imitation jewelry and simulated pearls. Marvella Pearls, Inc. was the name adopted about 1950 and changed to Marvella, Inc. around 1965.

The post WWII Marvella jewelry consists primarily of simulated pearls, and plain and faceted beads jewelry. The necklaces were made of multi-strands of brilliant faceted crystal beads, sometimes complemented by rhinestone roundels used as spacers. The beads are iridescent aurora borealis of highest quality, changing to different colors under light. Marvella advertisements of the 1950s emphasized this aspect of their faceted beads by actually listing the changing colors from red hot to cool pink with undercurrents of blues. In the mid 1950s, the earrings sold for under $10.00, single strand necklaces for about $15.00, and multi-strand pieces for $20.00 – 30.00. Marvella also offered simulated pearl jewelry as well as other types of jewelry combining beads or pearls with rhinestones, set on quality goldtone backings. One type of jewelry which is relatively rare is the multi-strands of simulated pearls with a very large central color stone. These are usually priced at about $200.00 – 400.00 per set at major shows. Marvella was purchased by Trifari in 1982 which itself became a subsidiary of Crystal Brands Jewelry Group in 1988. Marvella used many different trademarks, most of which include the company name or Marvell in a longer name such as Marvellesque, Marvellette, and Marvellier.

Marvella bracelet and matching earrings made of faceted iridescent glass beads. $45.00 – 65.00.

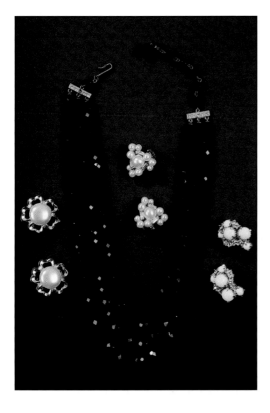

Left: *Marvella necklace made of three strands of faceted black glass beads. $30.00 – 45.00. Three pairs of typical Marvella earrings, especially the pair in the center. $15.00 – 25.00 each.*

Right: *Top: Goldtone Marvella pin and matching earrings in floral motif decorated with imitation jade beads. Good materials and workmanship. $40.00 – 60.00. Center: Two pairs of Marvella earrings with simulated pearls. $15.00 – 20.00. Bottom: Pair of Marvella earrings with opaque white glass beads. $12.50 – 20.00.*

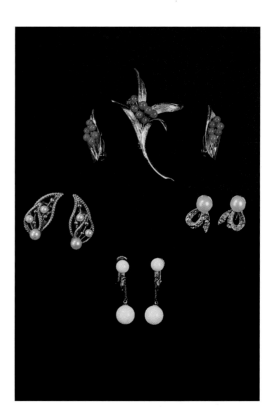

Mazer/Jomaz

Mazer Brothers was founded by Joseph Mazer and his brother Lincoln about 1927 in New York. Later, the company changed its name to Joseph J. Mazer and Company, Inc., and was listed as such in the 1950 *Jewelers' Circular.* The company went out of business in the late 1970s. Mazer manufactured high quality jewelry which sold at middle price range and is avidly sought in the collectible market today. The early 1950s jewelry was designed by Andre Fleuridas, and Adolfo designed some of the 1970s pieces for the company. The earlier jewelry is marked Mazer Bros., while the later pieces are marked Mazer or Jomaz.

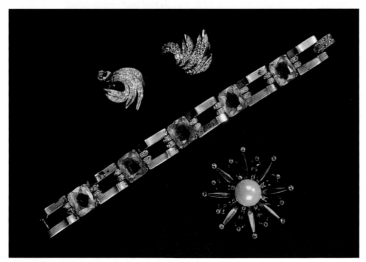

Top: Pair of pavé set rhinestone screw back earrings, marked Mazer. $35.00 – 50.00. Center: Early Mazer link bracelet with topaz rhinestones. $65.00 – 95.00. Bottom: Mazer pin in sterling vermeil set with rhinestones and a large pearl in the center. Note the balance and harmony between metal and rhinestones in this and the previous Mazer pieces. $65.00 – 90.00. Matching earrings, not shown. $50.00 – 65.00.

Pin and matching earrings made of metal leaves with a large central blue stone and scattered rhinestones. Marked JOMAZ. $75.00 – 100.00.

McClelland Barclay

If you ever come across a piece of jewelry marked McClelland Barclay, buy it without hesitation, for if you don't, you may never see it again. Barclay jewelry is not only extremely rare, but also among the very best costume jewelry ever made in America. McClelland Barclay was born in St. Louis, Mo., on May 9, 1891. He studied art with H. C. Ives, George Bridgman, and Thomas Fogarty and worked as an illustrator, sculptor, and painter. Barclay did illustrations for both *Cosmopolitan* and *Good Housekeeping* as well as posters for various agencies. Two of his posters, a U.S. Navy poster on national preparedness, and a Marine Corps recruiting poster, won national prizes.

Barclay extended his talents to making jewelry, and created beautiful sculpture-like jewelry in sterling silver and others set with rhinestones on gold plated metal. Unfortunately, Barclay's life came to an abrupt end during WWII, when a landing ship on which he was a passenger was destroyed by an enemy torpedo on July 18, 1943. His body was never found and he was reported as missing in action. The jewelry is usually marked McClelland Barclay. The *Jewelers' Circular* lists this trademark belonging to Rice-Weiner & Co., which may have been the producer or acquired the trademark after Barclay's death.

Middle right: *Necklace in Art Deco design made of three pieces of gold plated metal decorated with rhinestones. Marked McClelland Barclay. This is a typical McClelland Barclay piece in goldtone metal. Other necklaces are very similar to this piece with slight variation in the arrangement and color of rhinestones. Pins also show similar designs and can be easily recognized. $400.00 – 600.00.*

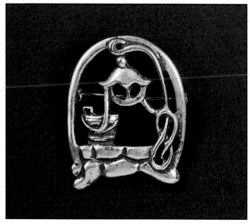

Bottom right: *Marked McClelland Barclay, sterling silver pin depicting a traditional well with bucket. This piece is also a typical example of M. Barclay jewelry in sterling silver. All sterling jewelry has almost three-dimensional sculptured look. $300.00 – 400.00.*

Miracle

Miracle is the trademark used by two different companies: Shiman Bros. & Co. and Albert S. Samuel and Co. Both firms are apparently out of business today. Shiman Bros. was manufacturer of fine jewelry and its history can be traced to the beginning of the twentieth century. Its name was changed to Shiman Bros./Colonial Inc. after its merger with Colonial Manufacturing Company in 1957. The trademark Miracle was used on both 14k as well as costume jewelry. The firm became a subsidiary of the Wasco Gold Products Corporation in the 1970s. Albert S. Samuel Co. operated from 856 Market Street, San Francisco, but the firm is neither at that address nor listed in the city phone directory. It is not clear whether the jewelry marked Miracle and displayed here was made by either company.

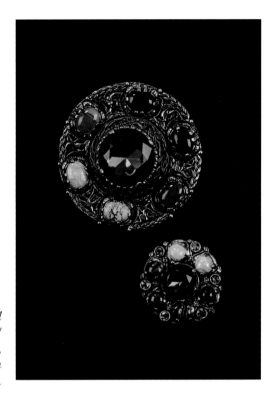

An exceptionally large brooch depicting a round hat in silvertone metal decorated with imitation gemstones. This brooch has a diameter of 3¼" and weighs three ounces. It most certainly had to be attached to heavy, thick fabric, such as a wool overcoat. $60.00 – 95.00. A small pin in somewhat similar material and design. $45.00 – 60.00.

Miriam Haskell

Miriam Haskell, born in 1899, began her professional career by opening a boutique, "Le Bijou de l'Heure," in 1924 in the chic McAlpine Hotel on posh Herald Square in New York City. The gift shop sold her unique jewelry to match and complement high fashion clothing, a WWI era concept popularized by Coco Chanel and similarly promoted by Hattie Carnegie; prior to the 1920s, only fine jewelry was considered suitable for high fashion attire.

Her success and the rising demand for her jewelry led to the founding of Miriam Haskell Co. with a wholesale division that was expanded when the company moved from Broadway to the 392 5th Ave. location. From the beginning, Haskell built a large clientele of the rich and celebrities who admired her handmade jewelry with creative and original designs produced in limited quantities. Haskell's principal

designer and collaborator was a man of exceptional talent and imagination, Frank Hess, whom she discovered while he was working as a display artist at Macy's. Their collaborative work lasted throughout her professional life and together they created some of the most original costume jewelry ever made, utilizing Czech and Austrian stones and glass beads, Japanese simulated seed pearls, and a variety of other materials arranged in a cluster of floral and abstract designs.

Miriam Haskell became ill in 1952 and passed the management of the firm to her younger brother, Joseph Haskell, who subsequently purchased it from her. It was then acquired by Morris Kinsler in 1954. Frank Hess continued as principal designer until 1954 when he retired. In 1983, Kinsler sold the enterprise to Sanford Moss, the firm's vice president, who began working for Haskell Jewels, Ltd. as a manager in 1958. The firm was then acquired by

Frank Fialkoff in 1990 and is still in business manufacturing Haskell jewelry, including reproductions that use original findings and are sold in fine department and specialty stores.

Most pre-war Haskell jewelry is not signed. The marks used since 1938 are script Miriam Haskell inside an oval frame or block Miriam Haskell within a crescent-shaped cartouche. The jewelry has such a distinctive look that even unmarked pieces can be identified by a knowledgeable collector, though they are often confused with DeMario and Robert jewelry. All Miriam Haskells, especially the early pieces, are collectible and expected to rise in prices. Haskell jewelry was always relatively expensive. In the mid 1950s, prices ranged from $15.00 to over $100.00. For example, a November 1951 advertisement in *Vogue* which introduced a new design, Gardenia, provides a price range of $12.00 to $100.00 per piece.

Above left: *An exquisite necklace and matching earrings in typical Haskell combination of excellent metalwork and pearls. Marked Miriam Haskell on an applied oval plaque. $250.00 – 300.00.*

Above right: *Left: Marked Miriam Haskell bracelet with three strands of opaque white glass beads highlighted with a floral clasp of seed beads decorated with clear rhinestones. $100.00 – 160.00. Upper right: Marked Miriam Haskell pin in filigree floral design decorated by simulated pearls. $80.00 – 120.00. Lower right: Marked Miriam Haskell brooch in floral design featuring faux turquoise. $150.00 – 200.00.*

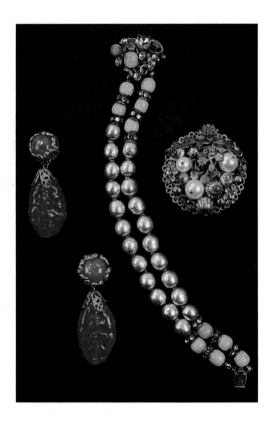

Top left: *Top left: Bracelet made of cork beads. Marked Miriam Haskell on attached metal tag. $75.00 – 100.00. Top right: Marked Miriam Haskell hinged bracelet decorated with fancy textured chain. $80.00 – 120.00. Bottom: Haskell "gold" coin bracelet demonstrating the skill and quality of workmanship which characterize all Haskell jewelry. Marked Miriam Haskell on the clasp. $250.00 – 350.00.*

Bottom left: *Left: Pair of screw back earrings with textured orange glass chunks. Marked Miriam Haskell on the fastener. $100.00 – 140.00. Center: Bracelet in two strands of simulated baroque pearls and Peking glass, terminating in an elaborate clasp decorated with beads and rhinestones. Haskell plaque mark. $125.00 – 165.00. Right: Impressive Haskell brooch with intricate floral design decorated with pearls and rhinestones. Excellent metalwork and finishing. Haskell plaque mark. $175.00 – 225.00.*

Opposite page, top left: *Necklace and matching earrings in lemon glass beads and pearls, in combination with green glass and goldtone metal leaves covering dark green dome-shaped glass stones. This set is unmarked, but it is similar to early Haskell jewelry and is shown in this chapter in hopes the readers can help identify its origin. This piece show signs of oxidization and repair. It may have more green glass leaves spaced between or behind the pearls. The author has seen several other similar pieces with slight variations. There is also a strong possibility that this set is a French import. $150.00 – 200.00. The necklaces are usually priced in the $100.00 – 150.00 range.*

Opposite page, top right: *Two Miriam Haskell pearl necklaces. Both with Haskell plaque mark. $120.00 – 160.00.*

Opposite page, bottom left: *Opaque white glass bead necklace marked Miriam Haskell on a metal tag. $100.00 – 140.00. Three pairs of marked Haskell earrings. $40.00 – 70.00 each.*

Opposite page, bottom right: *Very long necklace and matching earrings made of melon-shaped corrugated metal beads with excellent finishing. Marked Miriam Haskell on an attached metal tag and Haskell on screw back/clip earrings. $200.00 – 300.00.*

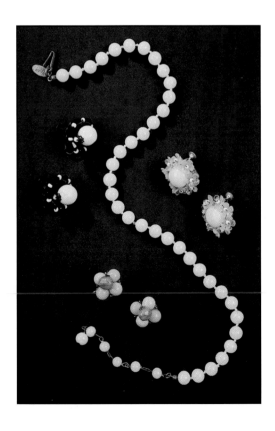

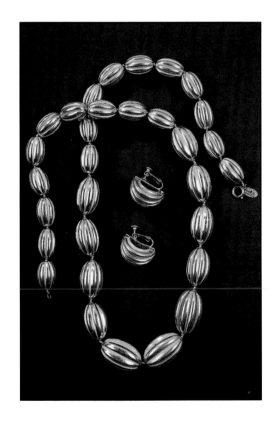

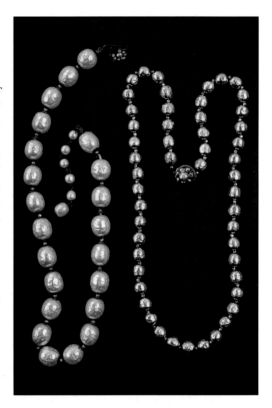

Left: *Top: Three strands of faceted black glass with red and green seed spacers make up this marked Miriam Haskell necklace. $100.00 – 150.00. Bottom: Marked Miriam Haskell necklace made of baroque pearls featuring cloisonne bead in the center. $200.00 – 250.00.*

Right: *Two typical Miriam Haskell pearl necklaces. Haskell plaque mark on both pieces. $100.00 – 150.00.*

Mizpah

As of this date, no information on the manufacturer, location, and dates of production of jewelry marked Mizpah was available. Over many years of collecting costume jewelry, the author has seen only a few pins marked Mizpah. The marked jewelry may have been presentation pieces given at time of parting rather than a manufacturer's trademark.

Mizpah was the name of several ancient cities in Palestine and is mentioned numerous times in the Bible. According to the Book of Judges, chapters 20–21, the Israelites assembled at Mizpah before the battle against the Benjamites. The possible site, now fully excavated, lies just north of Jerusalem. In ancient times, the word Mizpah meant "border" or "watchtower," but in today's common usage it means "farewell" or "God watch over you." Consequently, the jewelry marked Mizpah may have been given to a loved one at the time of departure. This is all speculative, but if true, it would explain the rarity as well as adding another dimension to the jewelry's history which some collectors may find appealing. Three Mizpah pins in the author's collection are all set with a relatively large colored stone and demonstrate quality workmanship.

Pin with exceptionally large amethyst stone mounted on silvertone metal with leaf pattern. Marked MIZPAH with an arrow going through two hearts. $60.00 – 100.00.

Monet

Monet's past is rooted in a company, Monocraft, founded in Providence, R.I., in 1929 by brothers Michael and Jay Chernow. Monocraft produced gold plated monograms which were set on handbags in the store at the time of purchase. The business expanded and the company became recognized as a manufacturer of durable and quality initials. The Chernow brothers, capitalizing on this advantage, began manufacturing jewelry under the name Monet around 1937.

Most Monet jewelry is made of gold plated metal with creative Art Moderne designs which were ahead of their time. Much of the 1940s jewelry used silver as the base metal. Monet was also responsible for several technological advancements in jewelry, such as the development of the friction ear clip which adjusted so it could firmly fit the ear without causing undue and painful pressure; and the barrel clutch for pierced earrings which replaced the butterfly clutch. The barrel clutch, now standard clutch in the industry, can be adjusted on the post to fit earlobes of any thickness, while the older clutches were not adjustable. Monet jewelry was sold at the middle price range. In the late 1940s – early 1950s, necklaces had an average price of $12.00 – 20.00 while earrings could be purchased at an average price of $4.00 – 7.50.

Monet was acquired by General Mills in 1968. In 1977, the company introduced a new line of jewelry named Ciani, with some pieces priced as high as $500.00. The firm was subsequently purchased by Crystal Brands Jewelry in 1989 and is still in operation. All Monet jewelry is marked on the back of the piece and/or on a metal tag attached to the necklace chain. Actually, the company was among the first to adopt the practice of marking their jewelry. Monet jewelry, especially the early and silver pieces, is sought by certain collectors, but not all collectors favor the jewelry and for this reason it is both underrated and underpriced in the market. Any collection of costume jewelry should include at least a few Monet pieces because of their durable and lasting quality and modern designs which were far ahead of their time.

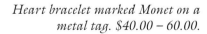

Heart bracelet marked Monet on a metal tag. $40.00 – 60.00.

Left: *Left: Monet slide necklace. $25.00 – 40.00. Right: Monet gold plated chain. $15.00 – 25.00. Center top: Monet pin and matching earrings in floral motif made of textured metal, displaying quality metal plating and workmanship for which Monet is famous. $40.00 – 65.00. Lower center: Monet dog figural pin. $30.00 – 45.00. Bottom: Monet white and gold metal flower pin. $25.00 – 35.00.*

Right: *Monet necklace. $45.00 – 65.00. Five pairs of marked Monet earrings. $20.00 – 35.00 each.*

Mylu

Mylu is the trademark used by Mylu Design Co. which ceased operations sometime in the 1970s. Most Mylu jewelry is in the form of novelty and figural pins, including a large amount of Christmas jewelry. The jewelry is usually in gold plated metal enhanced by rhinestones and/or enamel work. The quality of the material and gold plating is above average with most pieces retaining their gold luster. The jewelry is usually marked MYLU on the back of each piece.

Four figural pins marked MYLU. $25.00 – 40.00 each.

118

Napier

Napier Company was named after its president, James H. Napier, who led the company from 1920 to 1960. But the company's history can be traced back to 1875 when it was founded as Whitney and Rice in Attleboro, Mass., manufacturing silver products. The firm changed hands and name in 1882 and became Carpenter and Bliss and shortly thereafter, E. A. Bliss and Co., Inc. After rapid expansion in the late 1880s, the company moved to Meriden, Conn., in 1890. After WWI, the firm shifted emphasis from silver products to production of modern jewelry. James Napier became president in 1920 and the company adopted the name Napier-Bliss Co. In 1922, the name was changed to Napier Company. Napier is still in business today and a major producer of costume jewelry.

Most, but not all, Napier jewelry is simple, lacking fancy ornamentation and the embellished glitter of other costume jewelry. The designs are modern and simple in basic geometric forms and floral motifs. Some of the metalwork has a sculptured look somewhat resembling Mexican and Scandinavian silverwork. Today Napier jewelry is mass produced in large quantities and marketed through major department stores. The company used several trademarks, but they all include the name Napier.

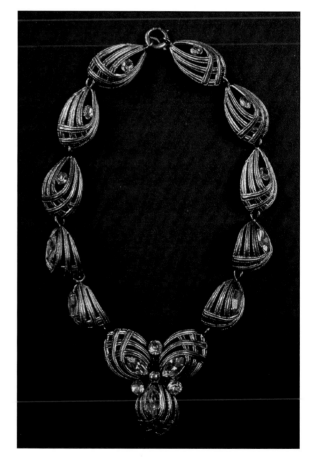

Above left: *Pavé set Napier heart pendant with matching screw back/clip earrings. Silver metal base. $40.00 – 65.00.*

Above right: *Exotic Napier necklace in silver and topaz rhinestones. $90.00 – 150.00.*

Left: *An exceptionally large (5" wide) Napier brooch and matching earrings in silver metal, depicting a bunch of grapes. $70.00 – 100.00.*

Bottom left: *Necklace and matching earrings with impressive Napier design, accomplished by combining silver and imitation lapis lazuli. $100.00 – 165.00.*

Bottom right: *Top: Napier leaf pin and matching earrings in sterling vermeil. $50.00 – 70.00. Center: Large Napier metal flower pin decorated with rhinestones. $30.00 – 50.00. Center right: Pair of Napier earrings made of simulated pearls. $15.00 – 20.00. Lower left: Napier poodle pin with moving head. $35.00 – 50.00. Lower right: Napier apple pin. $25.00 – 40.00.*

Opposite page, top left: *Center: Napier multi-strand metal bead necklace and possibly matching earrings. $45.00 – 60.00. Right: Two pairs of Napier earrings. $15.00 – 25.00 each.*

Opposite page, top right: *Outstanding Napier silver bracelet with simulated sharkskin backing that folds over the semicircle rings on the top. $95.00 – 145.00. Earrings. $30.00 – 45.00.*

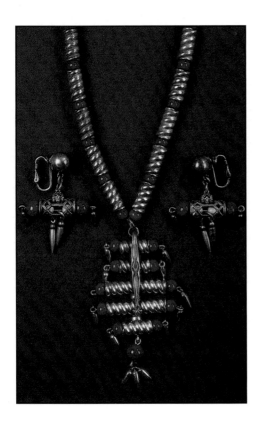

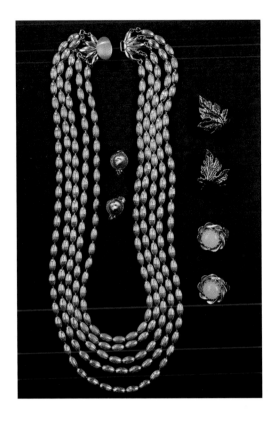

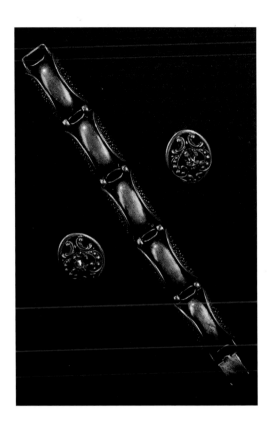

Nettie Rosenstein

Born in Vienna, Austria, Nettie emigrated with her family to the U.S. around 1892 when she was a small child. Like Carnegie, Rosenstein entered the world of fashion clothing and by the early 1930s had developed quite a reputation in the fashion world as a major designer, marketing her own fashion line and accessories. In 1961, Rosenstein discontinued her fashion line while the production of her jewelry and accessories continued for another decade. She died in 1980.

Rosenstein jewelry is of outstanding quality with unique designs which at the time sold at exceptionally high prices. Many pieces are in medal-like or figural form with imaginative designs, but not necessarily desirable by every collector as wearable jewelry. Many early pieces are in sterling silver and vermeil. The jewelry is usually marked with her name.

Attractive Rosenstein earrings with pavé set rhinestones and a central turquoise stone. Marked Nettie Rosenstein. Excellent material and workmanship. $50.00 – 85.00.

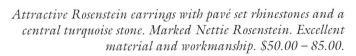

Newhouse

The jewelry marked Newhouse was possibly manufactured by J. L. Newhouse and Son, Inc. during the 1950s – 1960s period. Marked Newhouse jewelry is rare and this may be its first exposure in a book on costume jewelry. All of the pieces seen by the author are rhinestone jewelry of above average quality. Signed pieces are marked Newhouse on the earring clips.

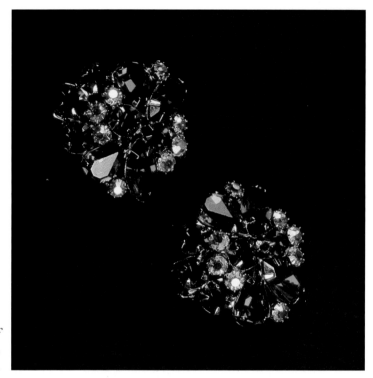

Pair of clip earrings decorated with rhinestones of three different colors. Marked NEWHOUSE. $30.00 – 45.00.

Ora

The trademark Ora belongs to the Chicago firm of Agnini and Singer, later Ralph Singer Company. The company was originally founded in 1921 by Oreste Agnini, a native of Naples, Italy. The firm was a manufacturer of costume jewelry, particularly novelties, shoe buckles, and hair ornaments in the 1930s, and a supplier of rhinestone buttons and pins for Eisenberg dresses before the latter undertook the production of Eisenberg jewelry. The Ora trademark was first used about 1951 and is more associated with Ralph Singer Company, Agnini's partner, which assumed control after the retirement of Agnini in 1952. Most of the Ora jewelry is small pieces set with quality rhinestones on gold or rhodium plated metal. Some of the jewelry combines the simulated pearls with rhinestones. The designs are subdued and traditional, but quite attractive. In early 1950s, Anne Geyer was the principal designer. Figural and novelty pins abound, notably, Shriner jewelry. But not all of the jewelry is set with rhinestones. Some of the later jewelry displays heavy metalwork accented with pearls. The mid 1950s advertisements by the company declared its jewelry as "Jewels of the Hour with a lifetime guarantee." An average price for a necklace was $10.00 – 15.00 while brooches sold for $7.00 – 10.00. The jewelry is marked ORA, sometimes within a rectangle frame, in small and hard-to-see letters. Always look for it on the back of the piece itself, not on the fasteners, such as earring clips or screws. Apparently Ralph Singer Co. is still in business and is listed in the 1994 *Jewelers' Circular*.

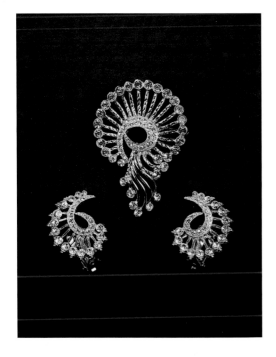

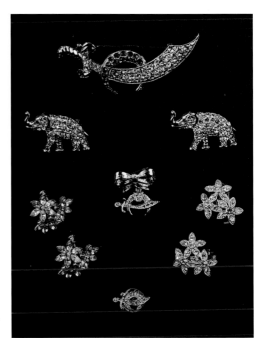

Top left: *Pin and matching earrings in clear rhinestones. Marked ORA. $40.00 – 60.00.*

Top right: *Center column: Three Ora Shriner pins. Top: $35.00 – 55.00. Center: $30.00 – 40.00. Bottom: $20.00 – 30.00. Second row: Two Ora rhinestone elephant pins. $25.00 – 40.00 each. Third row: Two pairs of Ora rhinestone earrings. $20.00 – 35.00 each.*

Bottom left: *Top: Ora flower brooch in goldtone metal and pearl with matching earrings. $30.00 – 45.00. Bottom: Two pairs of Ora rhinestone earrings. $25.00 – 35.00 each.*

Bottom right: *Exceptionally attractive necklace and matching earrings in floral design, utilizing faceted clear and blue stones. All pieces marked ORA. $135.00 – 185.00.*

Pakula

Pakula and Company was founded in Chicago about 1940. The company specialized in production of charms and identification bracelets, pearl jewelry, and compacts. Pakula jewelry is not very common and most of the pieces seen by the author are of average or below average quality. The firm produced pearl jewelry as well as others employing plastic inserts and rhinestones. These look like Lisner and lower priced Coro jewelry. The company is still in business.

Pakula used various trademarks including Aloha used exclusively on pearl jewelry; Enchantress within an oyster shell; Golden Key with a large key between the two words; and the letter P in a shield.

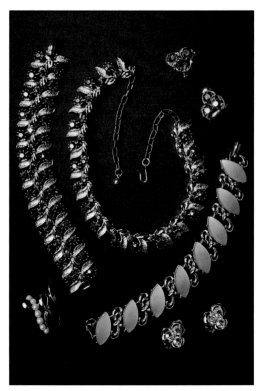

Top left: Matching necklace and bracelet with aurora borealis stones. Marked PAKULA. $60.00 – 95.00. Lower left: Pakula monogram pin with simulated pearls. $15.00 – 20.00. Right: Pakula bracelet with pastel plastic inserts. $25.00 – 40.00. Upper and lower right: Two pairs of marked Pakula earrings set with aurora borealis stones. $15.00 – 25.00 each.

Pam

Some jewelry found in the collectible market is marked PAM with a copyright symbol, but as of this date, the author has not been able to identify the manufacturer. The jewelry is almost identical to average Coro jewelry, giving the initial impression that the trademark may be one of the unregistered marks used by Coro. But careful examination indicates that the findings used by PAM are not identical to Coro findings. PAM jewelry is very scarce and this may be its first exposure in a book on costume jewelry.

Necklace with iridescent stones and enameled leaves in floral motif. Marked PAM. $35.00 – 50.00.

Panetta

Beneditto Panetta was already an accomplished jeweler engaged in the manufacture and retail sale of fine jewelry when he left Naples, Italy, for the United States. Once settled in New York City, Panetta began manufacturing fine jewelry which he wholesaled to jewelry stores. He also worked briefly for the Trifari and Pennino companies. After WWII, Panetta and his two sons Amedeo and Armand founded Panetta in 1945, and began manufacturing costume jewelry. Panetta jewelry demonstrates workmanship of highest quality. Some of the jewelry is in clear rhinestones mounted on rhodium plated base in classic or Edwardian designs. Others employ stones of various colors and shapes mounted on gold plated metal bases showing heavy metalwork. The firm also manufactured enchanting enamel jewelry complemented with pavé set rhinestones. Panetta was acquired by a Japanese concern in the late 1980s and is still in business at 25 W. 36th, NYC. The jewelry is usually signed Panetta.

Top: Pair of Panetta rhinestone earrings. $30.00 – 40.00. Bottom: Large pin/pendant with a central aquamarine stone mounted on openwork goldtone metal decorated with clear rhinestones. Marked PANETTA. $60.00 – 95.00.

Pastelli

Pastelli was the registered trademark of Royal of Pittsburg located in Pittsburg, Penn. The firm was in business from the mid 1950s to the mid 1980s. Pastelli jewelry is quite attractive and distinguishable. The firm manufactured primarily rhinestone jewelry often combined with frosted and translucent pastel stones and enameled pieces in pastel colors without stones. When signed, the jewelry is marked Pastelli. The mark Pastelli in script signature form under a crown and the word Royal is found on tags, and the author strongly suspects that much of the jewelry was not marked.

Enameled leaf pin and somewhat similar pair of enameled earrings. All pieces marked Pastelli. $20.00 – 30.00 each.

Pell

This company was founded in 1941 by the Gaita brothers in New York. Apparently, the company suspended production during WWII and resumed its operations after the war in the mid 1940s. Most of the jewelry found in the collectible market is figural pins with the earlier pieces employing primarily round and baguette clear rhinestones. As of 1990, Alfred Gaita, the youngest of the four founding brothers, was leading the company. The firm under the name of Pell Jewelry Co. is located in Long Island City, N.Y.

Three marked figural pins by Pell. All pieces well constructed with quality material. Cat. $45.00 – 65.00. Dog. $35.00 – 50.00. Swan. $45.00 – 70.00.

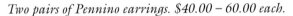

Pennino

Pennino is the trademark of Pennino Brothers founded by Oreste Pennino in the late 1920s in New York City. The firm manufactured jewelry, watch cases, and possibly watches. It was listed in the 1950 *Jewelers' Circular* and continued operations until about 1961.

Pennino jewelry demonstrates fine workmanship. The firm employed top quality stones mounted on sterling silver or heavily gold plated metal in traditionally classic designs. The jewelry is quite scarce in the collectible market and much of the jewelry seen by the author appears to have been made in the 1940s – 1950s period. Pennino jewelry is highly collectible and avidly sought by most collectors, especially the pre-war pieces. For this reason, it is sold at high prices which are expected to rise in the future. When signed, the jewelry is marked Pennino in script signature form or Pennino, sometimes with Pat. Pen. mark. The author strongly suspects that not all of the jewelry was marked.

Two pairs of Pennino earrings. $40.00 – 60.00 each.

Polcini

Polcini is a trademark used since about 1960, but the manufacturer's history can be traced back to the early 1900s when an accomplished Italian master jeweler, Ralph Polcini, emigrated to the U.S. and founded a small company in New York to manufacture costume jewelry. The original name of the company was Leading Jewelry, but after WWII, the company name was changed to Ledo. After Ralph's death in 1954, his son Damon Polcini assumed the leadership of the firm and the name was changed to Polcini. Damon Polcini died in the mid 1980s, but the company continued its operations on a smaller scale. The Polcini trademark is apparently unregistered and the firm is not listed in the *Jewelers' Circular*.

Polcini jewelry is of high quality and relatively scarce. Most of the jewelry combines excellent metalwork with high quality rhinestones in traditional and classic designs. Ledo jewelry is even more scarce and a find prized by any collector.

Elegant rhinestone pin in classic floral motif. Marked Polcini. $45.00 – 65.00.

Regency

As of this date, no definite and reliable information on dates, location, and manufacturer of jewelry marked Regency was available. Several companies used somewhat similar Regency trademark. Based on the material and designs of the jewelry available on the collectible market, the jewelry was manufactured between the 1940s to possibly early 1960s. Regency jewelry exhibits quality designs, superior material, and fine workmanship. The manufacturer employed top quality and unique rhinestones similar to those found on Florenza and Hollycraft jewelry. Much of the Regency jewelry found in the collectible market is decorated with multicolored rhinestones, sometimes combined with opaque and frosted imitation stones. Another type of jewelry combines beads and baroque pearls with antiqued metalwork in floral motifs.

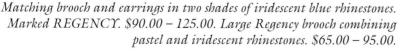

Matching brooch and earrings in two shades of iridescent blue rhinestones. Marked REGENCY. $90.00 – 125.00. Large Regency brooch combining pastel and iridescent rhinestones. $65.00 – 95.00.

Left: *Necklace with glass moonstones and iridescent rhinestones. Marked REGENCY. $100.00 – 150.00.*

Right: *Necklace and matching earrings with typical Regency iridescent rhinestones. Marked REGENCY. $100.00 – 150.00.*

Reinad

No definite information concerning the manufacturer, location, and dates of production of jewelry marked Reinad was available at the time of this publication. The 1950 *Jewelers' Circular* lists Reinad as a trademark used by Reinad Fifth Avenue of New York City, and there was also Reinad Novelty Company which operated from New York City during the same period. The latter also collaborated with Sceptron Jewelry Creations in the 1940s, manufacturing costume jewelry marked Sceptron.

Reinad jewelry is extremely rare and consists primarily of large brooches displaying excellent craftsmanship. These combine quality metalwork with clear and/or colored rhinestones. On most of the pieces seen by the author, the designer attempts to create a balance between the display of metalwork and imitation stones, with neither overwhelming the other. Based on the designs, the jewelry was manufactured possibly no later than the mid 1950s. If you see a piece of Reinad jewelry and like it, try to buy it, for you may never get a second chance; it will not be cheap when purchased from an informed dealer.

Large 3" wide brooch with sculptured floral design and emerald green rhinestones. Marked Reinad. $250.00 – 300.00. Reinad floral spray brooch with sapphire blue rhinestones. $175.00 – 235.00.

Richelieu was the trademark used by Joseph H. Meyer and Bros., founded in New York at the turn of the century. The Richelieu mark was first used in 1911. The firm specialized in production of simulated pearls and other costume jewelry incorporating pearls. It also manufactured men's jewelry. The mark is still used by Lisner-Richelieu Corporation on gold plated and silver jewelry employing cultured pearls.

Richelieu jewelry is not widely collected and has been totally neglected in other books on costume jewelry. This is largely due to the fact that much of the jewelry was not marked and most of the artificial pearl jewelry is by now damaged or discolored, losing its original luster. But the jewelry must have looked beautiful at the time of the purchase. Current Richelieu jewelry employs cultured pearls, especially freshwater pearls, which are more durable. This newer jewelry is beautiful and will certainly become collectible in the future. Relative to other costume jewelry, Richelieu jewelry was not expensive. A 1955 advertisement in *Vogue* lists a single strand choker at $3.00 and earrings at $2.00 a pair.

Above left: *Right: Richelieu simulated pearl and turquoise necklace with matching earrings. $25.00 – 50.00.*
Left: Three pairs of Richelieu simulated pearl earrings. $15.00 – 25.00 each.

Above right: *Early Richelieu simulated pearl necklace. $75.00 – 100.00.*

Robbins

This company was founded by Charles M. Robbins in 1892 in Attleboro, Mass. The firm owes its origin to manufacturing campaign buttons, but eventually became a major producer of badges, medals, and emblems as well as novelty and costume jewelry. In 1910, Ralph Thompson assumed the ownership of the company and it was incorporated in 1912 as Robbins Company, Inc. In 1963, the company was acquired by Continental Communications and is still in business manufacturing jewelry for both men and women.

Cameo pin. White on black plastic. Marked Robbins & Co. Attleboro Mass. $25.00 – 40.00. Two tie tacks marked Robbins. The lower piece has the General Electric trademark and the words "key man." $15.00 – 30.00 each.

Robert

Robert or Original by Robert is the mark used by Fashioncraft Jewelry Company. The firm was founded in New York City, in the 1940s by Robert Levey, David Jaffe, and Irving Landsman. Landaman left in 1951 and the company changed its name to Robert Originals, Inc., about 1960. Robert jewelry is sometimes confused with Miriam Haskell jewelry because of the similarity of designs and materials. Most of the designs have natural and floral motifs employing faux pearls, colored glass, crystal beads, and quality imported rhinestones set on gilded filigree open wire and openwork mountings. The 1940s advertisements claim that the jewelry was entirely hand crafted and so finely detailed that expert jewelers would often mistake them for genuine precious jewels. Robert jewelry was never cheap; in the mid 1940s, a pin and earrings set would usually cost around $50.00. The firm supplied jewelry to the motion picture industry, including the jewelry for the 1952 Oscar nominated Elia Kazan movie, "Viva Zapata," featuring Marlon Brando and Jean Peters. Levey retired in 1975.

Brooch with gold metal leaves and simulated pearls. This piece is a typical Robert piece. Note similarities with Haskell, Eugene, and Reynold and Helen Art jewelry. $200.00 – 250.00.

Top left: *Left: Earrings with green beads and rhinestones. Marked Robert. $50.00 – 75.00. Right: Robert enamel earrings. $60.00 – 80.00. Top: Robert enameled tin brooch. $40.00 – 65.00.*

Top right: *Simulated pearls and rhinestones are combined with gold plated floral metal base to create this 3" wide classic Robert brooch. $225.00 – 285.00.*

Lower right: *Top: Marked Sarah Cov, brooch and matching earrings in leaf-shaped design set with aurora borealis rhinestones. $30.00 – 45.00. Right: Marked Sarah Cov, clear rhinestone pin in snowflake motif. $20.00 – 30.00. Center: Marked Sarah Cov, blooming flower pin decorated with rhinestones. $20.00 – 30.00. Bottom: Necklace in combination of goldtone metal and rhinestones, marked Sarah Cov. $25.00 – 40.00.*

Sarah Coventry

Sarah Coventry was founded in 1949 by Charles H. Stuart in Newark, N.Y., shortly after the establishment of the sister company, Emmons Jewelers, Inc. Like Emmons, Coventry was successfully marketed through home parties (see Emmons for details). The company discontinued home party plans and operations in 1984, but the rights to the name were purchased by a Canadian manufacturer.

There is an abundance of Sarah Coventry jewelry in the market at low prices. Although never sold cheaply, most of the jewelry has the look of cheap costume jewelry with simple and unimaginative designs. In the 1960s and 1970s, Coventry jewelry prices were comparable to Trifari and better than average Coro jewelry. It is evident that the parties attended by millions of women across America were more responsible for its sale than the beauty or elegant designs of the jewelry itself. Better pieces are expected to rise in price and every collector should have at least a few pieces in their collection.

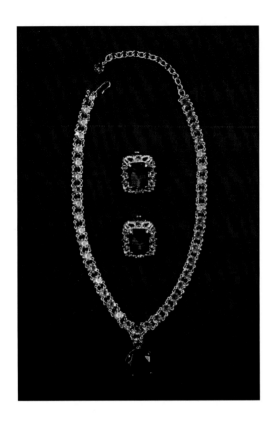

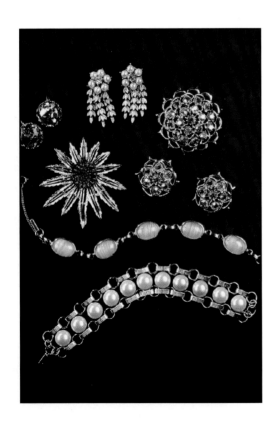

Opposite page, top left: *Pendant with large handset smoky gray stone and rhinestone decorated chain. Marked Sarah Cov. $25.00 – 35.00. Pair of possibly matching earrings with large handset smoky gray stones. $15.00 – 25.00.*

Opposite page, top right: *Upper left: Marked Sarah Cov, pendant and matching earrings featuring a large, faceted iridescent stone. $35.00 – 45.00. Upper right: Marked Sarah Cov, pendant and matching earrings featuring cabochon stones. $25.00 – 50.00. Lower left: Bar pin, marked Sarah Cov. $5.00 – 10.00. Lower right: Sarah Cov turtle pin/compact. $15.00 – 25.00.*

Opposite page, bottom left: *Top left: Screw back earrings with plastic "stones" of iridescent flakes. $10.00 – 15.00. Top center: Pair of better quality Sarah Cov earrings combining goldtone metalwork and simulated pearls. $15.00 – 25.00. Top right: Matching pin and earrings with aurora borealis stones, marked Sarah Cov. $25.00 – 35.00. Center left: Sarah Cov flower head pin. $20.00 – 35.00. Center: Sarah Cov link bracelet with glass quartz stones. $25.00 – 35.00. Bottom: Sarah Cov link bracelet with simulated pearls. $20.00 – 30.00.*

Opposite page, bottom right: *Top center: Pair of clip earrings featuring pearls with rhinestone accent. Marked Sarah. $10.00 – 15.00. Sterling silver Sarah Cov bracelet with foil-less stones. $35.00 – 55.00. Center right: Pair of S. Cov earrings. $15.00 – 20.00. Sterling silver Tinkerbell pendant marked Walt Disney Production, Disneyland. This piece came in a Sarah Coventry box, but it is not marked by the company name and is most likely a transplant. No price. Bottom left: Round rhinestone decorated Sarah Cov pendant. $20.00 – 30.00. Bottom right: Sarah Cov metal link bracelet in grape leaf link motif. $20.00 – 32.50.*

Top: *Two sets of Sarah Cov cuff links and matching tie tack. Left: $15.00 – 25.00. Right: $25.00 – 40.00.*

Center: *Two marked Sarah Cov rings. $15.00 – 25.00 each.*

Bottom: *Left: Better quality Sarah Cov pin and matching earrings in floral design, combining gold leaves and buds. $40.00 – 60.00. Top right: Sarah Cov pin with plastic inserts. $15.00 – 25.00. Center: S. Cov bracelet featuring multicolored cabochon stones. $25.00 – 40.00. Lower right: S. Cov spray pin with plastic stones simulating pearl and jade. $20.00 – 35.00.*

Schauer

Schauer Fifth Avenue, not to be confused with C. Schauer, was the distributor or possibly manufacturer of a large volume of costume jewelry in the 1960s and possibly 1970s. The jewelry was usually tagged with the company name. The firm employed quality rhinestones in a variety of colors and shapes. Linked bracelets and necklaces, particularly with large square and baguette stones, are the Schauer hallmark.

Schauer necklace in chain link with large purple stones mounted on the central portion covered with goldtone metal leaves. $35.00 – 55.00.

Schiaparelli

Born in Rome in 1890, Elsa Schiaparelli ventured into the garment industry by opening her first couture house in Paris, soon expanding to London and New York City. As an exceptionally talented and innovative designer as well as an acute businesswoman, Schiaparelli became a major rival and competitor of Coco Chanel in pre-war France and played a significant role in the development of the fashion industry for several decades.

Like Chanel and many other fashion designers, Schiaparelli extended her business into manufacturing fashion jewelry and accessories which she successfully continued in the U.S., after leaving France in 1940. Although she returned to France after the war, Schiaparelli was never able to re-establish her pre-war fame and prominence and was forced by the mid 1950s to discontinue her enterprises and limit her business to licensing agreements for the use of her name on accessories for several more years. She died in Paris in 1973.

Much of Schiaparelli jewelry was designed by many different designers and produced by different manufacturers. For this reason, there is great variation in quality and designs. There are many exceptional pieces displaying superior design, material, and workmanship. But there is also jewelry that can be ranked just above average. The jewelry is marked Schiaparelli in script signature form on an applied plaque, but not all pre-war pieces are marked.

The 1984 *Jewelers' Circular* lists this trademark belonging to Time Craft Industries with no current address, but the 1994 issue lists 1300 Galaxy Way, Concord, Calif., as the current address.

Left: *Parure consisting of necklace, bracelet, and earrings with faceted iridescent stones. Schiaparelli signature mark. $150.00 – 250.00. There is a great variation in prices. The asking price may be much higher. The author has two sets plus an additional bracelet and earrings. The second set was purchased at about 30 percent of the price paid for the first set. The earrings with the second set have a slightly thinner metal fringe than the pair shown here.*

Right: *Pair of Schiaparelli earrings with sculptured stones and pearl accent. Unusual sculptured stones were frequently used by Schiaparelli. $45.00 – 65.00. The asking price may be as high as $90.00.*

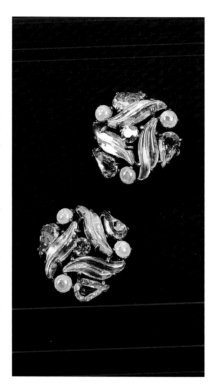

Schreiner

The company was founded by Henry Schreiner after WWII and after his death in 1951, operated under the leadership of his daughter Terry Schreiner and her husband Ambrose Albert until the late 1970s. Some Schreiner jewelry exhibits outstanding designs and craftsmanship employing unusual stones and is seldom encountered in the market. Many such pieces from the Terry Schreiner Albert Collection are displayed in Nancy Schiffer's book, *Rhinestones,* and Harrice Miller's book, *Costume Jewelry.* But much of the jewelry found on the collectible market consists primarily of pins and earrings with about average designs employing unusual and distinct stones, sometimes reverse mounted. Most brooches and earrings can be purchased in the $50.00 – 100.00 range. Schreiner jewelry is expected to rise in prices, particularly due to the recent attention it has received in several books on costume jewelry.

Two tier pin with opaque white and cloudy blue stones and clear rhinestone accent. Marked Schreiner. Schreiner frequently used unusual stones in elaborate designs. This is a common lower priced piece. $65.00 – 90.00.

Selini

The author could not find any definite and reliable information on the manufacturer of the jewelry marked Selini. Selini jewelry is of better quality, employing superior multicolored cabo-chon and faceted stones, sometimes combined with simulated pearls, in somewhat traditional designs. Both white and plated metal were used by the firm. Based on the material and designs of the jewelry seen by the author, the firm may have been in business in the 1930s – 1950s.

Selini jewelry is very scarce and has received little exposure in books on costume jewelry. Signed pieces are marked Selini followed by the copyright symbol on a raised portion on the back of each piece, not on the clasps or clips. Not all of the jewelry may have been marked.

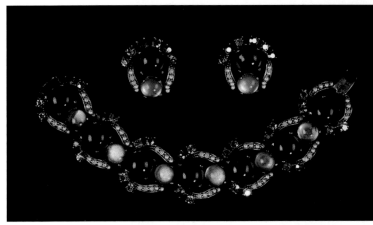

Linked bracelet of horseshoe design with dome-shaped stones in two shades of green, surrounded by seed pearls and rhinestones. Quality design and construction. All pieces marked Selini in script form. $100.00 – 150.00.

Sherman

Background information on the manufacturer of the jewelry marked Sherman is scarce and sketchy. The jewelry is of high quality, employing superior multicolored rhinestones usually mounted on gold plated metal often in floral motifs. Sherman jewelry is relatively scarce and has received little exposure in other books on costume jewelry. When signed, the jewelry is marked Sherman in script signature form on the earring clips and sometimes on an applied oval plaque on the back of pins.

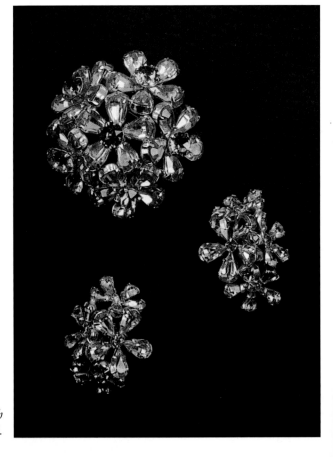

Matching pin and earrings in striking floral arrangement with yellow topaz rhinestones. Marked Sherman. $65.00 – 95.00.

Sorrento

Sorrento is the registered trademark of the Uncas Manufacturing Co., established in 1911 by Vincent Sorrentino in Providence, R.I. Most of Sorrento jewelry is either gold plated or sterling silver with delicate and somewhat classic designs. This jewelry is now attracting collectors' interest and is much more desirable than the common and lower quality Uncas jewelry with the famous U and arrow trademark. For additional background information on the company, see Uncas in this chapter.

Above left: *Matching necklace, bracelet, and earrings with lacy metalwork decorated with clear rhinestones. Marked sterling and SORRENTO. This set came in a fancy expensive box. $100.00 – 150.00.*

Above right: *Top: Sterling silver pendant and matching earrings with hematite stones. Marked SORRENTO. $60.00 – 95.00. Center: Sterling silver necklace with lacy metal work. Marked sterling and SORRENTO. This type of metalwork characterizes much of Sorrento jewelry and makes it easily identifiable. $50.00 – 90.00. Lower left: Sorrento pin with genuine jade stones. $45.00 – 65.00. Lower right: Sorrento gold plated pin with cabochon onyx and coral stones. $45.00 – 65.00.*

Star

Costume jewelry marked STAR may have been distributed, and possibly manufactured, by L. Heller & Son, Inc. The firm is listed in the 1904 and 1915 *Jewelers' Circular* with over a dozen trademarks and was possibly the wholesaler, not manufacturer, of simulated pearls and imitation stones jewelry. Two trademarks used in the 1940s and 1950s were La Tausca and Star, the former usually found on a tag on simulation pearl jewelry. Much of Star jewelry employs plastic inserts in floral or Deco designs similar to those of Lisner and Coro which were popular in the 1950s, except the quality is not as good as average Coro or Lisner. In fact, Star jewelry is usually found in poor condition with worn metal backings and scratched or missing plastic stones. The jewelry is usually marked STAR on back of earring clips.

Necklace and matching earrings in floral design mounted by cabochon and faceted purple stones. Marked STAR. This is an above average Star set. $50.00 – 75.00.

Left: *Marked Star, necklace and matching earrings in silvertone metal and blue plastic inserts. $35.00 – 50.00.*

Right: *Top: Round Star pin combining white plastic and clear rhinestones. $20.00 – 27.50. Center: Star earrings with yellow plastic flowers and rhinestone accent. $17.50 – 25.00. Bottom: Attractive Star earrings with multicolored rhinestone. $20.00 – 25.00. Left and right: Two pairs of Star earrings. $10.00 – 17.50 each.*

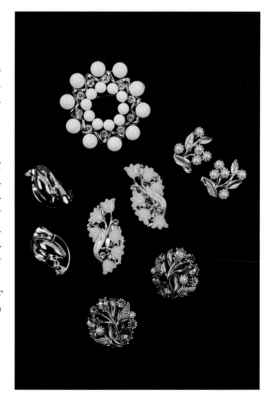

Steiner

Steiner jewelry was manufactured by a New York based company founded by Ernest Steiner. The jewelry is marked Ernest Steiner Original in script form on an applied half oval plaque. The firm manufactured both rhinestone and metal jewelry in somewhat modern designs. Steiner jewelry is relatively scarce and this may be its first exposure in a book on costume jewelry.

The Ernest Steiner Original jewelry is sometimes attributed to Ernest Steiner and Sons Inc., located in Fort Lauderdale, Fla. Apparently, the founders of both companies had identical names, though the actual trademarks are not exactly the same. According to Richard Steiner, an executive of the Steiner and Sons in Florida, this firm manufactures only fine jewelry using 14k gold and gemstones and is in no way related to the Steiner business in New York.

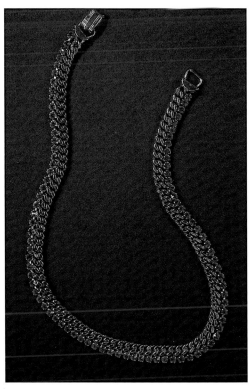

Steel chain flanked by ruby red rhinestones. Marked Ernest Steiner Original on an applied plaque. $40.00 – 65.00.

Swank

Swank, Inc., the world's largest producer of men's jewelry, was originally a women's jewelry manufacturer founded by Samuel M. Stone and Maurice J. Baer in Attleboro, Mass., in 1897 as Attleboro Manufacturing Co. In 1908, an agreement was concluded with the Aber and Wild Co. to manufacture men's jewelry. In 1914, the Kum-A-Part cuff button was developed and production expanded so rapidly that by the end of WWII, the company discontinued the manufacturing of women's jewelry in order to focus exclusively on the production of men's jewelry. By the late 1920s, the company was offering a complete line of men's jewelry under the name Swank. In 1936, the firm incorporated as Swank Products Inc., and in 1940 changed its name to the current "Swank, Inc." In the mid 1970s, Swank began experimenting with women's jewelry, but it continues today principally as a men's jewelry manufacturer.

Men's jewelry by Swank. The firm was such a prolific manufacturer that even a dozen photographs could not capture the range of jewelry it produced over so many decades. $10.00 – 35.00 each or pair.

Swoboda

Swoboda of California has been manufacturing jewelry since at least the 1950s. The jewelry is characterized by magnificent gold plated metalwork set with semiprecious stones and cultured pearls. The designs are exceptional, showing Victorian and Oriental influences. Swoboda jewelry is extremely rare, especially the more elaborate pieces, and highly prized by its owners. For these, expect to pay near $800.00 per set or above $400.00 for a necklace. The lower end pieces consist of figural pins, often with carved jade or other semiprecious stones set on gold plated metal. It is because of these lower priced pieces which were manufactured in relatively larger quantities that Swoboda jewelry is not ranked the highest on the value scale in Chapter 1. When Swoboda jewelry presents itself, buy it with no hesitation.

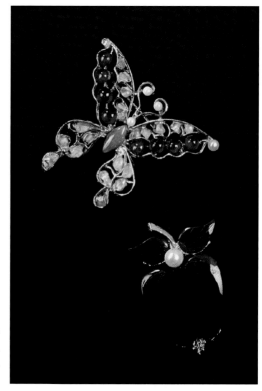

Two figural pins marked SWOBODA. Butterfly decorated with cultured pearls and semiprecious stones. $60.00 – 95.00. Carved jade in shape of apple with a cultured pearl accent. $70.00 – 100.00. Swoboda routinely used semiprecious stones in its jewelry.

Symmetalic

Symmetalic is the registered trademark of W. E. Richards Company, founded about 1900 in North Attleboro, Mass. The firm was the manufacturer of 10k gold and silver jewelry, particularly rings, pins, and pendants. The trademark Symmetalic was first used in 1936. Symmetalic jewelry is usually made of sterling silver, showing Edwardian and Art Deco influences. Some of the jewelry is in sterling vermeil, set with cultured pearls and top quality stones. In general, all of Symmetalic jewelry exhibits quality designs, quality materials, and fine workmanship. Symmetalic jewelry is relatively rare and highly collectible. W. E. Richards is still in business.

Sterling vermeil necklace with a large cultured pearl in the center. Marked SYMMETALIC. $300.00 – 450.00.

Top: Sterling silver brooch with faceted aquamarine stones and a central cultured pearl. Marked SYMMETALIC. $250.00 – 300.00. Center left: Marked Symmetalic fleur-de-lis pin. $50.00 – 75.00. Center right: Sterling silver pin. Marked SYMMETALIC. $70.00 – 100.00. Bottom: Sterling silver vermeil brooch with faceted aquamarine stones and a cultured pearl in the center. $150.00 – 225.00. Marked SYMMETALIC. All of the above pieces are typical Symmetalic jewelry. Look for Art Deco and Art Nouveau designs in sterling silver, sometimes enhanced with moonstone, aquamarine, and cultured pearl.

Tara

Tara is the trademark of Tara Jewels Co. located in Los Angeles, Calif. The firm manufactured a variety of rhinestone jewelry often mounted on goldtone metal bases. Plastic inserts were also used, though in a conversation with a spokesperson of the company, she could not recall the use of plastic in more recent jewelry. The quality of the jewelry varies drastically with the rhinestone pieces displaying higher quality of plating, material, and workmanship. The jewelry is usually marked Tara on a metal tag attached to the necklace chain or back of each piece (not on clasp or clip). It should be pointed out that the same trademark was also used by Art Carved, Inc., located in Austin, Texas, but the author's inquiries to this company were unanswered. The firm is no longer at its last listed address or in the Austin phone directory.

Necklace in floral motif with clear rhinestones. $35.00 – 50.00. Marked TARA. Pair of rhinestone earrings, marked TARA. $20.00 – 25.00.

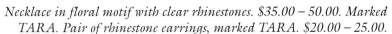

Bracelet and matching earrings with plastic inserts. Marked TARA. $30.00 – 40.00.

30 W. St. Inc.

Little is known about the manufacturer of the jewelry marked 30 W. St. Inc. Much of the jewelry seen by the author must have been manufactured no earlier than the 1960s. The firm's jewelry is about average quality, employing cabochon, faceted, and sculptured stones mounted on silvertone metal bases. The company's mark is on a raised portion on the back of each piece and is seldom fully legible.

Left: Figural bird brooch with clear and red rhinestones. This piece was manufactured in several colors. Marked 30. W. St. Inc. The mark is not always legible. $35.00 – 60.00. Right: Bracelet in floral design using sculptured iridescent stones and clear rhinestones. Marked 30 W. St. Inc. $30.00 – 45.00. Matching earrings, not shown. $15.00 – 25.00.

Tortolani

Tortolani was the manufacturer of costume jewelry from 1960 to 1975. The firm produced better quality jewelry in antiqued silvertone metal that usually has a three-dimensional sculptured look and is seldom seen with ornamental stones. Tortolani also manufactured enameled gold plated metal jewelry, sometimes using simulated pearls or stones as an accent. When signed, the jewelry is marked Tortolani in script signature form on a raised portion on the back, or on a paisley or teardrop-shaped applied plaque and/or a metal tag attached to the necklace chain.

Top: Enameled cable car pin with pearl accent. Marked Tortolani. $35.00 – 60.00. Center: Oxidized silver pin marked Tortolani. $25.00 – 50.00. Bottom: Tortolani oxidized silver necklace in floral design. $50.00 – 80.00.

Tortolani cross with filigree work. $40.00 – 55.00.

Trifari

The history of Trifari can be traced back to the mid 1800s in Naples, Italy, and a small workshop founded by Luigi Trifari, a goldsmith and producer of fine jewelry. Luigi's grandson, Gustavo Trifari, born in 1883, learned the trade in his grandfather's workshop before emigrating to America in 1904. For several years, Gustavo Trifari worked as a designer for Weinberg and Sudzen in New York City before establishing the firm of Trifari & Trifari about 1910 in partnership with his uncle, Ludovico Trifari. The firm produced costume jewelry but lasted only two years, after which Gustavo founded his own company, Trifari, which produced primarily hair ornaments and accessories decorated with rhinestones.

In 1917, Leo Krussman joined the company as sales director and later a partner, forming the Trifari and Krussman Company. The firm expanded production to include a wide variety of rhinestone jewelry. A third partner, Carl Fishel, an experienced and well-known salesman, was added in the early 1920s and the company changed its name to Trifari, Krussman & Fishel.

Trifari became one of the largest and best known producers of costume jewelry, manufacturing a broad range of jewelry at different price levels. Trifari jewelry displays superb designs and workmanship. It has a distinctive look, resembling fine jewelry, which can easily be recognized by collectors. Much of this is due to the work of a great designer, Alfred Philippe, who worked and designed jewelry for Trifari from 1930 to 1968. As a designer of fine jewelry, including jewelry for Cartier and Van Cleef & Arpels, Philippe brought to Trifari many imaginative ideas and is largely responsible for the creation and development of Trifari's distinctive and classic look. There were also other well-known designers who joined Trifari: Jean Paris (1958 – 1965), Andre Boeut (1967–1979), both from Cartier, and Diane Love (1971 – 1974), who designed the company's modern and contemporary jewelry in the early 1970s. In the early 1950s, Trifari necklaces were priced at $10.00 – 20.00 and a pair of earrings could be purchased for about $7.50.

Trifari was sold to Hallmark Cards, Inc. by the founders' sons who had assumed the leadership of the firm in 1964. In 1988, Crystal Brands acquired the company which is still in operation as one of the largest mass producers of costume jewelry.

Trifari used many different trademarks. The post WWII jewelry is always signed, with the exception of those pieces that carried a paper tag. The earlier marks are T under a crown (since 1939) and KTF (since 1935). If the letter T in KTF mark is saddled with a crown, the mark is of later date (first used 1954). The trademarks Trifari and Jewels by Trifari are primarily post WWII marks, though the latter was first used in 1920 and is often found on tags attached to the jewelry.

The Trifari jewelry pieces avidly sought by collectors are: early Trifari, especially those marked KTF which sometimes include carved pastel stones; pavé set and real-looking jewelry of the 1940s – 1950s; and figurals, particularly animals with a clear Lucite central stone known as a jelly belly. Like Coro, Trifari produced a broad range of jewelry in large volume and at different price levels. Some of the metal or plastic jewelry produced in the 1960s and 1970s is not as collectible and can be purchased at reasonable prices.

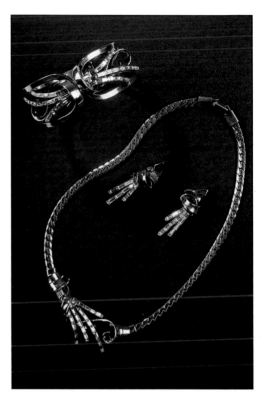

Top left: *Trifari necklace and matching earrings, with enameled leaves and turquoise blue plastic inserts. $60.00 – 85.00.*

Top right: *Trifari necklace, earrings and hinged bracelet decorated with baguette rhinestones. $165.00 – 200.00. Asking price at East Coast specialized shops may be as high as $350.00.*

Bottom left: *Top: Trifari brooch with matching earrings. Note the slender marquise rhinestones which were also frequently used by Weiss and Florenza. $65.00 – 95.00. Bottom: Fancy and classic Trifari necklace in floral motif. $75.00 – 100.00.*

Bottom right: *Trifari faux turquoise necklace. $40.00 – 65.00.*

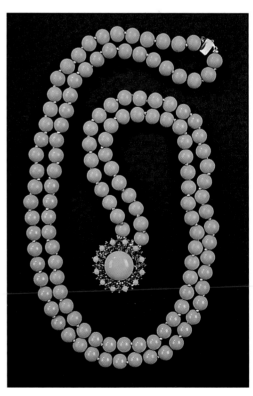

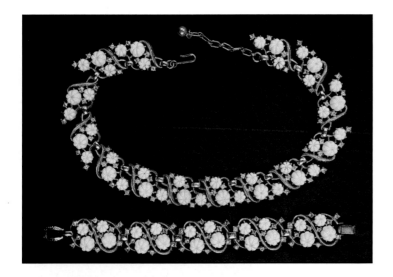

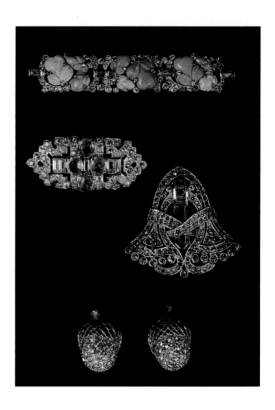

Top left: *Necklace and matching bracelet combining plastic flower inserts and rhinestones. Marked Trifari. $50.00 – 70.00.*

Middle right: *Top: Early Trifari bar pin with carved stones and rhinestones. Marked KTF. $250.00 – 300.00. Center left: Art Deco Trifari rhinestone pin highlighted with foil-less aquamarine stones. Marked KTF. $90.00 – 120.00. Center right: Early Trifari dress clip. Marked KTF. $65.00 – 95.00. Bottom: Trifari earrings depicting acorn. $40.00 – 60.00.*

Bottom left: *Sterling vermeil Trifari eagle pin in red, white, and blue rhinestones. $175.00 – 225.00.*

Opposite page, top left: *An elegant necklace by Trifari using carved, textured metal decorated with rhinestones. $95.00 – 135.00.*

Opposite page, top right: *Top: Trifari bracelet with multi-strand chains and hanging pearls. $30.00 – 50.00. Bottom: Trifari bead necklace. $30.00 – 50.00.*

Opposite page, bottom left: *Necklace and matching earrings with floral design, combining gold metal leaves and pearls. Marked Trifari. $75.00 – 100.00.*

Opposite page, bottom right: *More pearl jewelry by Trifari. Top left: Earrings. $20.00 – 35.00. Upper center: Crown pin. $35.00 – 45.00. Lower center: Pair of higher quality Trifari earrings decorated with pearls. $35.00 – 45.00. Bottom: Trifari necklace with geometric metalwork combined with pearls. $45.00 – 65.00.*

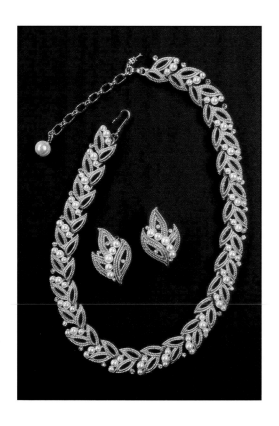

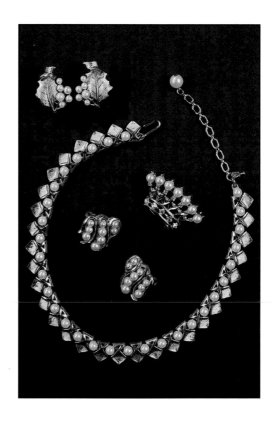

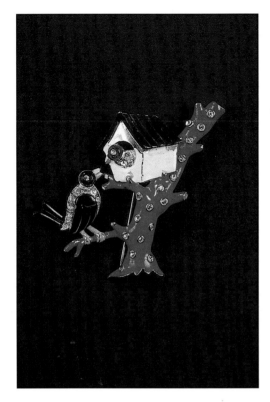

Top left: *Trifari enamel fur clip depicting nesting birds. $250.00 – 350.00. Asking price may be over $1,000.00.*

Top right: *Left & center: Trifari necklace and matching bracelet with pearl-like inserts. $75.00 – 100.00. Center: Simulated pearls and rhinestones are used to enhance the swirling metal gold leaf design of this Trifari brooch. $35.00 – 50.00. Bottom: This pair of Trifari earrings displays somewhat similar floral motif. $25.00 – 40.00.*

Bottom left: *Top left: Two small Trifari butterfly pins. $25.00 – 35.00 each. Lower left: Pair of Trifari rhinestone earrings in shape of flower heads. $30.00 – 45.00. Top center: Round dome-shaped Trifari brooch with delicate floral motif. $75.00 – 100.00. Center: Trifari brooch utilizing multicolored rhinestones in enchanting floral arrangement. $100.00 – 150.00.*

Bottom right: *Top left: Trifari circle pin decorated by green rhinestones. $35.00 – 45.00. Center left: Trifari butterfly pin using white plastic. $25.00 – 35.00. Lower left: Daisy pin and matching earrings in opaque white glass. $40.00 – 55.00. Top center: Trifari pin. $35.00 – 45.00. Center: Flower head brooch made of opaque white glass petals and beads. $40.00 – 60.00. Upper right: Pair of Trifari earrings displaying large blue topaz stones. $20.00 – 30.00. Center right: Trifari owl scarf pin. $15.00 – 20.00. Lower right: Pair of Trifari earrings with red plastic and baguette rhinestones. $30.00 – 45.00.*

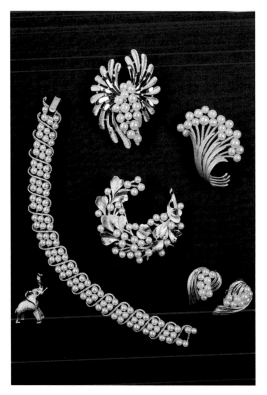

Top left: *Lower left: Trifari elephant pin. $15.00 – 20.00. Left: Trifari bracelet combining silvertone metalwork and simulated pearls. $35.00 – 50.00. Center: Trifari crescent-shaped pin with silvertone metal leaves complemented by imitation pearls. $35.00 – 50.00. Lower right: Trifari earrings. $25.00 – 40.00.*

Top right: *Center: Elegant Trifari necklace. $85.00 – 125.00. Bottom: Bracelet marked Trifari. $40.00 – 65.00. Upper left & lower right: Two pairs of Trifari earrings with similar design. $30.00 – 45.00 each.*

Bottom left: *Top: Trifari pin and matching earrings with baguette rhinestones. $60.00 – 90.00. Center: Wide Trifari brooch. $35.00 – 50.00. Bottom: Trifari bracelet. $40.00 – 65.00.*

Bottom right: *Center: Trifari necklace with baguette rhinestones. $80.00 – 110.00. Top and bottom: Trifari bracelet and matching earrings. Excellent metalwork. $65.00 – 95.00.*

Uncas

Uncas is the registered trademark of the Uncas Manufacturing Co., established in 1911 by Vincent Sorrentino in Providence, R.I. According to Stanley Sorrentino and internal company newsletters, Vincent formed a partnership with John E. Lanigan, and named the company Sorrentino & Lanigan. Later he bought out his partner and changed the company name to Sorrentino Ring Co. and finally Uncas Manufacturing Co., in 1915.

Known for its finger rings, Uncas became a major U.S. ring manufacturer marketing its products through a variety of retail outlets, including five and dime stores such as the Woolworth and Kresge chains. Uncas' success was largely due to selling its jewelry at affordable prices, including its famous ten cent wedding rings. During the 1930s, the firm continued its growth and expansion through acquisition of 12 different companies and offering a broad range of products with a worldwide distribution. In the 1950s, Uncas added an extensive line of religious jewelry.

Vincent Sorrentino retired in 1960 and his son, Stanley Sorrentino, became the president of the company. Under Stanley's leadership, the firm continued its process of diversification. In the mid 1980s, Uncas became a supplier of character and theme merchandise for the Disney Corp. Uncas is still in business, owned and operated by John Corsini, an Uncas veteran, who became the firm's president in 1991. Stanley Sorrentino continues to serve the company as chairman of the board.

Uncas Manufacturing Co. used many trademarks among which are Coronado, Christian, Heritage, Vincenzo, Sorrento, Corsini, and the letter U with an arrow passing through it or between two arrows pointing towards it. The last two marks are most often found on gold plated rings. Jewelry marked Sorrento which is primarily in sterling silver is shown elsewhere in this chapter.

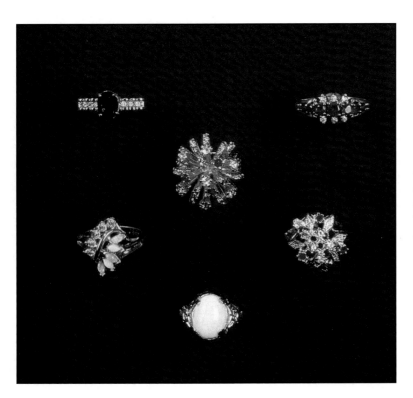

Six Uncas rings with diverse designs and stones. All marked with an arrow through the letter U. The bottom ring is in sterling silver with a genuine opal stone. $40.00 – 60.00. All others. $15.00 – 25.00.

Van Dell

Van Dell Corporation was founded in Providence, R.I. in 1943. The firm manufactured sterling and gold plated jewelry set with rhinestones and other imitation stones simulating gemstones. Van Dell also used both cultured and faux pearls. The jewelry is usually of high quality with classically traditional designs resembling fine jewelry. Van Dell jewelry is not cheap and enjoys high book prices, but because of the limited exposure in the collectible costume jewelry books, it can still be purchased at reasonable prices at most shows and flea markets. The author expects steady rise in prices in the future. Van Dell Jewelry is marked with the company name and fineness of the gold plating. Other trademarks used by the firm were Precious All and Younger Lady.

Above left: *Top: Gold filled floral pin with pearl accent. Marked Van Dell, ¹/₂₀ 12kt G.F. $45.00 – 60.00. Center: Gold filled Van Dell earrings with milky glass balls. $20.00 – 25.00. Bottom: Gold filled Van Dell pin in floral motif with blue rhinestone accent. $30.00 – 40.00.*

Above right: *Polished onyx stones are combined with textured sterling silver leaves and rhinestone accent to create this appealing necklace and matching earrings. Marked Van Dell. $75.00 – 100.00.*

Left: *Van Dell sterling vermeil pin and matching earrings in floral motif with pink faceted rhinestones. $65.00 – 95.00.*

Right: *Top: Van Dell brooch in sterling vermeil with a blue rhinestone and three simulated pearls. $50.00 – 75.00. Center and bottom: Three pairs of marked Van Dell earrings in gold filled and sterling silver. $20.00 – 40.00.*

Vargas

Vargas Manufacturing Company was founded in Providence, R.I., about 1945. The firm specialized in production of children's jewelry, but it also manufactured ornamental and costume jewelry for adults. These include rings, earrings, bracelets, and necklaces. Some of the jewelry is in sterling silver, but most of it uses gold plated metal, sometimes set with good quality rhinestones. Designs are usually traditional. The firm is still in business and expanded in 1980 by acquiring McGrath-Hamin, Inc., manufacturers of rings since 1907. Vargas jewelry is usually marked Vargas or with a V over a geometric diamond. Children's jewelry may be marked Cradle Craft.

Left: *Attractive Vargas necklace combining goldtone metal and blue rhinestones. $40.00 – 60.00. Matching earrings, not shown. $20.00 – 28.00.*

Right: *Top: Pair of Vargas earrings with guilloche style central stone framed by clear rhinestones. $15.00 – 20.00. Center: Child's heart pendant. Marked inside ⅟₂₀ 10kt G.F. and Vargas. $20.00 – 25.00. Bottom: Rhinestone studded Vargas ring. Marked 18kt G.E.P. next to Vargas V trademark. $20.00 – 35.00.*

Vendome

Vendome was established as a subsidiary of Coro to manufacture a superior line of jewelry. The mark was used as early as 1944 on charm bracelets and faux pearl jewelry, but the Vendome line which began in 1950s did not become popular until the early 1960s, largely due to beautiful designs introduced by Helen Marion, Vendome's principal designer. Basically, Vendome replaced Corocraft which up to that time marked the higher quality jewelry made by Coro. Vendome jewelry used the best of imported rhinestones and faceted crystal beads. The clarity and brilliance of the stones and top quality metalwork combined in artistically expressive designs were the main factors behind Vendome's success. The jewelry is highly collectible and should continue to rise in prices.

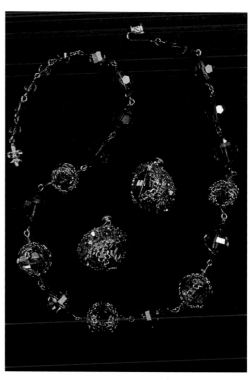

Attractive necklace and matching earrings with irregular and geometric cut iridescent glass beads wrapped in goldtone flower leaves. Marked Vendome. $90.00 – 135.00.

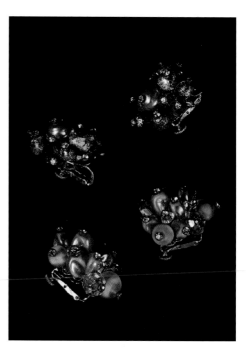

Left: *Vendome pendant in outstanding floral design covered with top quality blue and red rhinestones. $80.00 – 120.00.*

Right: *Two pairs of marked Vendome earrings combining beads and rhinestones. $25.00 – 40.00 each.*

Vogue

The trademark Vogue was first used by Park Importing Co., founded in New York City, about 1915. The firm specialized in simulated pearls and beads jewelry. But Vogue jewelry traded in the collectible market today was manufactured in the late 1930s to early 1970s by Harold Shapiro and his two partners, Jack Gilbert and George Grant. Actually Shapiro left the company in 1961 and his son Bernard founded Les Bernard, Inc., in 1963. Vogue jewelry is beautiful, demonstrating original and innovative designs, and is relatively scarce in the collectible market, particularly the earlier 1930s – 1940s pieces.

Four pairs of marked Vogue earrings in diverse materials and designs.
$25.00 – 35.00 each.

Bead necklace and matching earrings marked Vogue.
$60.00 – 85.00.

Waldman

Waldman jewelry was manufactured by Waldman Corporation which was in business no later than the 1970s. The firm may have not marked all of its jewelry and those that are marked are often illegible. Marked Waldman jewelry is scarce and pieces seen by the author are figural rhinestone jewelry.

Elephant pin decorated with clear rhinestones. Marked WALDMAN. Waldman mark is seldom legible. This is among three identical elephant pins that have legible mark. $35.00 – 50.00. The asking price may be higher.

Warner

The background information on Warner jewelry is scarce and incomplete. Based on the designs and material used, the company was probably established in the 1950s by Joseph Warner and continued operations into at least the early 1970s. Warner jewelry exhibits quality workmanship, superior materials and stones, often mounted on japanned (black) metal setting. Apparently not all Warner jewelry was marked, and some collectors and dealers tend to attribute many unmarked pieces with japanned metal backing to Warner. But it is important to note that not all Warner jewelry has blackened metal backing, and that not all unmarked jewelry with black backing is Warner jewelry. Other manufacturers such as JJ, Weiss, and Lewis Segal, also used japanned metal backings and many unmarked pieces do not demonstrate the workmanship or brilliant stones which distinguish the marked Warner pieces. All of the jewelry shown here lacks japanned backing and was intentionally selected for this purpose. Warner jewelry is not very common and since it is also of better quality, it commands solid and above average prices in the collectible market.

Large Warner brooch in combination of white satin, frosted, and clear rhinestones. $60.00 – 90.00.

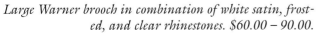

155

Pair of marked Warner earrings decorated with pearl and rhinestones. $25.00 – 35.00. Marked Warner bracelet made of framed amber glass hearts and beads. $50.00 – 75.00.

Weiss

Weiss Company was founded in New York City in 1942 by a former Coro employee, Albert Weiss. The company flourished during the 1950s – 1960s period, offering high quality costume jewelry with excellent Austrian rhinestones of exceptional quality and clarity. Weiss jewelry has somewhat traditional designs, including floral and figural jewelry. Its beautiful rhinestone studded figural jewelry, such as Weiss butterflies and insects, is avidly sought by collectors. Also desirable is Weiss "black diamond" jewelry replicating the German smoky quartz, set in typical Weiss designs. Weiss jewelry, highly underrated and underpriced, is comparable to Eisenberg and Bogoff jewelry. Without a doubt, the company manufactured some of the most beautiful and appealing rhinestone jewelry of the post WWII era. In the mid 1950s, an expandable rhinestone bracelet by Weiss sold for $10.00 to $15.00.

Weiss prices are rising rapidly and soon collectors who have missed the chance to add this type of jewelry to their collection will regret not taking advantage of the opportunity. Weiss jewelry is usually marked with the company name. Tags may also be marked A.W.Co with the large central letter W in shape of a crown. After Albert's retirement, his son Michael Weiss assumed the leadership of the company, but the firm ceased operations in the early 1970s.

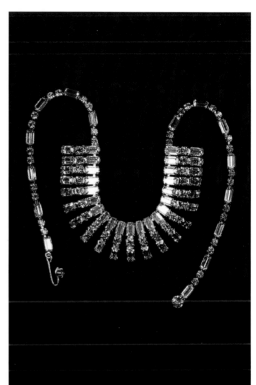

Top left: *Parure consisting of pendant, pin, and earrings displaying famous Weiss smoky diamond and clear rhinestones in an elegant, timeless arrangement. Marked Weiss. $165.00 – 200.00.*

Top right: *Necklace in a classic Weiss design showing off the firm's superior and brilliant rhinestones. $120.00 – 150.00.*

Bottom left: *Marked Weiss, Maltese cross brooch and matching earrings. $125.00 – 175.00.*

Bottom right: *Marked Weiss, rhinestone bow tie choker which is relatively rare compared to other Weiss jewelry. $150.00 – 200.00.*

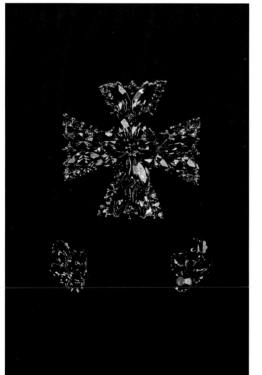

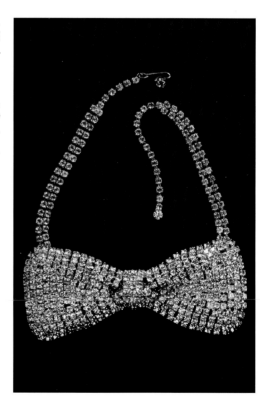

Top left: *Left: Top to bottom. Pair of Weiss earrings with blue rhinestones. $25.00 – 35.00. Marked Weiss brooch. $65.00 – 95.00. Weiss earrings set with emerald green baguette stones. $35.00 – 50.00. Center: Marked Weiss bracelet with opaque red glass and clear rhinestones. $50.00 – 85.00. Right: Top to bottom. Marked Weiss earrings. $40.00 – 50.00. Weiss brooch. $75.00 – 95.00. Pair of possibly matching earrings. $40.00 – 50.00.*

Top right: *Marked Weiss, blooming daisy pin and matching earrings. Similar pins were manufactured by several companies, some unmarked. It is not clear who set the trend, but the jewelry must have sold very well to motivate so many manufacturers. $90.00 – 135.00.*

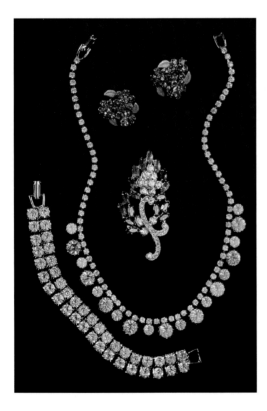

Bottom left: *More marked Weiss jewelry. Bracelet. $60.00 – 85.00. Necklace. $80.00 – 120.00. Pin with sapphire blue and clear rhinestones. $75.00 – 100.00. Earrings. $40.00 – 60.00.*

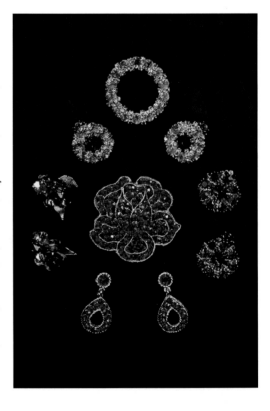

Bottom right: *Left: Pair of marked Weiss earrings. $35.00 – 45.00. Right: Pair of marked Weiss earrings. $40.00 – 50.00. Note that these are the same as the green earrings shown in the top photo. They were manufactured in several different colors. Center: Two sets of brooches and matching earrings by Weiss. Top set. $85.00 – 120.00. Bottom set. $90.00 – 135.00.*

Top left: *Left: Two pairs of Weiss earrings, one with tiger's eye and cultured pearl, and the other with enameled petals and the center pavé set with black stones. $35.00 – 50.00 each. Center: Enameled yellow flower pin with large opaque glass stone, marked Weiss. $35.00 – 50.00. Top right: Marked Weiss flower pin with opaque white glass stones. $45.00 – 65.00. Bottom right: Marked Weiss, enameled tin flower pin with a visiting ladybug. $30.00 – 45.00.*

Top right: *Left: Marked Weiss, necklace and matching earrings. $90.00 – 125.00. Right: Marked Weiss, necklace with light amethyst rhinestones. $75.00 – 100.00. Weiss pin with rhinestones of similar color. $35.00 – 50.00.*

Bottom left: *Left: Large Weiss brooch with faceted rhinestones of various shapes. $80.00 – 120.00. Pair of marked Weiss earrings. $35.00 – 50.00. Right: Marked Weiss strawberry pin. $40.00 – 55.00. Similar earrings. $40.00 – 50.00.*

Bottom right: *Top row: Three pairs of marked Weiss earrings. $30.00 – 45.00 each. Bottom: Large marked Weiss brooch and matching earrings. $90.00 – 125.00.*

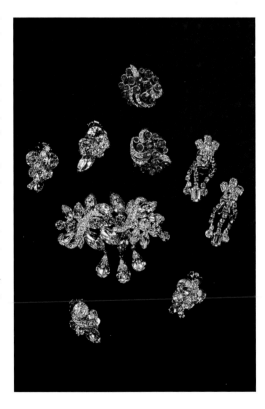

Top left: *More marked Weiss jewelry. Left: Earrings. $30.00 – 45.00. Bottom left: Necklace with double rows of brilliant rhinestones. $70.00 – 100.00. Bottom right: Bracelet with clear rhinestones. $45.00 – 60.00. Top left: Earrings with clear rhinestones. $30.00 – 40.00. Right: Triangular brooch. $85.00 – 125.00. Triple leaves brooch set with yellow topaz rhinestones. $60.00 – 90.00. Center: Brooch and matching earrings. $60.00 – 95.00.*

Top right: *Top right: Matching pin and earrings, marked Weiss. $65.00 – 95.00. Top center: Marked Weiss, floral brooch featuring enameled metal inserts framed by blue rhinestones. $65.00 – 95.00. Matching earrings, not shown. $40.00 – 50.00. Top left: Another famous Weiss strawberry pin. $40.00 – 60.00. Upper left: Marked Weiss enameled floral pin. $30.00 – 45.00. Bottom: Marked Weiss bracelet and matching earrings with enameled petals and simulated turquoise stones. $50.00 – 70.00. Lower right: Weiss brooch and matching earrings with black opaque stones. $60.00 – 90.00. Center: Weiss earrings with goldtone*

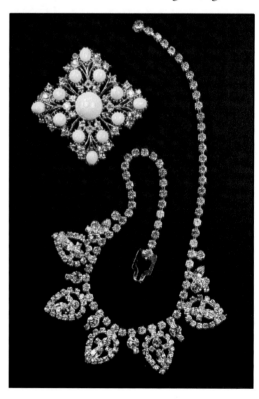

twisted rope metal base accommodating rhinestones of different colors. $35.00 – 50.00. Center right: Multitude of enameled metal flowers complemented by rhinestones make up this marked Weiss pin. $35.00 – 50.00.

Bottom right: *Marked Weiss necklace in clear rhinestones. $70.00 – 95.00. Weiss pin with painted yellow cabochon stones. $25.00 – 40.00.*

Bottom left: *Top right: Enameled flower pin and matching earrings, marked Weiss. $50.00 – 75.00. Lower right: Weiss flower head brooch. $40.00 – 60.00. Center: Weiss bracelet with blue rhinestones. $60.00 – 85.00. Left: Weiss pin. $35.00 – 50.00. Pair of Weiss earrings. $30.00 – 45.00.*

Whiting & Davis Co.

C. W. Whiting began working as a young boy for a chain manufacturing company founded in 1876 by William Wade and Edward P. Davis. As he learned the trade, he soon became a partner and eventually owner in 1907. The company expanded rapidly, largely due to the development of a chainmail mesh machine which enabled it to cheaply manufacture a variety of mesh products, including mesh handbags.

Famous for its silver mesh handbags and purse accessories, the company also produced jewelry throughout most of this century, including high quality reproductions of antique jewelry. As a silver manufacturer, most costume jewelry made by Whiting & Davis utilizes silver or silver plated metal and is usually signed with the company name, sometimes in a cartouche. The firm used at least two other trademarks, W.C.Co, standing for Whiting Chain Company, and W. & D., but the author has not seen these marks used on its costume jewelry.

Whiting & Davis plastic cameo set, including pendant, bracelet, and earrings. $150.00 – 200.00.

Left: *Whiting & Davis glass cameo pendant and two pairs of similar earrings with gold-tone and silvertone frames. Pendant marked Whiting & Davis. $50.00 – 80.00. Earrings. $25.00 – 45.00 each.*

Right: *Assorted Whiting & Davis earrings. The two pairs at the center left and right feature hematite stones, one of which is carved while the other is highly polished. $35.00 – 50.00. Glass cameo earrings. $25.00 – 45.00 each. All others. $20.00 – 30.00 each.*

Wiesner

Nothing is known about the manufacturer of the jewelry marked Wiesner. Several firms had similar names, including Wiesner of Miami and Joseph Wienser of New York, but it is not clear which, if any, of them manufactured the jewelry marked simply Wiesner. Wiesner jewelry is scarce and the author suspects that not all pieces were marked or that the firm was in business a relatively short period. Much of the marked jewelry is in both clear and multicolored rhinestones and is generally of better than average quality.

Dome-shaped pin with faceted clear rhinestones, marked Wiesner. $45.00 – 65.00.

Wingback

This trademark was used by Wingback Company founded in New York City, about 1946. The jewelry is extremely rare and identifiable by its "Wingback" fastener on the earrings and the Wingback mark on the wire. This type of jewelry is primarily found with simulated pearls or rhinestones of different colors, possibly of Czechoslovakian origin, and must have been manufactured for only a short period. In the 1950s, Danecraft aggressively promoted its Wingback earrings as "a totally new way to wear earrings," but the company's relationship with Wingback Company and this earlier jewelry is not clear.

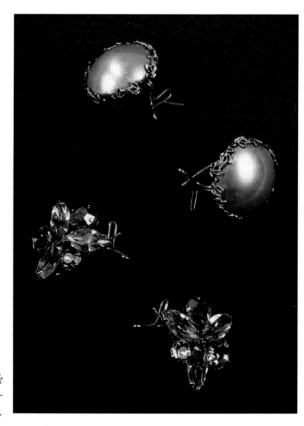

Two pairs of Wingback earrings photographed so the Wingback fastener is visible. Both are marked Wingback on the wire fastener. $25.00 – 40.00.

Chapter 4

Unmarked Costume Jewelry

Much of the costume jewelry found on the market is unmarked. Many pre WWII manufacturers did not sign their jewelry and used marked boxes or tags which were removed after the purchase. Others marked only one piece in a set, which, once separated, made identifying the unmarked pieces difficult. Many collectors frown at unmarked jewelry and collect only signed jewelry. Of course, by doing so they deny themselves the pleasure of owning some of the best jewelry made by the industry which usually can be purchased at bargain prices.

Evaluating unmarked costume jewelry should be based on the five criteria discussed in Chapter 1, especially design, originality, workmanship, and quality of the materials used. You can be more successful in your hunt for quality, unmarked costume jewelry by studying the signed costume jewelry you own and those shown in this and other books on costume jewelry. Try to become familiar with the design and the look which typifies the jewelry made by each manufacturer. Examine the metal, its color and plating, stamping on the back, the types of stones and beads used, and the way they are usu-

ally arranged as part of the design. Carefully compare the chains, hooks, and clasps on necklaces and bracelets, the screw and clips on earrings, the pin backs, and the way the pin stem is fastened. After a while, you will be able to identify many unmarked jewelry pieces or at least attribute them to few possible producers. Of course, without positive documentation, we would not know for certain the identity of the manufacturer, but being half certain is better than complete uncertainty.

Because of the problems with attribution, all unmarked jewelry shown in this section is identified just as "unmarked" jewelry without lengthy attempts to attribute pieces to a possible manufacturer. Currently, the author is undertaking a systematic study of the literature, designs, and findings to document the attribution of unmarked jewelry. Readers can be of great assistance in this regard by providing the author with information on unmarked jewelry. The information, such as a signed piece you own, which identifies an unmarked piece pictured in this or other books and literature; old jewelry ads and company promotions; and history would be of great assistance in documenting the history of the costume jewelry industry and recognizing the contributions of its many great manufacturers.

Some unmarked jewelry has patent numbers which can be researched to identify the manufacturer. The following table provides the approximate dates that correspond with patent numbers, but the readers should note that the date of the patent issue is not necessarily the same as the date the jewelry was manufactured.

PATENT NUMBERS (Million)	PATENT DATE
0.95 – 1.17	1910 – 1915
1.17 – 1.36	1916 – 1920
1.36 – 1.57	1921 – 1925
1.57 – 1.79	1926 – 1930
1.79 – 2.03	1931 – 1935
2.03 – 2.23	1936 – 1940
2.23 – 2.40	1941 – 1945
2.40 – 2.54	1945 – 1950
2.54 – 2.73	1951 – 1955
2.73 – 3.12	1956 – 1963

Matching Sets of Unmarked Costume Jewelry

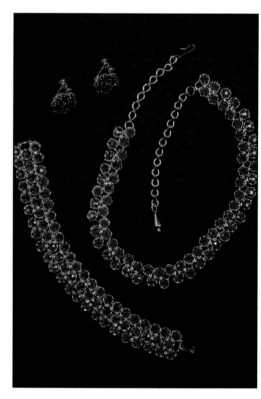

Left: *Matching necklace, bracelet, and earrings, showing open metalwork enhanced by blue rhinestones and simulated pearl fringe. Somewhat similar to some marked Barclay jewelry. $80.00 – 120.00.*

Right: *Matching necklace, bracelet, and earrings with rows of ruby red rhinestones. $80.00 – 110.00.*

Top left: *Black opaque glass and clear rhinestones are combined with gold plated metal leaves to create this pleasant and possibly not very old set. $75.00 – 115.00.*

Top right: *Opaque green glass and light green flowers mounted on goldtone metal base make up this set. $70.00 – 100.00.*

Right: *A set in combination of enameled metal leaves and pink rhinestones with simulated pearl accent. $85.00 – 125.00.*

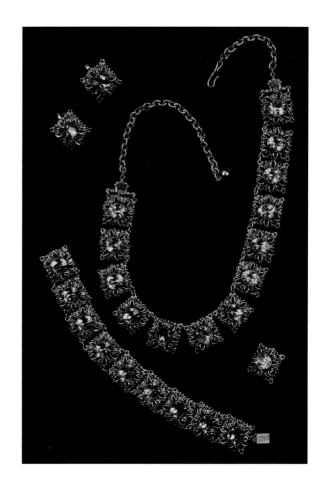

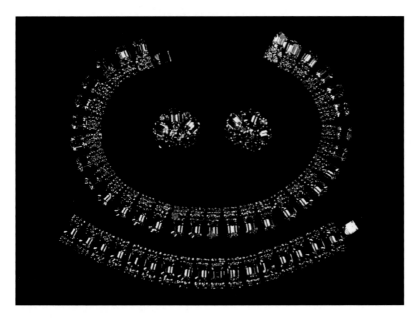

Top left: *A complete set with floral design that is very similar to Coro jewelry except that the hook, chain, and the drop are different. $95.00 – 135.00.*

Top right: *A matching set with quality topaz rhinestones mounted on filigree goldtone metal base. $95.00 – 135.00.*

Left: *Matching set with blue rhinestones similar to both Coro and Kramer jewelry. $100.00 – 150.00.*

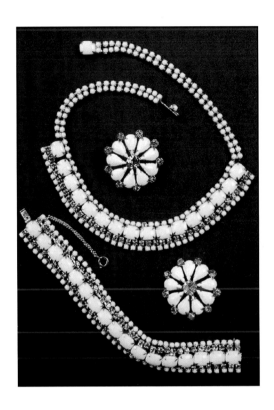

Top left: *Three different matching sets, possibly made by the same manufacturer, all exhibiting elegant designs and quality workmanship. Left: Bracelet and clip earrings in antiqued gold metal and green marbleized plastic "stones" accented by pearl and lavender rhinestones. Center: Necklace and earrings of the same combination and construction. Three-piece link bracelet with screw back earrings. $150.00 – 200.00 per set.*

Top right: *Handset opaque white glass stones are combined with blue rhinestones to create this set which was very popular in the 1940s and early 1950s. $100.00 – 150.00.*

Right: *Three unmarked sets of large brooches and matching earrings. Left: Rhinestones of various colors are combined with gold mesh knots in this attractive design. Center: Flat conical stones of iridescent green are used to create this stunning and eyecatching set. The earrings to the right use similar stones combined with slender gold leaves. Right: Rhinestones of diverse colors and size are attractively arranged to create this set. $85.00 – 135.00 per set. Extra earrings. $30.00 – 45.00.*

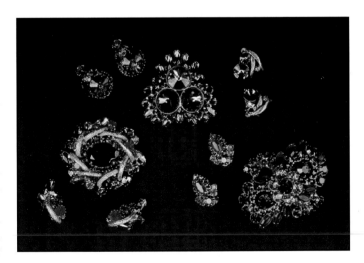

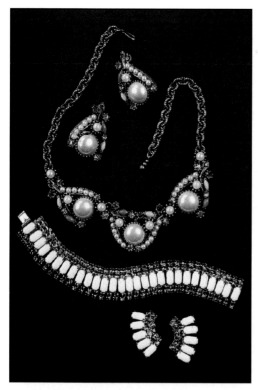

Top left: *Top: Necklace and matching earrings featuring simulated pearls complemented by imitation turquoise, coral, and rhinestones in an imaginative and novel design. $90.00 – 125.00. Bottom: Opaque white glass stones flanked by smoky gray rhinestones make up this simple but attractive bracelet and earrings set. $50.00 – 85.00.*

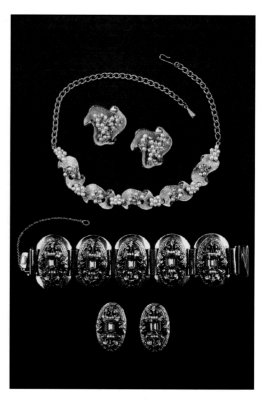

Top right: *Top: Pearl clusters in floral motif, wire mounted on textured gold metal flowers, in a highly skilled and artistic design. Fine material and craftsmanship similar to Miriam Haskell jewelry. $150.00 – 200.00. Bottom: Well-constructed bracelet and matching earrings in gilded brass, set with emerald cut topaz and seed pearl accent. The author has several other sets of similar construction with similar findings, but has not yet been able to identify and document its manufacturer. $100.00 – 150.00.*

Bottom left: *Three sets of pins and matching earrings. Top: Enameled metal flowers and leaves combined with rhinestones make up this set. $60.00 – 90.00. Right: Enameled metal complemented by frosted and glittering rhinestones in floral design. $50.00 – 80.00. Left: Opaque yellow glass stones combined with goldtone metalwork create this novel and somewhat abstract floral design. $50.00 – 80.00.*

Bottom right: *Necklace, bracelet, and possibly matching earrings in handset opaque white glass stones and blue rhinestone accent. $90.00 – 125.00.*

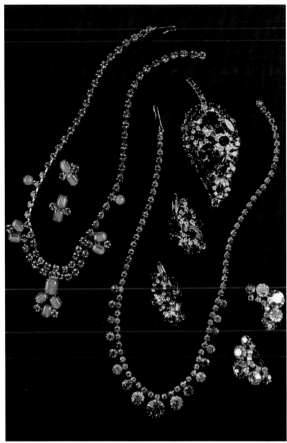

Top left: *Left: Necklace and matching screw back earrings with opaque blue glass stones and a lighter shade of blue rhinestones. $50.00 – 70.00. Top: Leaf-shaped pin and matching earrings decorated with rhinestones of assorted shapes and colors. $55.00 – 75.00. Bottom: Necklace and earrings with aurora borealis stones. $60.00 – 95.00.*

Top right: *Four matching sets in different shades of green and blue. All of high quality construction with superior rhinestones; all possibly manufactured by well-known producers. Left: Pin and earrings. $40.00 – 70.00. Lower center: Necklace and earrings in a classic, timeless design. $80.00 – 125.00. Upper center: Large brooch and earrings. $55.00 – 85.00. Upper right: Pin and earrings. $50.00 – 80.00.*

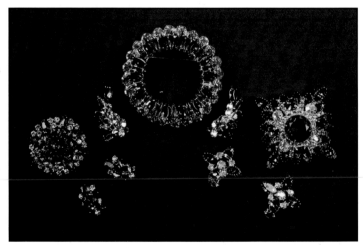

Right: *Left: Dome-shaped pin and matching earrings. $45.00 – 60.00. Center: Circle pin and matching earrings, combining marquise and round green rhinestones. $50.00 – 85.00. Right: Spotted black and iridescent rhinestones make up this nearly square brooch and matching earrings. $45.00 – 70.00.*

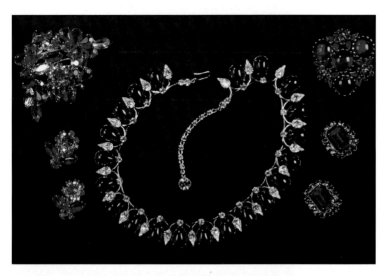

Top: *Left: Brooch and earrings combining handset red and iridescent rhinestones. $50.00 – 65.00. Center: Very attractive necklace emphasizing the contrast between handset red cabochon stones and brilliant clear rhinestones. $65.00 – 85.00. Top right: Pin with round red cabochons and enameled metal leaves, decorated with red rhinestones in a floral arrangement. $30.00 – 45.00. Lower right: Earrings with classic look featuring large, handset red stones. $30.00 – 40.00.*

Middle: *Left: Large, older flower brooch with creative combination of multicolored stones. $50.00 – 70.00. Bottom: Pair of round rhinestone earrings with blue and clear rhinestones. $15.00 – 20.00. Top center: Large floral brooch decorated with round baguette rhinestones, enhanced by simulated pearls. $50.00 – 70.00. Center: Attractive floral necklace with quality central pink rhinestones. Unmarked, but certainly the work of a known manufacturer, such as Bogoff. $55.00 – 90.00. Right: Handpainted flower brooch enhanced by chartreuse rhinestones. $50.00 – 70.00.*

Bottom: *Top: Geometric plastic pieces alternating with cabochon stones are combined and complemented by rhinestones to create this attractive bracelet; it was also made with butterscotch plastic. $50.00 – 85.00. Center: Bracelet with an Old World look, made of gilded brass featuring a large central piece holding a carved carnelian intaglio surrounded by round cabochon and faceted stones. $90.00 – 140.00. Bottom: Link bracelet set with pearl and cabochon stones simulating semiprecious stones. $35.00 – 45.00. Pair of earrings with genuine jade and coral stones mounted on a high quality and well-constructed base. $60.00 – 85.00.*

Above: *Top center: Large brooch with handset marquise rhinestones in three shades of blue. $40.00 – 60.00. Top left and right: Two smaller rhinestone pins. $15.00 – 25.00. Bottom: Three link bracelets. $35.00 – 60.00 each.*

Bottom left: *Top left: Pair of earrings with green rhinestones and textured metal drops. $15.00 – 25.00. Top right: Pair of earrings with fruity plastic stones. $20.00 – 25.00. Center: A large topaz stone is the highlight of this floral pin. $20.00 – 30.00. Lower right: Locket displaying intricate metalwork enhanced by enameled flowers, pearls, and rhinestones. $45.00 – 65.00. Lower left: Bracelet with two shades of faceted green plastic stones and a similar necklace above it in two shades of amber, both unmarked, but certainly made by the same manufacturer. Metal backing shows Ciner characteristics. Bracelet. $20.00 – 40.00. Necklace. $30.00 – 45.00.*

Bottom right: *Top: Goldtone link bracelet and earrings showing openwork and plastic inserts, complemented by simulated pearls and turquoise. $45.00 – 70.00. Bottom: Plastic is employed to simulate carved coral in this floral bracelet. $30.00 – 45.00. Similar earrings. $10.00 – 15.00.*

Top left: *Top left: Simulated pearls and coral are used to create this pair of Haskell-like earrings. $35.00 – 50.00. Top center: Iridescent stones of different colors and shapes are combined to create this attractive pin. $40.00 – 60.00. Earrings with gold leaves and iridescent stones. $25.00 – 35.00. Bottom: Two goldtone necklaces in floral design enhanced by simulated pearl and rhinestones. $25.00 – 35.00 each. Round brooch with iridescent rhinestones. $25.00 – 35.00.*

Bottom left: *Top: Pin with enameled leaves and flower heads set with rhinestones. $25.00 – 40.00. Pair of earrings with frosted and canary yellow rhinestones. $12.00 – 18.00. Center: Two link bracelets. The upper piece has plastic inserts simulating jade. $30.00 – 45.00. The lower piece employs large white opaque glass stones alternating with blue rhinestones. $35.00 – 45.00. Bottom: Two rhinestone brooches. $30.00 – 45.00.*

Below: *Top left: Attractive hinged bracelet decorated with black and white beads. $30.00 – 50.00. Top center: Leaf-shaped earrings with imitation ruby rhinestones. High quality material and construction. $25.00 – 35.00. Top right: Dangling blown glass is combined with hand painted metal leaves to create the innovative design of this pin and matching earrings. $60.00 – 90.00. Bottom: Wide link bracelet with plastic inserts simulating tortoise shell. $25.00 – 35.00.*

Top: *Early 1900s crown made of handset clear rhinestones mounted on white metal. Tiaras were popular in 19th century Europe and turn of the century U.S., but theater productions, pageants and beauty contests were the primary source of demand for both tiaras and crowns. $150.00 – 200.00. This is a roughly estimated price since insufficient numbers are traded.*

Middle: *Top: Matching pin and earrings with diverse pastel stones. $40.00 – 65.00. Bottom: Two rhinestone studded bracelets. $35.00 – 50.00. Center: Rhinestone necklace, $35.00 – 50.00.*

Bottom: *Top: Necklace of better quality, combining simulated pearls and rhinestones. $45.00 – 70.00. Bottom: Bracelet and matching earrings in combination of pearl and rhinestones. $40.00 – 60.00.*

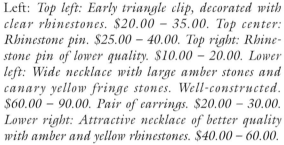

Left: *Top left: Early triangle clip, decorated with clear rhinestones. $20.00 – 35.00. Top center: Rhinestone pin. $25.00 – 40.00. Top right: Rhinestone pin of lower quality. $10.00 – 20.00. Lower left: Wide necklace with large amber stones and canary yellow fringe stones. Well-constructed. $60.00 – 90.00. Pair of earrings. $20.00 – 30.00. Lower right: Attractive necklace of better quality with amber and yellow rhinestones. $40.00 – 60.00.*

Bottom left: *Bottom: Charming green bracelet with opaque glass and rhinestones. $35.00 – 50.00. Lower left: Blooming flower head pin in opaque glass and two shades of pink rhinestones. $30.00 – 50.00. Top right: Necklace in floral motif. Though unmarked, the drop at the end of the chain limits possible manufacturers to only three firms. $35.00 – 55.00. All others: Five pairs of earrings. All except the upper right pair use opaque glass stones. $20.00 – 30.00 each.*

Bottom right: *Top: Three large rhinestone brooches. Right: $40.00 – 60.00. All others: $30.00 – 45.00. Center: Foil-less glass stones are mounted on chromium plated filigree metal base to create this slender bracelet. $45.00 – 65.00. Bottom: Attractive slender pin with large black opaque glass and clear rhinestones. $25.00 – 35.00.*

Top left: *Left: Three pairs of well-constructed rhinestone earrings.
$20.00 – 35.00 each. Center: Necklace with a large iridescent
stone and gold plated metalwork which resembles an owl. $35.00 –
60.00. Lower right: Delicate, thin metal leaves embrace large
stones in this appealing pin and matching earrings. $40.00 –
60.00. Upper right: Good quality rhinestones are mounted on
black plastic base to create this flower pin and matching earrings.
$30.00 – 45.00.*

Top right: *Three different matching sets featuring white opaque
glass. $45.00 – 65.00 per set.*

Right: *Bejeweled pieces set with diverse rhinestones simulating
gemstones. All of high quality material and workmanship. Lower
left: Hinged bracelet completely covered with handset imitation
stones. The inner rim engraved BEKX and M 4217. $100.00 –
165.00. Upper left and right: Two pairs of earrings. $35.00 –
50.00 each. Top: Large, impressive 3" brooch with handset multicolored faceted stones. $90.00 – 135.00. Center: Necklace made of
three pieces in a floral motif decorated with multicolored rhinestones. $65.00 – 90.00.*

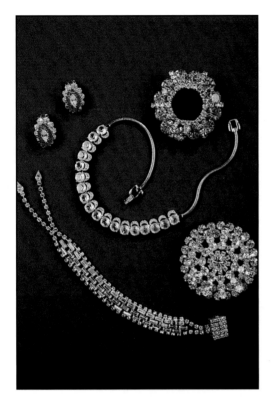

Top left: *Top: High quality circle rhinestone brooch. $45.00 – 60.00. Rhinestone earrings. $30.00 – 45.00. Center: Foil-less stones with crescent-shaped crowns make up this enchanting necklace. $50.00 – 85.00. Left: Adjustable rhinestone bracelet. The clasp box at the end when opened reveals four indentations which would allow placing the two teardrops at the other end through the box. When locked, the two teardrops will dangle on the side of the box. The total length is 9", allowing the bracelet to be adjusted between 6½ to 8" in length. $50.00 – 75.00. Lower right: Brooch. $40.00 – 55.00*

Bottom left: *Top left: Pendant with goldtone filigree work decorated with simulated pearls and possibly matching earrings. Pendant. $20.00. Earrings. $15.00 – 20.00. Center: Victorian style pendant and matching earrings exhibiting quality metalwork, complemented by rhinestones, simulated pearl, and turquoise. $50.00 – 70.00. Upper right: Chain link necklace with rhinestones. $25.00 – 40.00. Bottom: Chain necklace with rhinestone fringe. Quality construction. $25.00 – 45.00. Bracelet not shown. $20.00 – 30.00.*

Opposite page, top left: *Upper left: Flower pin. $20.00 – 35.00. Upper center: Attractive red floral pin with cabochon stones. $40.00 – 60.00. Earrings, not shown. $20.00 – 30.00. Upper right: 1930s brooch in bow motif with clear rhinestones. $27.50 – 45.00. Center: Bracelet. $45.00 – 70.00. Bottom: Assorted group of rhinestone pins and dress clips. $20.00 – 45.00.*

Opposite page, top right: *Upper left: Rhinestone earrings. $15.00 – 25.00. Upper center: Large flower pin with red rhinestones. $60.00 – 90.00. Lower left: Bracelet featuring conical brown stones, complemented by faceted rhinestones. $35.00 – 55.00. Lower right: Bracelet with emerald cut red stones. $30.00 – 45.00.*

Opposite page, bottom left: *Early pieces displaying superior gilded metalwork and topaz stones. Top: Large dress clip, $50.00 – 85.00. Center: Pin. $30.00 – 40.00. Lower center: Necklace. $65.00 – 95.00. Bottom: Bracelet. $40.00 – 60.00.*

Opposite page, bottom right: *Top left: Two early 1930s triangular dress clips. $25.00 – 40.00. Top center: 1930s rhinestone pin. $35.00 – 45.00. Top right: Fan-shaped rhinestone earrings. $20.00 – 30.00. Lower left: Pin with large pink stone covered with floral metalwork, set with rhinestones. $25.00 – 40.00. Center: Four bracelets. $25.00 – 40.00 each. Center right: Round pin. $25.00 – 40.00. Lower right: Pair of rhinestone earrings. $15.00 – 20.00.*

Left: *Top, left to right: Large rhinestone brooch. $35.00 – 45.00. Round pin with central star motif and pink rhinestones. $25.00 – 45.00. Pin and matching earrings with stylized leaf-shaped fluted metal holding iridescent rhinestones. $35.00 – 50.00. Center: Attractive necklace with rigid center in rhinestone decorated floral motif. $40.00 – 60.00. Bottom center: Gold plated metal and clear rhinestones are combined to create this bracelet. Heart charm for engraving, $25.00 – 40.00. Center right: Large brooch with marquise topaz stones and unopened flower buds. $30.00 – 45.00.*

Bottom left: *Top: Leaf-shaped pin decorated with brilliant rhinestones. $40.00 – 65.00. Necklace in stylized floral motif with topaz rhinestones. $30.00 – 45.00. Center left: Bracelet. $35.00 – 50.00. Lower left: Round and dome-shaped rhinestone pin. $20.00 – 35.00. Lower right: Wide bracelet featuring large topaz rhinestones. $35.00 – 55.00.*

Bottom right: *Top: Large 2½" square brooch with aurora borealis stones. Excellent quality and construction. $90.00 – 140.00. Bottom: Pair of earrings with large imitation emerald stones. Unmarked, but certainly the work of a renowned manufacturer. $50.00 – 80.00.*

Top left: *Top: Three blooming flower brooches. Left: With green rhinestones similar in design to those produced by Weiss, Schreiner, and several other manufacturers. $40.00 – 60.00. Center: An exceptionally large and early brooch with a delightful design. $80.00 – 125.00. Right: Pavé set on silver base metal. $40.00 – 60.00. Bottom: Two rhinestone bracelets. $35.00 – 55.00 each.*

Top right: *Left: Wide bracelet. $30.00 – 45.00. Top center: Pin in lacy pattern with handset multicolored rhinestones. $40.00 – 60.00. Center: Delicate necklace with gold leaves and two shades of green stones. $35.00 – 50.00. Bottom: Rhinestone brooch. $30.00 – 45.00. Right: Bracelet with alternating yellow and brown cabochon stones framed by multicolored stones. $40.00 – 60.00.*

Right: *Top left: Leaf-shaped brooch in three shades of iridescent rhinestones. Unmarked, but it can probably be identified since only three companies used these shades of rhinestones. $30.00 – 45.00. Lower left: Bracelet with cabochon central stones flanked by iridescent marquise rhinestones. $50.00 – 65.00. Top center: Large brooch in two shades of green with aurora accent. $40.00 – 55.00. Center: Flower pin. $30.00 – 45.00. Lower center: Necklace with foil-less smoky gray stones and aurora accents. Quality material and workmanship. $60.00 – 95.00.*

Top left: *Top left: Necklace and matching earrings. $40.00 – 60.00. Lower left: Goldtone mesh metal decorated with a large brown rhinestone. $25.00 – 35.00. Upper right: Oxidized metal featuring plastic on glass cameo in imitation of earlier pieces. $30.00 – 45.00. Lower right: Very large two tier brooch with handset green rhinestones. $50.00 – 85.00.*

Top right: *Top center: Triangle dress clip. $25.00 – 35.00. Center: Attractive necklace tastefully combining metalwork with two shades of blue rhinestones. $60.00 – 90.00. Center left: Flower pin with foil-less aquamarine stones. Mazer, Trifari, and several other manufacturers produced this type of jewelry. $45.00 – 65.00. Center right: 1930s Art Deco style rectangular brooch. $40.00 – 60.00. Bottom: Very large 3½" wide early brooch with cobalt blue rhinestones of various shapes. $70.00 – 100.00.*

Left: *Handset opaque white glass jewelry. Necklace. $50.00 – 80.00. Bracelet. $35.00 – 50.00. Pins. $35.00 – 50.00. Earrings. $20.00 – 30.00.*

Above: *Upper left: Hinged bracelet and matching earrings with floral motif set with clear rhinestones highlighted by an enameled cross. Rare. $60.00 – 90.00. Center: Exceptionally large 1930s brooch with clear rhinestones depicting a tree with blooming flowers. $45.00 – 70.00. Top right: Hinged filigree bracelet with two large simulated aquamarine stones. Late 1920s – early 1930s. $45.00 – 70.00 Asking price may be as high as $150.00. Center right: Pair of 1930s rhinestone earrings. $15.00 – 25.00. Bottom: Wide rhinestone bracelet, possibly of a more recent origin. $25.00 – 35.00.*

Right: *Top: Pair of dress clips decorated with round moonstones. $50.00 – 75.00. Upper left: Milky opaque glass stones are combined with pale pink rhinestones to create this attractive pair of earrings. $25.00 – 40.00. Top center: Pair of earrings. $25.00 – 35.00. Center: Necklace with antiqued goldtone metalwork, enhanced by marbleized plastic and rhinestones. $50.00 – 85.00. Bottom: Bracelet with purple plastic inserts, pearls and rhinestones mounted on antiqued goldtone metalwork. $40.00 – 65.00. Right: Pair of earrings with handset opaque glass stones. $15.00 – 25.00.*

Opposite page, top left: *Top left: Pin with handset aurora borealis stones. $30.00 – 45.00. Center: Necklace. $40.00 – 60.00. Right: Rhinestone pin. $25.00 – 40.00. Bottom: Exquisite brooch and matching earrings decorated with brilliant aurora borealis rhinestones. $60.00 – 90.00.*

Opposite page, top right: *Top: Pin and matching earrings with handset sculptured stones combined with faceted rhinestones. $45.00 – 65.00. Center: Art Deco style rhinestone bracelet. $70.00 – 100.00. Bottom: Two rhinestone brooches. $35.00 – 50.00 each.*

Opposite page, bottom left: *Top left: Pair of screw back earrings. $20.00 – 35.00. Top center: Pair of dome-shaped earrings with pavé set clear rhinestones and protruding faux pearls. $17.50 – 25.00. Upper right: Necklace in floral design featuring cabochon green plastic stones on white metal base. Marked with Pat #125,355. $35.00 – 50.00. Center: Bracelet and to its left, matching earrings with alternating glass cabochon stones and simulated pearl. Good quality and workmanship. The metalwork on the back is similar to Ciner. $45.00 – 65.00. Bottom: Rhinestone spray pin. $25.00 – 32.50.*

Opposite page, bottom right: *Lower left: Pair of clip earrings. $15.00 – 20.00. Bottom: Delightful necklace set with multicolored cabochon and faceted stones. Good quality and construction. Certainly the work of a major manufacturer. $50.00 – 75.00. Center: Unmarked Coro-like necklace in floral design, decorated with topaz rhinestones. $35.00 – 50.00. All others: Three pairs of screw back rhinestone earrings. $15.00 – 20.00 each.*

Top right: *Top left: Small horn of plenty pin, $15.00 – 20.00. Center left: Wreath rhinestone pin. $15.00 – 25.00. Center: Matching necklace, bracelet, and earrings with enameled disk and clear rhinestones. $50.00 – 75.00. Top right: Pair of earrings. $15.00 – 20.00. Center right: Delicate rhinestone pin. $20.00 – 30.00.*

Below: *Outstanding bracelet with green glass cabochon stones and baroque pearls mounted on the back of gilded brass dragons and inside fancy lotus-like shells. The clasp suggests Oriental or continental origin. $125.00 – 175.00.*

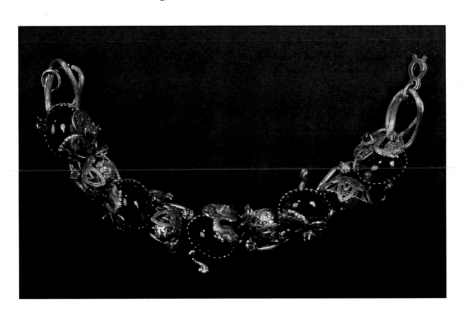

Top left: *Unmarked figural pins for dog lovers. The two bottom pieces in the middle column and the second and third pieces in goldtone metal in the right hand column are of much higher quality. $25.00 – 45.00. All others. $8.00 – 30.00.*

Top right: *Bugs and butterflies. Top row: Two large butterflies. $30.00 – 45.00 each. Center: Older and scarce spider and a bee. $50.00 – 75.00 each. Bottom center: Pair of insect earrings with clear central stones. $45.00 – 75.00. Near exact replicas are still manufactured today and can be bought in department stores for $10.00 – 15.00. All others: $8.00 – 30.00 each.*

Bottom left: *Creatures of the deep seas. Top right: Two matching sterling vermeil fish. $35.00 – 55.00 each. Center left: An early sailfish in pavé set blue and white rhinestones. $25.00 – 45.00. Two early enameled fish fur clips. $30.00 – 40.00 each. Bottom left: Metal turtle sweater guard with enameled back and Pat. #2,853,761 (ca. 1958). $20.00 – 35.00. All others: $10.00 – 25.00 each.*

Bottom right: *Diverse group of figural pins. $15.00 – 60.00 each.*

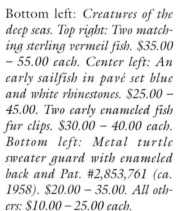

Top left: *A group of figural pins consisting primarily of cats and birds. $15.00 – 60.00 each.*

Top right: *Figural animal pins and a pair of horsehead earrings. $10.00 – 60.00 each.*

Bottom left: *Diverse group of pins. The lower left pair are actually clips with moving tails used as bookmarks. $10.00 – 45.00 each.*

Bottom right: *More figural pins, earrings, and cuffs. $10.00 – 40.00 each or matching set.*

Top left: *Figural jewelry with political campaign and patriotic theme. The center pieces are shoe buckles. $15.00 – 50.00 each or pair.*

Top right: *Figural birds. Top right: Flying bird pin of quality workmanship. $50.00 – 80.00. Top left: Exotic bird brooch. $45.00 – 65.00. Top center: An older penguin pin/clip with cabochon stone belly. Scarce. $80.00 – 120.00. All others: $10.00 – 45.00 each.*

Left: *Figural insects. The center piece is made of foil-less faceted stones mounted on silver. $40.00 – 60.00. Top center: Well-made piece with pavé set body and enameled wings. $20.00 – 35.00. All others: $10.00 – 20.00 each.*

Opposite page, top left: *Figural bird pins and earrings. $15.00 – 45.00 each or matching set.*

Opposite page, top right: *Early large figural bird brooches. $60.00 – 100.00 each.*

Opposite page, bottom left: *Figural butterfly pins. The three larger, older pieces, $45.00 – 65.00 each. All others: $10.00 – 25.00 each.*

Opposite page, bottom right: *Delicious figural fruit pins and earrings. $20.00 – 45.00 each or matching set.*

Left: *Two fruit necklaces. $35.00 – 65.00 each.*

Right: *Center: Grape necklace and matching earrings with green cabochon stones. $40.00 – 60.00. Other three pins: $20.00 – 40.00 each.*

Below: *More fruits for the amusement of figural jewelry collectors. The top row shows enameled fruit pendants made in the 1970s. $6.00 – 10.00 each. Lower right: Matching pin and earrings. $25.00 – 35.00. All others: $6.00 – 12.00 each.*

Above: *Hinged bracelet with the upper part covered by ruby red rhinestones planted in a field of smoky gray rhinestones. $60.00 – 90.00.*

Below: *Large black opaque stones with streaks of gold surrounded by multicolored stones decorate this hinged bracelet. $65.00 – 95.00.*

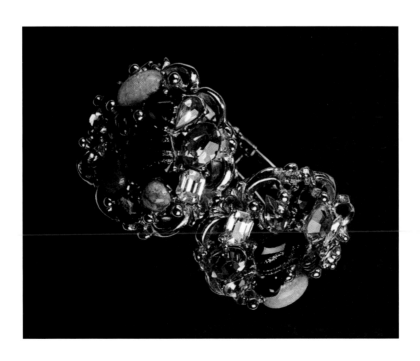

Top left: *Left: High quality locket with ornamental metal-work decorated with turquoise. $60.00 – 90.00. Center: Pendant/compact with Victorian style plastic cameo. Marked Napier. $30.00 – 45.00. Right: Locket with repoussé flower and three pop-up miniature picture frames mounted inside on a spring. Sterling silver book chain. $100.00 – 150.00.*

Bottom left: *Left: Early locket with transfer painting of a lady's portrait surrounded by glass beads. Complementary decorative chain. This same piece also comes in form of flat pendant and false locket. $40.00 – 65.00. Center: Locket with plastic cameo mounted on black glass. $60.00 – 90.00. Right: Early locket with Victorian design and book chain. $100.00 – 165.00.*

Opposite page, top left: *Left: Three early, good quality imitation cameo pins. Top piece is made of molded slag glass. $45.00 – 70.00. Others made of plastic. $35.00 – 50.00. Center: Locket displaying elaborate ornamental metalwork. Floral engraving on the back side. Photos of 1930s couple inside. $60.00 – 90.00. Upper right: Large pin with molded plastic flower cameo. $15.00 – 25.00. Center right: Cameo pin with illegible mark. Similar pin with legible mark identifies this pin as a Robbins piece, also shown in Chapter 2 as an unmarked piece. $15.00 – 25.00. Lower right: Jet cameo pin. Damaged rim. $50.00 – 75.00.*

Opposite page, top right: *Upper left: Pair of plastic cameo earrings. Pat. #3,176,475 (ca. 1965). $20.00 – 30.00. Jet cameo pin. $90.00 – 135.00. Center left: Glass intaglio pin/pendant, imitation of jet and hematite carvings. $40.00 – 60.00. Lower left: Celluloid imitation cameo pin. $20.00 –35.00. Center: Cameo pendant with white glass profile of a lady on black glass in gilded brass frame. $45.00 – 60.00. Upper right: Good quality molded plastic cameo. Possibly hand-finished. $50.00 – 80.00. Center right: Low quality molded plastic pendant of more recent origin. $10.00 – 12.50. Lower right: Molded white glass profile of a lady on black glass cameo mounted on filigree silvertone base. $30.00 – 45.00.*

Opposite page, bottom right: *Exquisite hinged bracelet and matching earrings decorated with multicolored rhinestones. $90.00 – 135.00.*

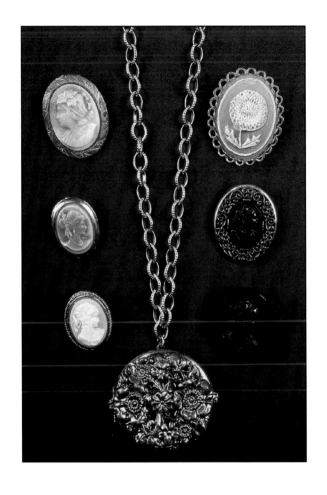

Chapter 5

Imported Costume Jewelry

Austrian Costume Jewelry

Austria has been a major source of rhinestones and crystal beads for the costume jewelry industry throughout the twentieth century. One major supplier, of course, has been the famed Swarovski Corporation established by Daniel Swarovski in a small mountain village, Wattens, in 1895. The Austrian manufacturers were in direct competition with the Jablonec area manufacturers who were the main suppliers of the well-known Czechoslovakian rhinestones. As a result, rhinestone jewelry production also grew in Austria and much of it was exported.

The Austrian costume jewelry common in the U. S. collectible market today consists of rhinestone jewelry, Austrian glass beads, and cut crystal jewelry. Most of the rhinestone jewelry is small, delicate pieces in floral designs displaying a glittering rainbow of colors. The mountings are usually goldtone or plated metal, frequently accented with enamel work. Most of this type of jewelry is of above average construction with, of course, top quality rhinestones. Large and elaborate jewelry of exceptional quality resembling expensive fine jewelry was also manufactured, but it appears that these were intended primarily for the European market and is more difficult to find in the U. S. collectible market. Austrian costume jewelry is usually marked Austria or Made in Austria on the reverse side, sometimes in difficult-to-see places.

Top left: *Large brooch with ruby red aurora borealis rhinestones, marked Austria. $60.00 – 90.00. Three pairs of earrings, all marked Austria. $20.00 – 30.00 each.*

Top right: *Left: Enameled pin with ruby red rhinestones. Marked Austria. $30.00 – 45.00. Top: Brooch with multicolored rhinestones, marked Austria. $35.00 – 50.00. Right: Three pairs of earrings, all marked Austria. $20.00 – 30.00.*

Bottom left: *Brooch and matching earrings. Marked Austria. $90.00 – 125.00.*

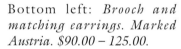

Bottom right: *Top: Matching pin and earrings showing typical Austrian combination of enamel and rhinestones with floral motif. $40.00 – 60.00. Bottom left: Pin, marked Austria. $20.00 – 30.00. Center: Floral pin with frosted marquise stones and rhinestones. Marked Austria. $20.00 – 35.00. Right: White enamel floral pin, marked Austria. $20.00 – 30.00.*

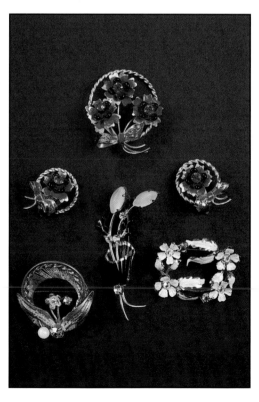

Top left: *Top: Pair of earrings with a pearl center surrounded by flowers of turquoise, blue, and pink rhinestones. $30.00 – 40.00. A small flower pin with plastic inserts. $20.00 – 30.00. Center: Turtle pin covered with green rhinestones of different shades and pearl accent. Marked Austria. $50.00 – 75.00. Pair of earrings with opaque white glass and aurora rhinestones. $20.00 – 25.00. Bottom: Earrings with multicolored iridescent rhinestones. $20.00 – 27.50.*

Top right: *Top: Flower basket pin and matching earrings, marked Austria. $40.00 – 60.00. Center: Enamel floral pin and a pair of enamel earrings, both marked Austria. Pin. $25.00 – 35.00. Earrings. $15.00 – 20.00. Bottom: Pair of blue enamel and rhinestones earrings. $15.00 – 20.00.*

Bottom left: *Plastic sundial bracelet. Functional piece with instructions. $40.00 – 60.00.*

Bottom right: *Top: Austrian pin with baguette and round rhinestones. $30.00 – 50.00. Top right: Circle pin. $15.00 – 25.00. Bottom: Three pairs of rhinestone earrings, marked Austria. $20.00 – 30.00 each..*

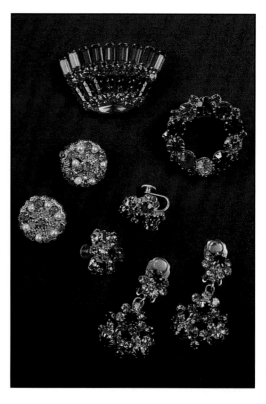

Czechoslovakian Costume Jewelry

Some of the most beautiful and exquisite costume jewelry was produced in Czechoslovakia. The country was formed in 1918 after WWI, incorporating the territory known as Bohemia, long known for its superior porcelain, glassworks, garnet, and bead jewelry. Czechoslovakia was occupied by the Germans during WWII. Exports resumed after the war, but the country fell under the Soviet sphere of influence during the cold war years. Not long after the disintegration of the Soviet Union, the country was peacefully divided into two separate nations: Slovakia and Czech Republic.

A large volume of jewelry was exported during the two world wars and if you have a piece of jewelry marked Czechoslovakia, it was probably made between 1918 and 1939. Some of the Czech export jewelry was in the Victorian tradition, but much of it shows Art Deco influence, incorporating quality rhinestones, molded and faceted glass beads, and geometrically cut colored glass imitating gemstones. Bohemian garnet jewelry set in gilt silver was also exported. Czech jewelry has such a distinct look that it can easily be recognized by trained eyes, though some jewelry made in other countries, especially France, may look similar at first glance since they used imported Czech stones and findings.

Czech jewelry is often marked in hard-to-see places, requiring a magnifying glass to find and read. On pins and brooches, the mark could be on the pin stem or side of the catch which holds the pointed end of the pin stem. On necklaces, the mark could be on back of the clasp or safety catch, but is often found on the jump ring or the last chain link that is secured by the safety catch. Hallmarks on silver include a woman's head with scarf or bonnet and a rabbit or goat head. After 1955, the goat head was used for silver with fineness of 925 or better. Assay marks were also introduced in 1955. Among the five (initially six) assay marks used, one that is frequently encountered is the letter J in a square, standing for Jablonec, a major center of production. The readers should note that some of the Czech jewelry is shown in the beads and lockets section.

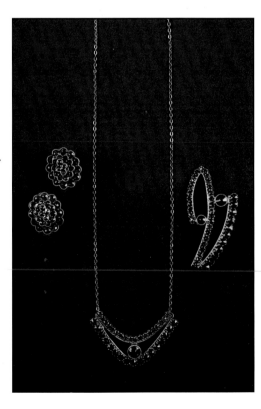

Left: *Early, transitional, Art Deco Czech necklace in enameled filigree work with simulated cabochon carnelian stones and beads. Eastern influence. $175.00 – 225.00.*

Right: *Parure consisting of necklace, pin, and earrings in sterling vermeil, set with genuine garnets. 1940s goat and 900 silver hallmark used for local production. One piece has Jablonec assay mark. Although similar jewelry was imported into the U. S., these pieces were most likely brought to the U. S. by post WWII Czech or German emigrants. $400.00 – 550.00.*

Top left: *Art Deco geometric cut glass necklaces. Both marked Czechoslovakia. Top: Covered with filigree work and set with marcasite. $100.00 – 145.00. Bottom: $80.00 – 120.00.*

Top right: *Left: Silver filigree and marcasite flower head brooch, marked Czechoslovakia. $90.00 – 135.00. Center: Silver filigree and marcasite pendant with a black glass cameo, marked Czechoslovakia. $90.00 – 125.00. Early Czech silver flower pin with rhinestones. $45.00 – 65.00.*

Bottom left: *Left: Molded amethyst glass pendant, marked Czechoslovakia. $35.00 – 50.00. Top center: Czech rhinestone necklace. $35.00 – 50.00. Bottom left: Early Czech brooch with molded plastic cameo in silver frame. $45.00 – 65.00. Bottom right: Early marked Czech clear plastic pendant with reverse carved floral motif enhanced by gold paint (Prystal plastic). $50.00 – 75.00. Center right: Marked Czech, metal alloy locket with engraved Victorian floral motif. $60.00 – 90.00.*

Bottom right: *Two marked Czech necklaces made of molded glass beads and a pair of screw back yellow art glass earrings. Necklaces. $45.00 – 60.00 each. Earrings. $40.00 – 60.00.*

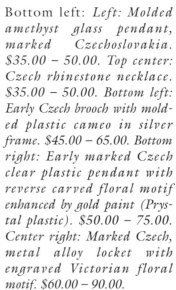

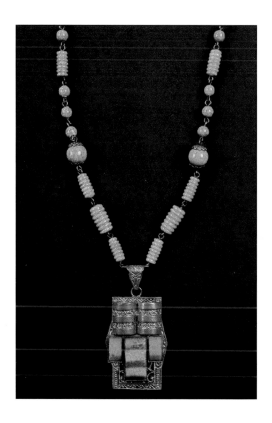

Top left: *Art Deco pendant with gilded metal combined with marbleized glass in geometric form complemented by molded glass beads. Marked Czechoslovakia. $100.00 – 150.00.*

Top right: *Lower left: Brooch with inlaid bird and berries on imitation lapis lazuli. Marked Czechoslovakia. The process involves carving the glass or stone base and filling the depressions with enamel, then sanding and polishing the surface. $60.00 – 95.00. Center right: Marked Czech, pin with multicolored cabochon and faceted stones. $35.00 – 45.00. Long rhinestone necklace marked Czechoslovakia. $40.00 – 60.00. Top left: Early marked Czech brooch set with multicolored rhinestones. Typical early Czech pin. $40.00 – 60.00.*

Right: *Five marked Czech pins. $30.00 – 55.00 each. Three pairs of marked Czech screw back earrings. $15.00 – 25.00 each.*

Above: *Large Czech brooch with wood beads held together with metal leaves decorated with rhinestones. $45.00 – 65.00.*

Bottom left: *Marked Czech pendant with dome-shaped marbleized glass mounted on gilded metal base with scroll design and green rhinestone accent. $80.00 – 120.00.*

Bottom right: *Top: Early 1900s, three tier brooch and possibly matching earrings made of genuine garnets mounted on sterling vermeil base. Tube hinge type of joint on the pin. Unmarked. Although unmarked, these are very similar to German and Czech garnet jewelry and were possibly manufactured in the same area that later became Czechoslovakia. Pin. $185.00 – 250.00. Earrings. $60.00 – 95.00. Bottom: Small Czech butterfly pin made of genuine garnets mounted on sterling vermeil base. Marks: 900 for silver fineness, goat mark and number 3 (ca. 1940s); and maker's initials EB. $90.00 – 140.00.*

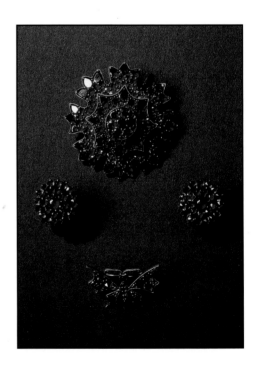

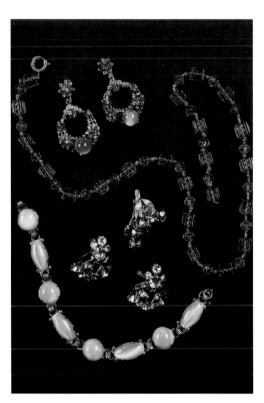

Top left: *Left: Art Deco bracelet with plastic inserts and chain links imitating lapis lazuli. Marked Czechoslovakia. $50.00 – 85.00. Center: Long rhinestone necklace. $40.00 – 60.00. Small Czech pin. $17.50 – 25.00. Top right: Large marked Czech dress clip. $40.00 – 65.00. Right: Two pairs of marked Czech earrings. $15.00 – 20.00.*

Top right: *Bottom: Art Deco Czech bracelet with cabochon glass stones. $40.00 – 60.00. Top: Marked Czech screw back filigree earrings with pink cabochon and faceted stones. $25.00 – 40.00. Right: Long Czech molded glass bead necklace. $45.00 – 65.00.*

Bottom left: *Center: Marked Czech necklace with dark amethyst rhinestones. $25.00 – 35.00. All others: Four pairs of screw back rhinestone earrings and a clip marked Czechoslovakia. $20.00 – 30.00 each.*

Bottom right: *Left: Unmarked necklace, possibly Czechoslovakian, with painted yellow glass cabochon stone and beads. $75.00 – 100.00. Right: Peking glass type necklace reflecting the Oriental influence on early Czech jewelry. Marked Czechoslovakia. Such pieces were made of carved jade, sometimes set with diamonds, during the Victorian era. $135.00 – 175.00.*

Imported costume jewelry from Germany covers the entire range of costume jewelry styles and designs popular in the U. S., particularly after WWII. Common among these are plastic and glass beads jewelry. The higher quality jewelry is made of clear or multicolored cut crystal beads in single or multi-strand necklaces with matching earrings. But molded glass bead jewelry in practically every shape and color, particularly red and black, was also imported in large quantities. The quality of this type of jewelry varies. Some is low quality jewelry not much different than their cheap Japanese counterparts which were also imported into the U. S. after WWII.

One category of German jewelry which is quite attractive consists of large colored glass stones with rhinestone or pearl accent mounted on filigree or openwork gold plated metal. Some of the pendants include a plastic or glass cameo, though the matching earrings may be in plain glass. The chains are usually elaborate, displaying similar metalwork and often complemented with faux pearls. This type of jewelry which has been manufactured in Germany since 1920s is relatively common in the collectible market, particularly post WWII pieces which were imported in large quantities beginning in the 1950s. They are also well underpriced. A pendant and earrings set can usually be purchased for $45.00 to $65.00. They are marked West Germany on the earring clip and/or on a small ring next to the pendant's safety catch.

Silver and other metal jewelry was also imported from Germany. The silver jewelry is usually marked Germany or West Germany, accompanied with 800 or higher silver fineness mark. The piece may also include the manufacturer's mark, but this mark should not be confused with the national German silver mark which may also be found on the product, particularly on older pieces. This is a crown and a crescent-shaped moon symbol used to mark silver jewelry after 1888.

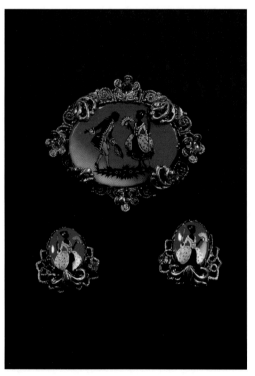

Left: *Brooch and matching earrings with painted porcelain portrait depicting a lady and gentleman. $75.00 – 100.00.*

Right: *Top: German rhinestone pin in two shades of blue. $30.00 – 50.00. Bottom: Five pairs of earrings showing use of transfer painting, rhinestones, and plastic on glass cameo, all common material in post WWII imported German jewelry. All marked West Germany. $15.00 – 20.00 each.*

Top left: *Top left: Two marked German pendants with glass cameo, goldtone filigree frame, and simulated pearl accent. $40.00 – 50.00 each. Bottom: Pendant with glass cameo surrounded by simulated pearls and matching pair of earrings. $40.00 – 60.00.*

Top right: *Lower left: Pendant with large faceted red stone mounted on goldtone filigree with pearl, rhinestone, and enamel accents. $40.00 – 60.00. Top left: Pair of clip earrings with rhinestone and pearl mounted on goldtone filigree metalwork. Marked West Germany. Possibly matches the above pendant. $15.00 – 25.00. Lower right: Pendant with typical goldtone German filigree combined with rhinestones and pearls. $35.00 – 50.00. Top right: Pair of earrings, possibly matching above pendant. Marked West Germany. $17.50 – 25.00.*

Bottom left: *Matching necklace and earrings made of pastel, black, and white molded plastic. Germany mark on the back of the center piece. $50.00 – 75.00.*

Bottom right: *Left: Pendant and matching earrings with imitation blue glass cameos. $45.00 – 65.00. Right: German pendant with a large faux turquoise surrounded by simulated pearls and turquoise. $30.00 – 45.00.*

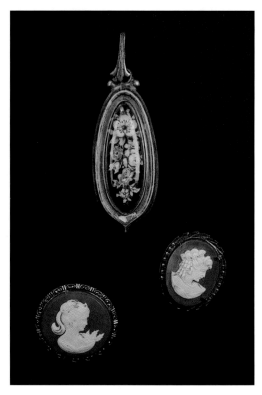

Top left: *Pearls combined with goldtone filigree metalwork make up this matching pendant and earrings, marked West Germany. $45.00 – 70.00.*

Top right: *Top: Hand-painted porcelain pendant marked Rosenthal with the company's crown trademark. Rosenthal is a German porcelain manufacturer founded in 1879 in Selb, Bavaria. $70.00 – 100.00. Bottom left: Top quality plastic cameo dress clip almost indistinguishable from real shell cameo. Marked Western Germany. $40.00 – 55.00. Bottom right: Pin/pendant. High quality shell cameo mounted on 800 silver frame decorated with marcasite. Back of shell has the carver's fancy script initials GL. Possibly German. 1920s – 1930s. $65.00 – 100.00.*

Bottom left: *Top: Large brooch and matching earrings painted blue with a large handset iridescent central stone and rhinestone accent. Marked West Germany. $40.00 – 60.00. Bottom: Matching pin and earrings with elaborate filigree metalwork enhanced by topaz rhinestones. $45.00 – 75.00.*

Bottom right: *Matching necklace and earrings made of blue Bohemian glass beads. Marked West Germany. $50.00 – 75.00.*

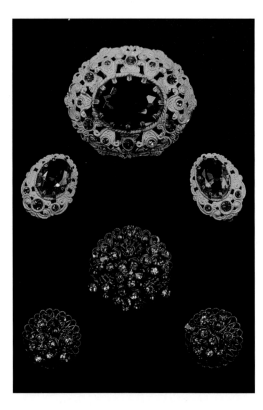

Top left: *German pendant and matching earrings with imitation tiger's eye glass stones. $45.00 – 65.00.*

Top right: *Top left: Pin with plastic inserts in imitation of mosaic work. $7.50 – 12.50. Center: Woven wire work. Left: Goldtone earrings. $5.00 – 7.50. Right: Heart-shaped silver enhanced by pearls. $12.00 – 18.00. Original price tag on the back is $7.50. Bottom left: Round silver pendant depicting a bunch of grapes. Marked Germany and 800 for silver fineness. $65.00 – 85.00. Bottom right: Small figural pin in goldtone metal and red rhinestones. Marked West Germany. $6.00 – 10.00.*

Right: *Top left: Pair of German earrings and closely matching pin of similar construction. $25.00 – 40.00 each. Top center: Pendant featuring handset mother-of-pearl in a frame of simulated pearls. Marked West Germany. $20.00 – 25.00. Bottom: Filigree metalwork in combination with imitation moonstones make up this pair of earrings, marked West Germany. $20.00 –25.00.*

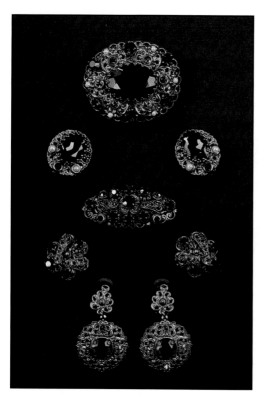

Top left: *Center: Necklace of faceted red glass beads marked West Germany. Large volume of glass bead jewelry similar to this necklace was imported in the late 1940s and 1950s. The common colors are black, red, and white. $20.00 – 30.00. All others: Seven pairs of earrings, marked West Germany. All except lower left pair, which is made of clear plastic, are made of various types of beads. This are low quality German bead jewelry imported in the 1950s, almost indistinguishable from their Japanese counterparts also imported during the same period, and possibly reflect the devastating effects of the war on Germany which had always produced quality products. The author believes that some of the bead jewelry of similar construction carrying the trademarks of American manufacturers was actually made abroad in either Japan or West Germany. $8.00 – 16.00 each.*

Top right: *Center: Necklace in three strands of faceted black glass beads. $20.00 – 35.00. Pin with sculptured frosted stones. $20.00 – 25.00. High quality earrings made of iridescent beads of uncommon shapes. $20.00 – 35.00. All others: Six pairs of earrings, marked West Germany. $15.00 – 25.00 each.*

Left: *Top: Brooch and matching earrings combining goldtone filigree metalwork and handset black faceted stones with pearl accent. Marked West Germany. $45.00 – 65.00. Center: Pin and matching earrings in silvertone filigree metalwork and handset iridescent rhinestones. $40.00 – 60.00. Bottom: Pair of screw back earrings with filigree metalwork, handset topaz central stone and smaller rhinestone accent. $20.00 – 30.00.*

Both Italian shell cameo and mosaic jewelry was produced in the early nineteenth century and became exceptionally popular during the Victorian era where classical subjects were in vogue. They were artistic creations of highly skilled Italian artisans and were usually set in 18k yellow gold. As such they would not fall within even our broad definition of costume jewelry. But, both shell cameo and mosaic jewelry are mass produced today for the tourist and export markets and, in general, no longer reflect the artistic expression and quality workmanship of the individual jeweler.

The early mosaic jewelry used minute pieces of hard stone or glass cemented together to create an artistic picture just as hundreds of pieces of a mosaic or jigsaw puzzle when put together create scenes. These are sometimes referred to as micromosaic. There were two types: Roman, which used hard stone and generally depicted classical themes such as ancient ruins; and Florentine, which used glass and had floral designs. The modern versions use larger stones depicting floral motifs and are set in goldtone metals. While the nineteenth century pieces were like beautiful miniature paintings, the modern versions, especially those made today, are generally of low quality. The difference between the early and modern mosaic jewelry is the difference between the fine and imitation costume jewelry.

Italian shell cameos also reached their zenith of popularity during the Victorian era, though the art itself can be traced back to ancient Greece and Rome. They were artistic creations of individual carvers who created miniature sculptures in relief, using the different colored layers of the shell to the best of advantage. Old cameos were frequently set in karat gold.

The modern cameos are largely mass produced for the tourist and export markets in the Italian city of Torre de Greco and lack the artistic creativity and quality workmanship of the nineteenth century individual carvers. Shell cameos and their glass and plastic imitations have been popular throughout the twentieth century. With the expanded import of Italian jewelry, shell cameos are making a comeback and are now sold in the jewelry sections of many department stores.

Another type of imported Italian jewelry is made of art glass beads known as Venetian glass beads which have been exported abroad for several centuries and once were used as trade beads in North America. The twentieth century versions are of much lower quality but still quite attractive. Venetian bead jewelry is also displayed in Chapter 9.

Two 1930s mosaic bracelets with glass pieces set in brass frame. Both marked Italy.
Top: $60.00 – 90.00. Bottom: $50.00 – 70.00.

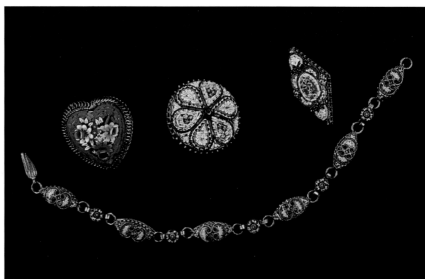

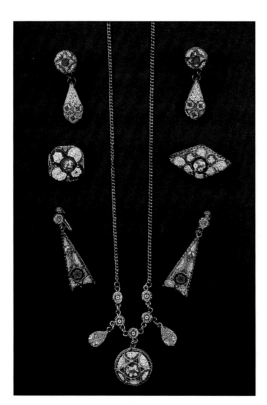

Top left: *Top left: Mosaic pin. $35.00 – 50.00. Center: Round mosaic pendant. $45.00 – 65.00. Lower left: Mosaic screw back earrings. $25.00 – 35.00. Lower right: Mosaic link bracelet. $40.00 – 60.00.*

Top right: *Top: Three mosaic pins. Left to right: 1950s heart-shaped pin. $25.00 – 35.00. Round early 1900s pin. $40.00 – 55.00. 1930s diamond-shaped pin. $30.00 – 45.00. Bottom: Link bracelet. $35.00 – 50.00.*

Bottom left: *Top to bottom. Pair of screw back earrings, 1930s. $30.00 – 45.00. Two small 1930s pins. $25.00 – 40.00 each. Earrings. 1920s – 1930s. $30.00 – 50.00 each. Early 1900s necklace. $65.00 – 90.00.*

Opposite page, top left: *Italian mosaic pins and earrings. All post WWII pieces. Note that the glass pieces are larger and designs less elaborate. Also new glass is somewhat shinier. Lower right: Large brooch with roses. $40.00 – 50.00. Center and right: Four pins. $25.00 – 40.00 each. Top: Two pairs of earrings with roses. $17.50 – 22.50.*

Opposite page, top right: *Top left: 1960s mosaic pin. $20.00 – 25.00. Top center: Pair of screw back earrings. $20.00 – 30.00. Top right: Small 1960s pin. $16.00 – 20.00. Center: Two pins with roses in the center, framed by mosaic work. $35.00 – 50.00. Bottom: Link bracelet. $35.00 – 50.00.*

Opposite page, bottom left: *Italian shell cameo pendant and matching earrings in 800 silver frame. $90.00 – 130.00.*

Opposite page, bottom right: *Left: Pair of cameo shell clip earrings on gold plated base. $30.00 – 40.00. Center: Shell cameo pendant in gold plated frame. $45.00 – 60.00. Top right: Shell cameo pendant in plastic frame imitating tortoise shell. $30.00 – 45.00. Right: Shell cameo pin. $40.00 – 50.00.*

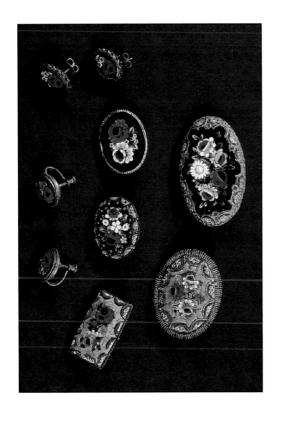

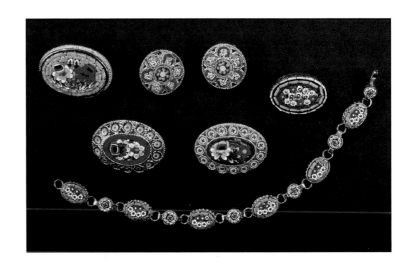

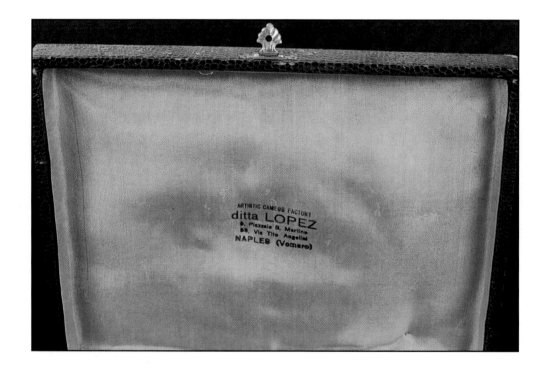

Opposite page, top: *Parure consisting of necklace, bracelet, pin, and earrings with carved shell cameos mounted on filigree 800 silver base, in the original box. $400.00 – 550.00.*

Opposite page, bottom: *Name and address of the manufacturer of the above set inside the lid of the original box.*

Right: *Top: Large shell cameo brooch in gold plated frame, 1920s – 1930s. $80.00 – 120.00. Center: Pair of shell cameo screw back earrings. $25.00 – 35.00. Bottom: Shell cameo mounted on 800 silver ring. Illegible maker's mark. $40.00 – 60.00.*

Bottom left: *Top: Shell cameo mounted on gold plated scarf pin. $30.00 – 45.00. Left: Turn of century coral cameo pendant (lavaliere) set on gold top metal mounting. $45.00 – 60.00. Right: Shell cameo pendant in gold plated frame. $30.00 – 45.00. Bottom: Shell cameo pin in gold plated frame. $45.00 – 60.00.*

Bottom right: *Shell cameo mounted on silver filigree base complemented by two aquamarine stones. This type of jewelry was made throughout the Victorian era to as late as Victorian Revival period in the 1930s. $150.00 – 225.00.*

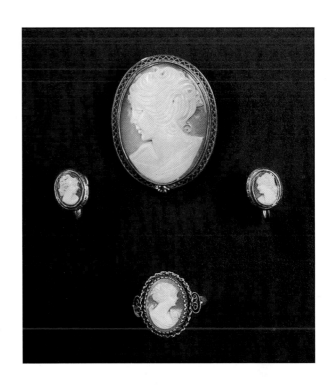

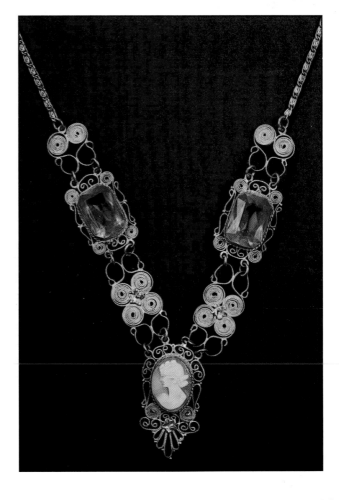

Top left: *Two porcelain cameos framed in 14k gold plated frame with 14k gold plated chains. Purchased in Italy in the 1960s. These are part of a set of twelve produced by the artist Tilton (first name not legible). Due to insufficient information and number traded, an accurate estimated price cannot be provided.*

Top right: *Top: Matching necklace, bracelet, and earrings made of Venetian glass beads. $80.00 – 120.00. Lower left: Pair of Venetian glass earrings. $20.00 – 25.00.*

Left: *Right: Venetian glass necklace and information tag by its importer, Oxford Co. $35.00 – 50.00. Top left: Pair of Venetian glass earrings. $20.00 – 25.00. Center left: Venetian glass pin. $20.00 – 35.00. Lower left: Pair of screw back Venetian glass earrings. $15.00 – 25.00.*

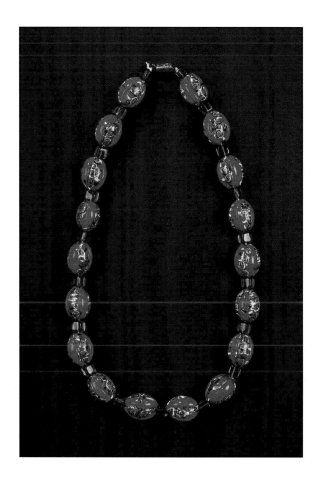

Top left: *Necklace. Venetian glass beads with faceted blue glass spacers. $30.00 – 45.00.*

Top right: *Venetian glass bead necklace with gold and mica inclusions. $60.00 – 90.00.*

Above: *Mosaic bracelet with ROMA in the center. $65.00 – 95.00.*

A significant amount of jewelry from the Orient has been exported to the United States since the 1930s. Imports from China ceased after the establishment of the Communist rule in 1949 and resumed again after the opening of trade in 1973; imports from Japan and Hong Kong increased after WWII.

Although the tradition of jewelry making dates back to ancient times in both China and Japan and beautifully designed pieces have been made for hundreds of years, this section will focus on twentieth century jewelry, particularly, the more common types made for the export market. Only jewelry with Oriental designs, motifs, and material are considered in this chapter. Japanese jewelry with faux pearl and beads which is practically indistinguishable from their western counterparts is shown in Chapter 9.

Among the Chinese jewelry readily available to U. S. collectors are ivory and bone carvings; jewelry employing jade and other semi-precious stones; and silver jewelry, frequently incorporating some type of good fortune statement as part of the design. Japanese jewelry includes both bone and ivory carvings, and mother-of-pearl pieces. One type of Japanese jewelry is handpainted miniature porcelain figural jewelry which is extremely rare.

Another type of Japanese jewelry is niello metal jewelry. The Meiji restoration in 1868 which ended the power of Shugonate in Japan and therefore employment of Samurai, led to the decline of the demand for swords. Facing a stagnant market, many Japanese swordsmiths began to produce other metal products such as metal vessels, boxes, and jewelry. One category of metal jewelry is known as Komai Jewelry named after a Kyoto family of swordsmiths which successfully transferred the art of inlay (zooan) used in making sword furniture to metal vessels and jewelry. Komai jewelry, which is quite rare, cannot be classified as costume jewelry because they were all handmade with fine gold and silver inlays using a highly labor intensive process. Imitations of this type of metalwork were however mass produced in Kyoto and are known as damascene or Kyoto jewelry. These often depict Oriental motifs in gold or silver inlay over a black field. Brass or steel is used as the base metal. Superior Kyoto pieces are still hand crafted and inlaid with 24k gold and pure silver.

The Japanese damascene jewelry can be easily confused with Toledo damascene jewelry which also employs similar Oriental motifs in addition to the traditional Toledo scroll and geometric designs. Some of the Japanese pieces and most of the Toledo pieces are not marked. In order to show the striking similarity, a few Spanish Toledo pieces are shown alongside the Japanese damascene jewelry. Both types of jewelry sell within the same price range.

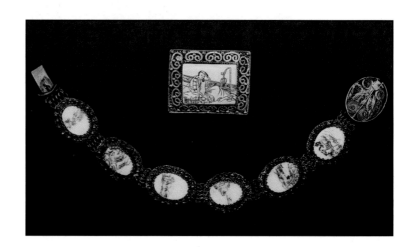

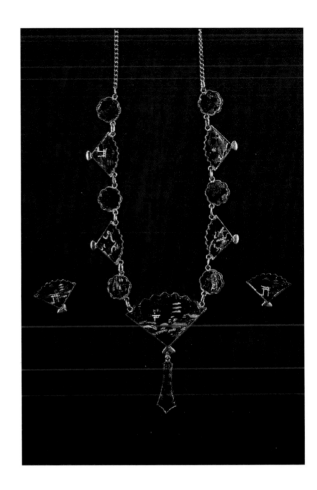

Opposite page, left: *Carved jade pendant.*
$50.00 – 80.00.

Opposite page, right: *Japanese pin with*
hand-painted scene on ivory, mounted on silver
filigree base. $50.00 – 70.00. Japanese link
bracelet with village scenes painted on bone in
filigree silver frames. $60.00 – 90.00.

Top left: *Matching necklace and earrings with*
lacquered wood and glass beads. $25.00 – 45.00.

Top right: *Japanese damascene necklace, match-*
ing earrings. Marked Japan. $40.00 – 65.00.

Right: *Left and right: Two Japanese damascene*
bracelets. One marked Japan on the clasp.
$20.00 – 40.00 each. Center and top right:
Unmarked pendant and hinged bracelet simi-
lar to Japanese damascene jewelry, but most
likely Toledo damascene. Shown in this section
to stress the similarities. More Toledo jewelry is
shown at the end of this chapter. Pendant.
$20.00 – 35.00. Bracelet. $35.00 – 45.00.

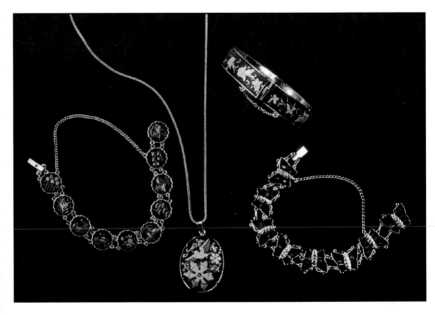

Top left: *Heart necklace and earrings made of mother-of-pearl. Necklace. $25.00 – 35.00. Earrings. $10.00 – 15.00 each.*

Top right: *Necklace in mother-of-pearl and white glass beads. $25.00 – 40.00. The asking price may be much higher. Pair of mother-of-pearl earrings. $10.00 – 15.00.*

Bottom left: *Three necklaces made of mother-of-pearl beads. Those with the rose shade are favored by some collectors. $15.00 – 45.00 each. The asking price may be much higher.*

Bottom right: *Upper right: Carved ivory earrings. $15.00 – 25.00. Mother-of-pearl pendants and earrings. $8.00 – 12.00 each.*

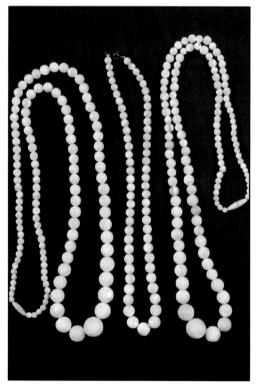

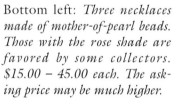

Top left: *Roses in carved bone and ivory. Top left: Pin/pendant featuring a rose carved from ivory. $30.00 – 45.00. Center: Pendant in carved bone marked Made in Switzerland, shown here to stress the similarity with Oriental pieces. Many Swiss pieces were also hand painted in realistic floral colors. $30.00– 60.00. Top right: Carved ivory rose mounted on gold plated metal base. $30.00 – 50.00. Lower right: Pair of carved ivory earrings. $25.00 – 35.00.*

Top right: *Top left: Pair of carved ivory earrings. $25.00 – 35.00. Lower left: Carved ivory pendant. Signed with the carver's initials. $35.00 – 50.00. Right: Carved bone necklace. $25.00 – 50.00. Asking price varies drastically.*

Below: *Right: Carved ivory pin. $40.00 – 60.00. Left: This brooch was purchased in Moscow, USSR, and is shown here for comparison in order to stress the fact that not all carved ivory is from India, China, and Japan. The practice is prevalent throughout the world, including North America. This brooch was probably made in Arkhangelsk, located in northwestern Russia, with a long tradition of sea mammal tusk carvings. $150.00 – 200.00.*

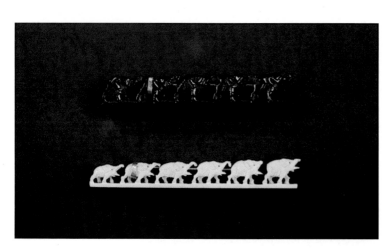

Top: *Top left: Pair of carved ivory earrings. $25.00 – 35.00. Top center: Chinese carved ivory with painted scenery. $40.00 – 60.00. Top right: Carved ivory dress clip marked Japan. These were imported in large volume made of both ivory and bone. $20.00 – 35.00. Bottom: Flexible bracelet in carved bone. $35.00 – 45.00.*

Middle: *Left: Jade earrings. $30.00 – 45.00. Top: Jade pin. $30.00 – 45.00. Center: Jade bracelet. This piece is also manufactured in imitation jade made of plastic and dyed soapstone. A hot needle test can determine whether it is plastic. A hardness scratch test with a knife can determine whether it is true jade. Most substitute stones will show a scratch mark. $50.00 – 90.00. Right: Jade scarf pin. $20.00 – 30.00.*

Bottom: *Top: Carved amber pin. Identical pieces also were made of carved plastic. A hot needle test and pine smell will determine whether it is amber. $75.00 – 125.00. Bottom: Carved ivory pin. Identical pieces were also made of carved plastic. $70.00 – 120.00.*

Opposite page, top: *Outstanding carved Peking glass link bracelet mounted on silver. It is not clear whether this bracelet is of Chinese origin. $125.00 – 165.00.*

Opposite page, bottom left: *Long Chinese neck-lace made of cloisonne beads. $45.00 – 70.00. This piece is probably from the 1970s. Add 20 to 50 percent for pre WWII cloisonne jewelry.*

Opposite page, bottom right: *Left: Two Chinese sterling silver earrings. The top piece reads: good health, happiness and wealth. $15.00 – 25.00 each. Top center: Gold plated pin with Oriental motif and imitation jade glass beads. $20.00 – 35.00. Center: pin with oriental dragon motif and cabochon glass stone. It is not clear whether this piece is of Chinese origin. Similar jewelry was made in Hong Kong, but this piece is not marked. $20.00 – 35.00. Bottom: Jade cross in sterling silver frame with sterling silver chain. Possibly from Hong Kong. $30.00 – 45.00.*

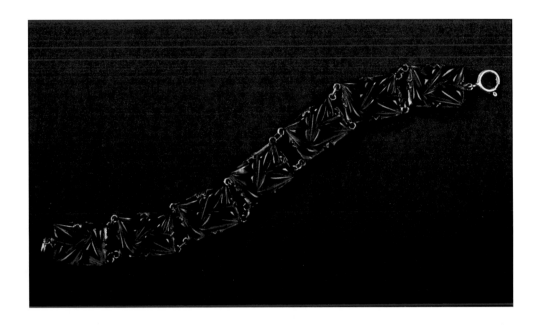

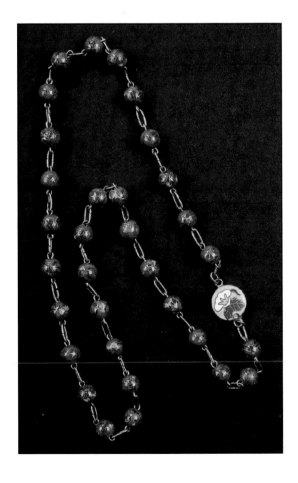

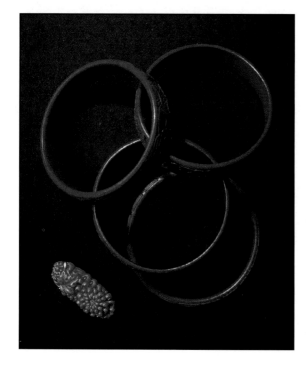

Top left: *Three butterflies and an insect pin made of carved or cabochon jade stones. The right piece may not be of Chinese origin. The left piece usually came in a Chinese silk pouch. $25.00 – 45.00.*

Top right: *Top left: Carved ivory pin with two flower heads. $20.00 – 35.00. Center left: Carved ivory rose pin/pendant. $25.00 – 40.00. Lower left and right: Two carved ivory fish pendants. $30.00 – 45.00. Top right: Carved ivory pin with a dragon motif. $45.00 – 65.00. Bottom: Carved ivory round pendant with a circle of elephants. $35.00 – 45.00.*

Left: *Top: Group of Chinese cinnabar bangles. Priced according to age and quality of carving. These are from the 1970s. $10.00 – 35.00 each. Pre-1930s pieces are at least three times higher in prices. Bottom: Carved coral on sterling silver mounting. Identical pieces were also made in porcelain and plastic. $95.00 – 135.00.*

Spanish Toledo Jewelry

Toledo, a major historic city in central Spain, has a long tradition of excellent metal work which has been successfully applied to jewelry manufacturing. For centuries the city was world famous for its Toledo Swords which were particularly favored in Europe and North Africa. But the local metal smiths also manufactured damascene metal vessels as well as jewelry which was also exported. Aside from minor technical differences, the process of manufacturing the damascene Toledo jewelry is similar to the Japanese damascene jewelry described in the previous section.

The jewelry identified as Toledo jewelry on the U. S. collectible market can be divided into two categories. One type of jewelry has a black field with naturalistic motifs in gold inlay, similar to and often mistaken for Japanese damascene jewelry. The other category consists of both men's and women's jewelry, displaying scroll or arabesque motifs which are perhaps rooted in the Moorish and Islamic influences on the arts and architecture of southern Spain. This type of metalwork which is sometimes combined with plastic inserts imitating mother-of-pearl has its own distinct look which easily identifies it as Spanish jewelry. Some of the damascene jewelry was shown alongside the Japanese damascene jewelry in the previous section in order to show the similarities. This section will focus on the second category which is usually referred to as Spanish Toledo ware. Most of the Spanish jewelry is unmarked and originally came with "Made in Spain" tags. But, the mark "Spain" can sometimes be found on the clasp or the clip.

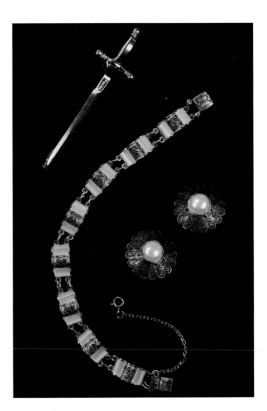

Left: *Link bracelet, unmarked. $35.00 – 50.00. Pair of clip earrings marked Spain. $20.00 – 30.00.*

Right: *Top left: Sword pin. Unmarked. $15.00 – 25.00. Center: Link bracelet. $35.00 – 45.00. Right: Pair of silver clip earrings with simulated pearl. $20.00 – 30.00.*

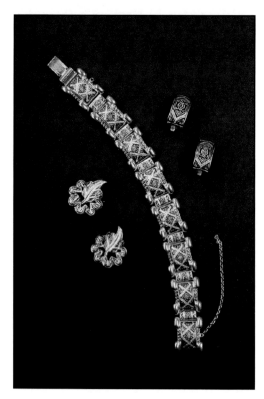

Top left: *Damascene pin with bamboo motif. $20.00 – 35.00.*

Top right: *Unmarked bracelet. $30.00 – 40.00. Two pairs of cuff links. $15.00 – 25.00 each.*

Bottom left: *Unmarked bracelet. $30.00 – 45.00. Two pairs of unmarked clip earrings. $15.00 – 25.00 each.*

Bottom right: *Bracelet with enameled flying bird motif. $35.00 – 50.00. Two pairs of cuff links. $15.00 – 25.00 each.*

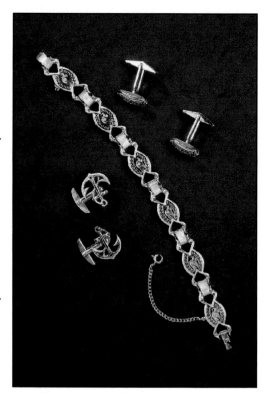

Chapter 6

Gold Filled and Silver Jewelry

Gold filled and plated jewelry was popular throughout the twentieth century. Technically there is a difference between the two technologies. Gold electroplate refers to application of 24k gold to a base metal using electrolysis. The industry-wide standard requires a minimum surface gold thickness of 7/1000 of an inch. The term gold wash is used for jewelry that does not meet this minimum surface gold thickness requirement.

Gold filled is a misnomer and should actually read gold body, filled with a base metal, or "gold, filled." The process dates back to the development of Sheffield silver by Thomas Bolsover in 1742. In case of gold filled or rolled gold, thin sheets of karat gold are fused to a thicker base metal and then rolled to create thin sheets or wires from which the jewelry is made. According to the standards used by the industry, the fineness of the gold layer dressing the base metal must be indicated as part of the hallmark, such as 14k G.F. or 1/20–12k G.F. The latter indicates that ⅟₂₀th of the metal is of 12k gold.

Many manufacturers of costume jewelry used gold filled and plated metal or similar patented alloys. Among these are Van Dell, Krementz's rolled gold, Trifari with patented Trifarium, and Hobe with patented "Formula 70", all of which are covered in Chapter 3. Others who produced exclusively gold plated and gold filled jewelry are identified and covered in this chapter.

With the discovery of silver mines in the Western territories and subsequent increase in its supply, silver provided a relatively low cost metal for jewelry in the U. S. By the turn of century, there was widespread use of silver in the manufacturing of jewelry, providing the population with a broad range of jewelry at affordable prices. Early silver jewelry usually was not marked, and sterling silver standard was not adopted in the U. S. until 1906. Prior to this date, American standard required 900 parts per thousand and both "coin" and "standard" marks indicate 900 fineness, though, several manufacturers such as Tiffany adopted the sterling standard, 925 silver, at a much earlier date.

The costume jewelry industry manufactured silver jewelry throughout the twentieth century, particularly during WWII when the supply of other metals was restricted. Many pieces covered in this chapter are simply marked sterling. Some are marked silver jewelry and not covered in

Chapter 3 under specific manufacturer's name, but are identified and shown only in this chapter. Furthermore, a significant amount of foreign silver jewelry was imported into the U. S., particularly after WWII. Among these imported jewelries are Mexican, Siamese (Thailand), Scan-

dinavian, and Middle Eastern silver jewelry which were popular at different times. Limited space permits showing only a few examples of each type in this chapter, but a forthcoming book on silver jewelry by this author will devote a chapter to each country's production.

Opposite page, top left: *Matching gold filled pendant and screw back earrings with geometric cut smoky gray glass stones. Marked A & Z, ⅟₂₀ 12k G.F. This trademark belongs to A & Z Chain Co., founded in 1905 by Carl Anshen and Saul Zeitlin in Providence, R.I. The company was purchased by Amtel, Inc., in 1970. $60.00 – 85.00.*

Opposite page, top right: *Top left: Gold filled pin decorated with clear and foil-less sapphire blue rhinestones. Marked M & S, ⅟₂₀ 12k G.F. Trademark of M & S Jewelry Manufacturing Co., operating in the 1940s in Providence, R.I. $25.00 – 35.00. Lower left: Gold filled and rhinestone screw back earrings. $20.00 – 25.00. Top right: Pair of gold filled screw back earrings. Marked dec, trademark of Curtis Jewelry Co. $20.00 – 30.00. Lower right: Circle pin with rhinestones and two gold hearts. Marked CC held in palm of a hand. Trademark of Curtman Company. $35.00 – 50.00. Center: Gold filled pendant decorated with blue rhinestones and three suspended tassels. Marked ⅟₂₀ 12k G.F. $30.00 – 45.00.*

Opposite page, bottom left: *Top left: Gold filled floral pin and matching screw back earrings with black enamel work, marked A & Z (see above). $40.00 – 55.00. Center left: round gold filled pin with three low grade, but genuine gemstones. Marked EKELUN, 14k G.F. This is the trademark of Ekelund Bros., Inc., founded about 1910 in Providence, R.I. $35.00 – 50.00. Center right: Round gold filled pin with a group of rhinestones giving the impression of a bouquet of flowers. Marked CARLA, the trademark of National Costume Jewelry Company, founded early 1950s in Buffalo, N.Y. The 1994 Jewelers' Circular lists CARLA as the trademark of Carla Corp., located in Providence, R.I. $35.00 – 45.00. All others: Three pairs of gold filled screw back earrings. The lower left pair is with cultured pearls and marked IPS, the trademark of IPS Inc., located in Seekonk, Mass. The firm is no longer in business. $25.00 – 35.00. All others: $20.00 – 30.00 each.*

Opposite page, bottom right: *Top: Pair of gold filled earrings with brilliant rhinestones. Marked DeCurtis, ⅟₂₀ 12k G.F. This is the trademark of Curtis Jewelry Manufacturing Co., Providence, R.I. $20.00 – 30.00. Center: Sterling vermeil pin decorated with cultured pearls and blue baguette stones. Marked B & O, sterling, ⅟₂₀ 12k G.F. This was the trademark of B & O Chain Co., operating around 1940 to the late 1960s. $50.00 – 75.00. Bottom: Gold filled sweater guard pin. Marked CM with the letter C embracing M. Trademark of Curtman Company, founded about 1936 in Providence, R.I. $40.00 – 50.00.*

Top right: *Center: Slender gold filled floral pin with blue stones. Marked White Co. $30.00 – 40.00. Lower center: White gold filled sweater guard pin. Marked M & S (see above). $35.00 – 50.00. Bottom: Two pairs of gold filled cuff links. The right pair with bowling ball and pins was made by Kreisler Manufacturing Corp., founded in 1913. The firm was located in North Bergen, N.J., but was moved to St. Petersburg, Fla., in 1977. $25.00 – 40.00. Left cuffs links $15.00 – 20.00. Top center: Two pairs of gold filled screw back earrings with cultured pearls. $25.00 – 30.00 each. All others: Two pairs of white gold filled screw back earrings with rhinestones. $15.00 – 20.00 each.*

Bottom right: *Three large sterling silver brooches. The two right pieces are in sterling vermeil. $45.00 – 70.00 each. The asking price varies drastically and may be as low as $35.00 or as high as $125.00*

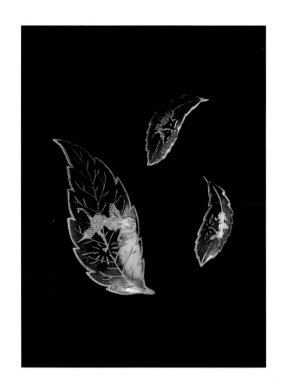

Opposite page, top left: *Upper left: Pair of sterling silver clip earrings with Pat. #156,452 with possibly the last digit missing (ca. 1925). $35.00 – 50.00. Center left: Pair of sterling silver screw back earrings. $12.50 – 20.00. Lower left: Slender sterling silver pin in shape of a flying bird. $20.00 – 30.00. Center: Sterling silver bracelet featuring topaz stones. $40.00 – 65.00. Top right: Floral sterling silver brooch. $40.00 – 60.00.*

Opposite page, top right: *Top left: Sterling vermeil screw back earrings with green and clear rhinestones. $25.00 – 40.00. Lower left: Sterling vermeil brooch in floral motif set with green rhinestones. Marked Courtly, the trademark of Swiss Harmony Inc., Chicago, Ill. $30.00 – 45.00. Center: Sterling silver bracelet with foil-less clear stones. $40.00 – 60.00. Top right: Heavy sterling vermeil brooch with topaz color stones. $40.00 – 65.00. Center right: Small sterling silver pin with red rhinestones. Marked with letter I superimposed over H, the trademark of Harry Iskin, later Iskin Manufacturing Company, Philadelphia, Penn. Out of business by the mid 1940s. $35.00 – 45.00.*

Opposite page, bottom left: *Top left: Sterling silver pendant with three birds, marked International with the trademark of the International Silver Co., Meriden, Conn. $40.00 – 65.00. Both book and asking prices vary drastically. Top right: Sterling silver charm bracelet. $60.00 – 85.00. Bottom: Sterling silver bracelet. $40.00 – 60.00.*

Opposite page, bottom right: *Matching sterling silver pin and earrings, marked Siam. Large volume was imported from Thailand in the 1940s and 1950s. There are significant variations in book and asking prices. $60.00 – 85.00.*

Top: *Sterling silver bracelet and earrings, marked Siam. Bracelet. $50.00 – 70.00. Earrings. $20.00 – 35.00.*

Bottom: *Center: Basse-Taille enamel pin. Marked Norway and with David-Anderson trademark. The company was a major manufacturer of this type of enamel jewelry. $35.00 – 50.00. Bottom: Basse-Taille enamel necklace made of slender leaves. Marked Norway and with David-Anderson Co. trademark. $65.00 – 95.00.*

Top: *Top left: Sterling silver enamel maple leaf pin. Marked BMCO. $40.00 – 60.00. Top center: Sterling vermeil brooch. $40.00 – 60.00. Top right: Sterling vermeil crown pin. $25.00 – 40.00. Bottom: Sterling silver bracelet set with rhinestones. $45.00 – 60.00.*

Bottom left: *Three silver coin bracelets. Top: Made of Australian WWII period coins. $45.00 – 70.00. Center: 1960s coins of Trinidad and Tobago. $30.00 – 45.00. Bottom: 1910 – 1920 Canadian coins. $50.00 – 75.00.*

Bottom right: *Persian silver bracelet with hand done miniature paintings on ivory. Miniature paintings on Persian jewelry contain similar themes as the famed miniature paintings of the Persian manuscripts dating back to as early as the twelfth century. This piece is circa 1920 – 1930s, but such jewelry was imported into the U. S. as early as the 1880s by Armenian and Persian Jewish emigrants who were primarily Oriental rug merchants. The jewelry is little understood on the collectible market and is often sold as Chinese jewelry. The author's forthcoming book on silver will display many pieces and identify the major artisans. $100.00 – 150.00. Asking price varies; such a piece can be purchased for as low as $25.00.*

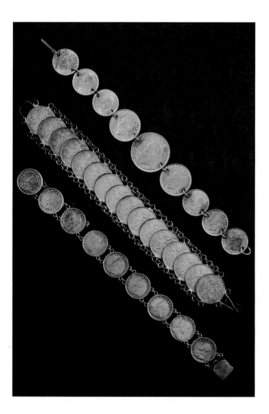

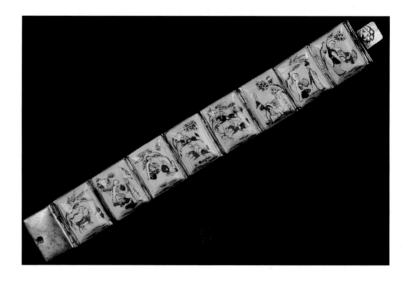

Above: *Silver bracelet with cactus and Mexican folk figures. Marked Hencho en Mexico with eagle stamp mark. Mexican jewelry is among some of the most beautiful silver jewelry imported into the U. S. Several Americans were influential in the revival of the industry in the Taxco area and the jewelry's popularity in the U. S. Large volumes were imported especially during and after WWII. Quality signed jewelry is extremely collectible and has experienced an astronomical rise in prices. The prices of unsigned or less desirable pieces are also expected to rise in the future. $125.00 – 160.00.*

Below: *Top left: Large Mexican silver leaf set with abalone shell. Marked 925 and Hencho en Mexico encircling the maker's initials MRS with eagle assay mark. $50.00 – 80.00. Top right: Small leaf-shaped pin made of silver and covered with abalone shell. Marked Hencho en Mexico encircling the maker's initials ASM. Also marked sterling, Cuern. $35.00 – 55.00. Center: Mexican silver bracelet with abalone shell. Marked 925, sterling, and Mexico. $60.00 – 90.00. Lower right: Leaf-shaped Mexican silver pin set with abalone shell. Marked with maker's initials MSR, 925 sterling, and Taxco. $35.00 – 50.00.*

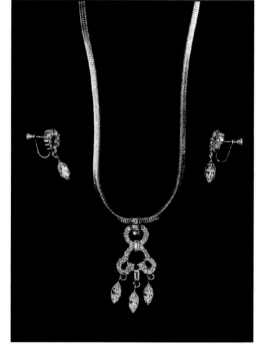

Top left: *Turbaned head in carved obsidian and matching screw back earrings. Marked sterling, Mexico. $95.00 – 145.00.*

Top right: *Necklace and matching earrings in sterling silver and rhinestone. All pieces simply marked sterling. $60.00 – 95.00.*

Bottom left: *Necklace and matching bracelet in silver filigree with floral design. $50.00 – 70.00. Similar silver pin. $20.00 – 25.00. This type of jewelry was manufactured in Mexico, Italy, and the Middle East. This set is possibly from Italy.*

Bottom right: *Scandinavian (Lappish) brooch in sterling silver and hanging gilded half domes and drops. Marked 830S for silver fineness with the maker's initial H. This type of jewelry which is still being made is based on traditional Lappish motifs and was brought to the U. S. by Scandinavian emigrants and American tourists. Like Persian silver and enamel jewelry, it is little understood and seldom correctly identified on the collectible market. Prices vary drastically. $85.00 – 125.00.*

Chapter 7

Brass, Copper, Pewter, Tin, and Other Metals

Many metals such as tin, brass, bronze, copper, aluminum, and polished steel were used in mass-produced costume jewelry. Among these, copper and tin were popular during the 1930s – 1950s period. Copper, the choice metal during the Arts & Crafts Movement, was frequently used in mass-produced costume jewelry of the 1950s, replicating the hand-hammered look of the earlier jewelry.

Many copper pieces are not marked, but among signed pieces several brands are highly collectible. Foremost among these is the copper jewelry made by Rebajes. The company was founded in New York City by Francisco Rebajes in 1932. Born in the Dominican Republic, Rebajes moved to New York in 1923 and while seeking employment, began making jewelry using borrowed tools and aluminum cans in a basement apartment. From this meager beginning, Rebajes' career rose rapidly, enabling him to establish a store on fashionable Fifth Avenue in

1942. By 1953, the firm was employing over 60 workers and its jewelry retailed throughout the United States. Many Rebajes designs are derived from nature, depicting leaves, birds, fish, and other animals. Others are Art Moderne, reflecting the contemporary interest in cubist and abstract designs and primitive African Art which partly inspired it. Rebajes stopped production in 1960. Recognized for the designer's talent and craftsmanship, jewelry by Rebajes is highly collectible and will continue to rise in prices.

Another manufacturer of copper jewelry is Renoir of California, Inc., founded in Los Angeles in 1946 by Jerry Fels. Most of the jewelry is signed Renoir and was inspired by contemporary abstract and modern art trends. Another company, Matisse, Ltd., also founded in Los Angeles by Jerry Fels and family in 1952, manufactured copper jewelry with surface enamel work. Both firms were out of business around 1964.

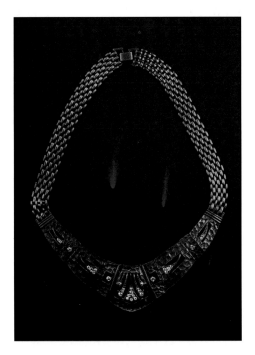

Top left: *Unmarked handmade copper necklace enhanced by rhinestones.* $150.00 – 200.00.

Bottom left: *Left: Copper bracelet marked Solid Copper with adjoining initials JP. $45.00 – 65.00. Center: Large copper flower pendant marked Solid Copper. $25.00 – 35.00. Right: Unmarked copper and imitation turquoise are combined to create this bracelet and matching earrings. $50.00 – 75.00.*

Bottom right: *Top left: Pair of unmarked copper earrings. $20.00 – 25.00 each. Top center and right: Two pairs of copper earrings, marked Renoir. $30.00 – 45.00 each. Bottom: Copper bracelet and matching earrings, marked Renoir. $75.00 – 100.00.*

Opposite page, top left: *Top: Copper pin and pair of earrings with enameled front. $5.00 – 7.50 each. Center: Unmarked pair of copper earrings. $20.00 – 25.00. Center right: Matching enameled copper pin and earrings. $10.00 – 20.00. Bottom: Unmarked copper necklace. $30.00 – 45.00.*

Opposite page, top right: *Matching set of copper necklace, bracelet, and screw back earrings with plastic crescents and rhinestones. Unmarked. $60.00 – 90.00.*

Opposite page, bottom left: *Top: Two pairs of copper earrings, marked Renoir. Basketweave and laurel patterns. $30.00 – 40.00 each. Top right: Brass flower head brooch, marked Kirschenbaum. $25.00 – 35.00. Center: Unmarked copper necklace. $35.00 – 50.00. Lower center: Wide Renoir bracelet in mesh pattern. Not a very common Renoir pattern. $50.00 – 75.00. Bottom: Pair of copper earrings, marked Renoir. $30.00 – 40.00.*

Opposite page, bottom right: *Top: Large copper brooch marked Hand Made. $35.00 – 45.00. Bottom: Unmarked copper necklace and matching screw back earrings. $50.00 – 70.00.*

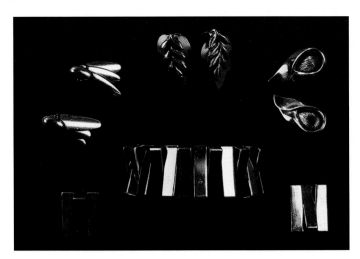

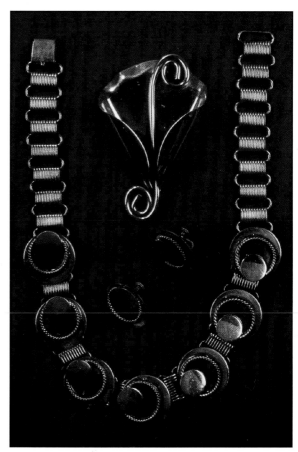

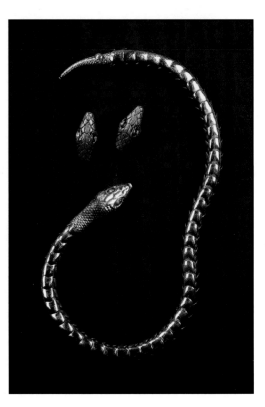

Top left: *Top to bottom: Metal cuff bracelet with 1933 Chicago World's Fair logo. $35.00 – 50.00. Silvertone hinged bracelet with goldtone Shriner symbol in the center. $30.00 – 45.00. Copper cuff bracelet with butterfly on the top highlighted by turquoise. Marked Solid Copper encircling a bell, the trademark of the Bell Trading Post Co., founded about 1932 in Albuquerque, N.M., later a division of Sunbell Corporation. $40.00 – 60.00. Hinged copper bracelet in leaflet pattern, marked Matisse Renoir. $45.00 – 70.00.*

Top right: *Gilded brass serpent necklace and matching earrings. $90.00 – 135.00.*

Bottom left: *Marked Rebajes, copper fish pin. $75.00 – 100.00. Asking price may be as high as $150.00.*

Bottom right: *Top left: Cuff bracelet, marked Coppercraft Guild. $45.00 – 65.00. Center left: Cuff bracelet, marked Solid Copper with the Bell Trading Post Co. trademark. $35.00 – 50.00. Lower left: Metal cuff bracelet, marked Sarah Cov. $15.00 – 30.00. Top right: Unmarked gold plated hinged bracelet. $40.00 – 65.00. Center right: Hinged bracelet with imitation cameo. Marked Coro. $30.00 – 50.00. Lower right: Gold washed hinged bracelet. $40.00 – 60.00.*

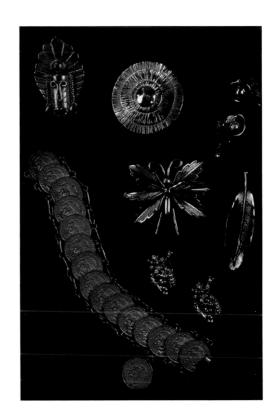

Top left: *Top left and right: Four pairs of marked Matisse earrings. $30.00 – 45.00 each. Bottom: Unmarked matching necklace and earrings in combination of copper and imitation goldstone. $35.00 – 50.00.*

Top right: *Top left: Pre-Columbian inspired copper face brooch, marked Hencho en Mexico. $25.00 – 40.00. Top center: Haitian copper circular pin, marked Chenet d'Haiti. $10.00 – 15.00. Top right: Pair of copper earrings, marked Copper by Bell with Bell Trading Post Co. trademark. $20.00 – 25.00. Lower left: Mexican coin bracelet. $15.00 – 25.00. Center: Bell copper insect pin. $15.00 – 20.00. Center right: Small leaf pin, marked with initials NYE in trefoil. This is the trademark of Stuart Nye Silver Shop located in Asheville, N.C., and in business since at least the 1950s. The firm's current name is Nye Hand Wrought Jewelry. $15.00 – 25.00. Lower center: Pair of goldtone screw back earrings with a knight in armor beneath a crown. Marked Coro. $20.00 – 30.00.*

Right: *Left: Unmarked silvertone tin metal necklace and matching earrings with rose head and leaves design and rhinestone accent. $25.00 – 40.00. This is a relatively common piece, but may have a much higher asking price. Center: Textured gold washed metal bead necklace. Unmarked. $15.00 – 30.00. Right: Pair of unmarked gold plated earrings. This pair has the same patent number as marked Marino jewelry. See Chapter 3. $15.00 – 25.00.*

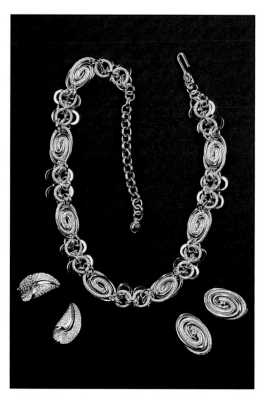

Top left: *Top row: Three small pewter pendants. All marked Norway. The right piece is also marked TPB and the other two with initial EH. $15.00 – 20.00 each. Center left: Pewter pin, marked Jorgen Jensen, Handmade, Denmark. Jorgen Jensen, a major Danish designer/manufacturer, worked primarily in pewter. $25.00 – 40.00. Center: Unmarked Art Moderne metal necklace. $35.00 – 50.00. The author has seen several variations of this piece. Center right: Round Swedish pewter pin, marked INGLINGE KLOT, EF, and N9. $20.00 – 35.00. Lower left: Pewter screw back earrings, marked Jorgen Jensen. $25.00 – 40.00.*

Top right: *Lower left: Pair of unmarked silvertone earrings. $5.00 – 7.50. Center: Featherweight aluminum necklace and matching earrings marked West Germany. $15.00 – 20.00.*

Bottom left: *Variety of painted tin jewelry. Many major manufacturers produced this type of jewelry, including Coro and Weiss. $10.00 – 25.00 each.*

Bottom right: *Copper/silvertone metal belt with Indian Chief head encircled by the motto Liberty – Equality – Fraternity – 1776. $40.00 – 65.00.*

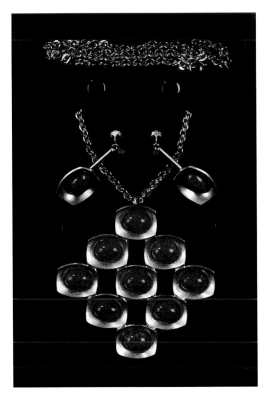

Top left: *Art Moderne pewter necklace and matching earrings with cabochon imitation lapis lazuli in velvet pouch and original box. Marked Jorgen Jensen. Many of the works of this accomplished Danish designer are easily recognizable and avidly sought by a limited number of collectors in the U. S. $200.00 – 250.00. This is a very rough estimate since insufficient numbers are traded.*

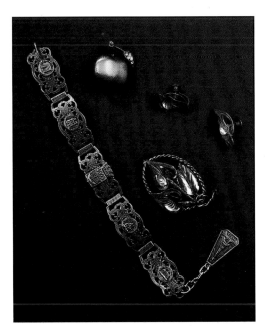

Top right: *Lower left: Silvertone French souvenir link bracelet. Marked France with illegible trademark. $40.00 – 60.00. Right: Matching pin and earrings in sterling silver and copper with natural display of leaves. Marked sterling and Copper. $40.00 – 60.00. Top: Copper apple pin with rhinestone accent. $10.00 – 20.00.*

Bottom left: *Top: Goldtone pin and matching screw back earrings in floral design, marked B.N. Several companies used these initials and as of this date, the author has not been able to definitely identify the manufacturer. This set is a very typical example of jewelry found on the collectible market with the same trademark. $30.00 – 45.00. Center: Floral pin and matching earrings in goldtone solid and mesh metal. $30.00 – 45.00. Left: Early repoussé and gilded metal link bracelet with floral design. $45.00 – 70.00.*

Bottom right: *Left and right: Two marked Art Moderne pewter pendants by the Swedish metalsmith R. Tennesmed. $50.00 – 90.00 each. Center: Scandinavian pewter pendant, signed Rolf Buodd. Also marked Norsk Hand Arbeide. $50.00 – 80.00.*

Chapter 8

Plastic Jewelry

Plastic was used in the production of costume jewelry because of its low cost and the fact that it could accommodate a rainbow of colors. It was also lighter than metals, thereby allowing production of bulkier pieces. Technically, there are three broad categories of plastic with different chemical properties: celluloid, Bakelite, and Lucite.

Celluloid's use in the production of jewelry and accessories dates back to the nineteenth century, but its use was limited to imitating other natural materials, such as tortoise shell or ivory. In fact, some of the patented products incorporated the word "ivory," such as French Ivory which was patented and produced in Rockford, Ill. A factor that limited the popularity of celluloid was its flammability. A nonflammable substitute under the trade name Lumarith was introduced in 1927 by the Celluloid Corporation. This combined with the development of injection-molding technology led to low cost mass production and widespread use of celluloid in the late 1920s and 1930s. Typical products were rhinestone studded bangles, pins, and hair ornaments such as haircombs, hatpins, and headbands.

In 1909, Leo H. Baekeland patented his accidentally discovered product, thermosetting phe-

nol formaldehyde resin which he labeled Bakelite. Later similar plastic was manufactured under various tradenames among which Catalin and Prystal, produced by the Catalin Corporation, are the most sought after. Although Bakelite was used in production of a variety of products, its widespread use in jewelry production did not take effect until the 1930s when cheap plastic jewelry was the only jewelry that many could afford to buy. Bakelite jewelry was produced in a variety of colors, some with carved designs, especially on bangles. Reverse carving, where the design was cut on the back of the piece and sometimes enhanced by gold paint to give it a three-dimensional look was used in the late 1930s and after Prystal, a clear Bakelite, was introduced by the Catalin Corporation.

During WWII, the rhinestone imports from Czechoslovakia were disrupted and the costume jewelry industry used plastic "stones" of various colors and shapes on metal mountings and created some of the most beautiful designs of the 1940s and 1950s. Coro, Lisner, Star, and Trifari were among the major manufacturers of this type of jewelry. It is yet to be appreciated by most collectors and is well underpriced, rendering it perhaps the best investment jewelry among plastic jewelry. However, the European collectors seem to favor this type of jewelry and simple Coro or Lisner sets are usually marked above $100.00. The 1997 *Miller's International Antiques Price Guide* lists an unmarked Coro-like pin and earrings set at $90.00 – 100.00 which usually would not fetch a price above $40.00 in the U. S. market. Many collectors avidly seek Bakelite jewelry, especially the figurals, carved pieces, and those in uncommon colors.

Lucite, a crystal clear plastic, was introduced by DuPont Corp. in 1937. Being more cost effective, Lucite replaced Bakelite by the 1950s, and was used in production of costume jewelry as early as 1940. The most collectible Lucite jewelry is "jelly belly" figurals with a central Lucite "stone." At this time, collectors and trend followers consider only clear bellies as "true" jelly bellies which has resulted in fantastic price increases. The readers should be warned that most jelly bellies found on the collectible market are reproductions even though some are actually signed pieces. Also collectible is Lucite jewelry tinted in a variety of colors, and clear reverse carved pieces with paint used to highlight the design.

Left: *A group of plastic bangles. Carved bangles. $60.00 – 120.00. All others. $30.00 – 60.00.*

Right: *Top left: Celluloid pin. $25.00 – 40.00. Top right: Plastic circle pin imitating pearls. $10.00 – 15.00. Bottom: Parure in stylized floral design with brown plastic inserts. This type of jewelry became popular after WWII especially in the 1950s. $60.00 – 90.00. The asking price varies drastically.*

Top left: *Top: Pair of plastic earrings in imitation tortoise shell. $15.00 – 25.00. Center: Pair of carved Bakelite earrings. $25.00 – 35.00. Two plastic bar pins. $30.00 – 45.00. Bottom: Plastic necklace with goldtone metal spacers. Mold marks indicate that this piece may have been made in Germany. See the section on German jewelry for a similar piece in different color with identical mold marks. $40.00 – 65.00.*

Top right: *Top and bottom: Mah jong bracelets. $60.00 – 95.00 each. The asking and book prices may be much higher. Center: Plastic pin and two dress clips. $30.00 – 45.00 each.*

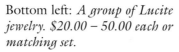

Bottom left: *A group of Lucite jewelry. $20.00 – 50.00 each or matching set.*

Bottom right: *Top left: Matching pin and earrings with plastic inserts and rhinestones. $30.00 – 45.00. Center: Three colors of molded plastic are used to create this unmarked necklace which was probably produced by a major manufacturer. $30.00 – 45.00. Bottom: Two plastic scarab link bracelets. $25.00 – 35.00 each.*

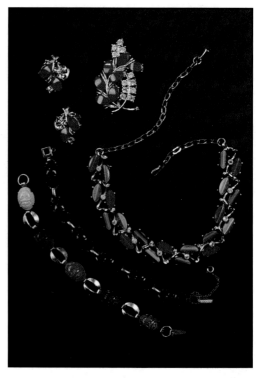

Top left: *Top left: Matching necklace and clip earrings with yellow plastic inserts. $35.00 – 50.00. Bottom: Matching necklace and bracelet with yellow plastic inserts and enamel accent. $35.00 – 55.00.*

Top right: *Top left: Blue metallic plastic pieces are combined with chrome to create this bracelet with modern design. $35.00 – 50.00. Top center: 1930s Bakelite cameo brooch. $60.00 – 90.00. Quality construction and material. The asking price may be as high as $120.00. Top right: Hat ornament enhanced by rhinestones. $20.00 – 40.00. Bottom: Plastic beads highlighted by floral clasp in imitation of Oriental jade jewelry. Quality material and construction. Metal backing has the characteristics of Ciner jewelry. $40.00 – 60.00.*

Bottom left: *Simple or elegant? Parure consisting of necklace, flexible bracelet, and screw back earrings made of plastic and gold plated spacer beads. $120.00 – 165.00.*

Bottom right: *Center left: Plastic bead necklace with carved center beads. $50.00 – 70.00. Center right: Plastic bead necklace with a plastic ring. $40.00 – 60.00. All others: Eight pairs of plastic earrings with diverse designs. $15.00 – 40.00 each.*

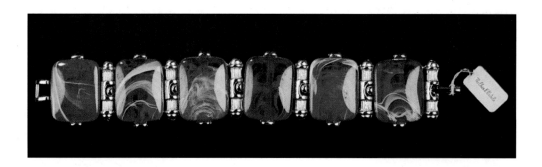

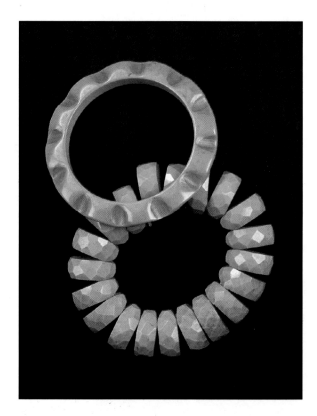

Top: *Most plastic jewelry was not marked and carried the retailer's tag such as this bracelet sold by Chas. W. Weise Co., now a defunct chain department store in Illinois. The original price was $2.50. $20.00 – 30.00.*

Above left: *A diverse group of U. S. made and imported Occupied Japan plastic pins. $10.00 – 45.00 each.*

Above right: *Early carved plastic bangle and flexible bracelet. Bangle. $80.00 – 125.00. Bracelet. $100.00 – 165.00.*

Chapter 9

Bead and Simulated Pearl Jewelry

Beads have been used as jewelry and ornaments throughout the world since prehistoric times. They were used in some societies as a form of money and by the early European settlers in North American as a tool for bartering with the Native Americans.

Beads used in the production of costume jewelry came from a variety of sources made in different shapes and colors using diverse materials. First and foremost were the Venetian glass beads produced on the island of Murrano which are usually referred to as milefiori (multiflower) beads. The cheaper versions are now mass produced in Purdalpur, India. Faceted and molded glass beads were produced in Bohemia, later Czechoslovakia, with its center of production in Jablonec. Here also began the mass production of rhinestones and cut crystals by the now renowned firm of Swarovski, which later relocated to the Austrian Tyrol near Innsbruck. In German Bavaria, post WWII Czech and German settlers created a new center of production called Nea Gablonz as a western source of supply of glass and crystal beads.

China was the source for porcelain, cloisonne, bone, ivory, and a variety of semiprecious beads. Japan provided the world markets with glass and plastic beads as well as seed and faux pearls. The industry also used a variety of stamped, embossed, and hammered metal beads.

Most manufacturers of costume jewelry used beads along with rhinestones in a variety of designs, and several of them produced some jewelry made exclusively of beads and faux pearls. Among these were Coro, Trifari, Robert, Haskell, Marvella, Laguna, and Pakula whose jewelry is shown in Chapter 3. This chapter covers a broad range of jewelry, both domestic and foreign, utilizing beads and faux pearls, not covered in other chapters under specific names.

Left: *Fringed necklace and matching earrings made of Bohemian beads and simulated pearls. $150.00 – 225.00.*

Bottom left: *Two Bohemian glass necklaces. $60.00 – 95.00 each.*

Bottom right: *Left and right: Two cut cube glass necklaces. $60.00 – 85.00 each. Center: Necklace featuring geometric amber glass. $60.00 – 90.00.*

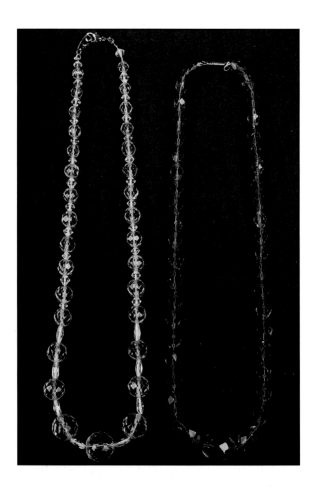

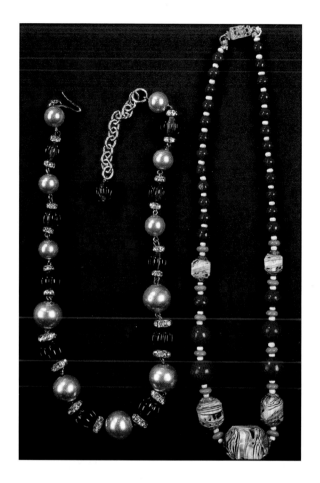

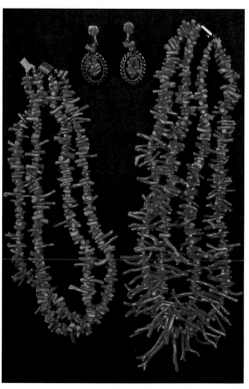

Left: *Multi-strand necklace made of Bohemian glass of different shapes. $150.00 – 200.00.*

Right: *Left: Simulated pearl, sculptured green beads, and rhinestone roundels are combined to create this attractive necklace. $100.00 – 150.00. Right: Necklace made of cut glass and glass beads. $60.00 – 90.00.*

Bottom right: *Two coral necklaces and a pair of screw back coral earrings. Left: $70.00 – 100.00. Right: $85.00 – 135.00. Earrings. $30.00 – 45.00. The asking prices vary drastically.*

Top: *Parure consisting of necklace, bracelet, and earrings made of cut glass and imitation coral glass beads. Unmarked, but possibly a Japanese import. $75.00 – 100.00.*

Bottom left: *Center: Imitation pearl necklace. $40.00 – 65.00. Left: Imitation pearl earrings. $15.00 – 25.00. Right: Earrings made of pearl and beads. Good quality material. $20.00 – 30.00.*

Bottom right: *Iridescent Bohemian glass beads. Left: Green necklace and matching earrings. $45.00 – 70.00. Right: Amber necklace. $30.00 – 45.00.*

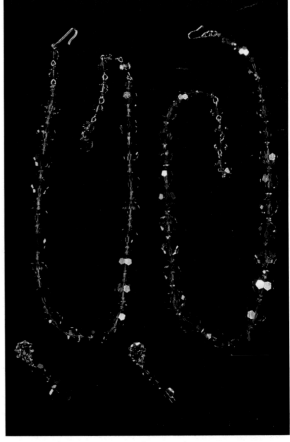

Right: *Unmarked bead jewelry possibly from Japan. Bracelet. $15.00 – 25.00. Flexible bracelet and matching earrings. $15.00 – 25.00. Earrings. $5.00 – 8.00.*

Bottom left: *Long cobalt blue cut glass necklace. $60.00 – 95.00.*

Bottom right: *Left: Baroque pearl necklace with a bunch of fruits in the center. Unmarked. $35.00 – 60.00. Right: Two strand pearl necklace. Unmarked. $25.00 – 45.00. Bottom: Pair of earrings. Unmarked. $7.50 – 12.50.*

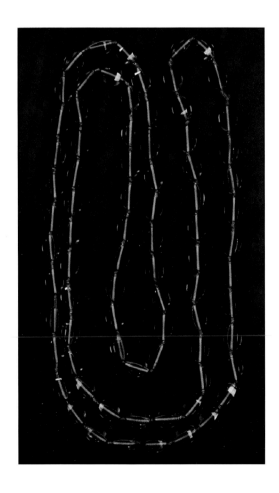

Top left: *Three different pearl necklaces and a pair of earrings. Necklaces. $25.00 – 40.00 each. Earrings. $5.00 – 7.50.*

Top right: *Simulated bead and jade necklace and matching earrings. Unmarked, but high quality production possibly by a major manufacturer. $50.00 – 75.00.*

Bottom left: *Genuine cherry amber necklace. $135.00 – 175.00.*

Top left: *Two white seed bead necklaces.*
$20.00 – 40.00 each.

Top right: *1950s bead jewelry imported from*
Japan. Necklace and matching earrings.
$20.00 – 35.00.
Pair of screw back earrings with beads made
of wood. $10.00 – 15.00.

Bottom right: *Necklace made of black mold-*
ed glass beads and two plastic bead necklaces.
All unmarked, but most likely Japanese
imports from the 1950s and 1960s. $15.00 –
22.50 each.

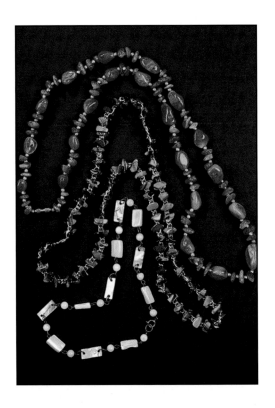

Top left: *Three necklaces made of genuine agate, tiger's eye, and mother-of-pearl. $25.00 – 45.00 each.*

Top right: *Necklace made of white glass beads and flowers. Unmarked, but most likely West German or Japanese import. $25.00 – 40.00.*

Bottom left: *Necklace made of white glass beads. Unmarked, but possibly from West Germany. $30.00 – 45.00. Two plastic bead necklaces, both unmarked, but most likely Japanese imports. $15.00 – 20.00 each.*

Bibliography

Baker, Lillian. *Art Nouveau & Art Deco Jewelry.* Collector Books, 1981.

*_____. *Fifty Years of Collecting Fashion Jewelry 1925 – 1975.* Collector Books, 1986.

_____. *100 Years of Collectible Jewelry.* Collector Books, 1978.

Twentieth Century Fashionable Plastic Jewelry. Collector Books, 1992.

*Ball, Joanne Dubbs. *Costume Jewelry, The Golden Age of Design.* Schiffer, 1990.

*Ball, Joanne Dubbs and Torem, Dorothy Hehl. *Masterpieces of Costume Jewelry.* Schiffer, 1996.

Baubles, Sibylle Jargstorf. *Buttons and Beads, The Heritage of Bohemia.* Schiffer, 1993.

Becker, Vivienne. *Fabulous Costume Jewelry.* Schiffer, 1993.

Bell, Jeanenne. *Answers to Questions About Old Jewelry.* Books Americana, Inc., 1985.

*Burkholz, Mattew and Kaplan, Linda L. *Copper Art Jewelry, A Different Luster.* Schiffer, 1992.

*Cera, Deanna Farneti, ed. *Jewels of Fantasy, Costume Jewelry of the 20th Century.* Harry N. Abrams, 1992.

Colliers magazine. Various issues.

Darling, Sharon S. *Chicago Metalsmiths.* Chicago Historical Society, 1977.

Davidov, Corinee and Dawes, Ginny Redington. *The Bakelite Jewelry Book.* Abbeville Press, 1988.

DiNoto, Andrea, "Bakelite Envy," *Connoisseur*, July, 1982.

*Dolan, Maryanne. *Collecting Rhinestone Jewelry, An Identification and Value Guide.* Books Americana Inc., 1989.

Ensko, Stephen. *American Silversmiths & Their Marks.* Robert Ensko, Inc., 1948.

Ettinger, Roseann. *Forties and Fifties Popular Jewelry.* Schiffer, 1994.

_____. *Popular Jewelry 1840 – 1940.* Schiffer, 1990.

Gold, Annalee. *75 Years of Fashion.* Fairchild Publications, Inc., 1975.

Gordon, Eleanor and Nerenberg, Jean. "Early Plastic Jewelry", *Antique Trader*, Nov. 26, 1974; and various issues.

**Harper's Bazaar.* Various issues.

Haslam, Malcolm. *Marks and Monograms of the Modern Movement, 1875 – 1930.* Scribner, 1977.

Hughes, Graham. *Jewelry.* E. P. Dutton and Co., 1966.

_____. *The Art of Jewelry.* Viking Press, 1972.

Jewelers' Circular. Brand Name and Trademark Guide. Jewelers' Circular Keystone, various years.

*Katz, Sylvia. *Early Plastics.* Shire Publications, Ltd., 1986.

*_____. *Plastic Common Objects, Classic Designs.* Harry N. Abrams, 1984.

Kelly, Lyngerda and Schiffer, Nancy. *Costume Jewelry, The Great Pretenders.* Schiffer, 1987.

Ladies' Home Journal. Various issues.

Lynnler, J. L. *All That Glitters.* Schiffer, 1986.

*Miller, Harrice Simons. *Costume Jewelry Identification and Price Guide.* Avon Books, 1994.

_____. *Official Identification and Price Guide to Costume Jewelry.* House of Collectibles, 1990.

*Mulvagh, Jan. *Costume Jewelry in Vogue.* Thames & Hudson, 1988.

Proddow, Penny, Heally, Debra, and Fasel, Marion. *Hollywood Jewels.* Harry Abrams, 1992.

*Rainwater, Dorothy T. *American Jewelry Manufacturers.* Schiffer, 1988.

_____. *Encyclopedia of American Silver Manufacturers.* Third Edition Revised. Schiffer, 1986.

*Romero, Christie. *Warman's Jewelry.* Wallace-Homestead Books Co., 1995.

Samberg, Ronben. "Costume Jewelry," *Fortune Magazine,* Dec., 1946.

Sears, Roebuck & Co. catalog. Various years.

*Schiffer, Nancy. *Costume Jewelry: The Fun of Collecting.* Schiffer, 1988.

_____. *Fun Jewelry.* Schiffer, 1991.

_____. *Rhinestones! A Collector's Handbook & Price Guide.* Schiffer, 1993.

_____. *Silver Jewelry Treasures.* Schiffer, 1993.

_____. *The Best of Costume Jewelry.* Schiffer, 1990.

Shields, Jody. *All That Glitters, The Story of Costume Jewelry.* Rizzoli International, 1987.

*Tardy International Hallmarks on Silver. Tardy, 1985.

*Trademarks of the Jewelry and Kindred Trades. Jewelers' Circular–Keystone Publishing Co. Various years.

*Untracht, Oppi. *Jewelry Concepts and Technology.* Doubleday, 1985.

Vogue magazine. Various issues.

*Sources that were directly used in writing this book are indicated with an asterisk before the name.

Index

COLLECTOR BOOKS

Informing Today's Collector

For over two decades we have been keeping collectors informed on trends and values in all fields of antiques and collectibles.

DOLLS, FIGURES & TEDDY BEARS

4707	A Decade of **Barbie** Dolls & Collectibles, 1981–1991, Summers	$19.95
4631	**Barbie** Doll Boom, 1986–1995, Augustyniak	$18.95
2079	**Barbie** Doll Fashions, Volume I, Eames	$24.95
3957	**Barbie** Exclusives, Rana	$18.95
4632	**Barbie** Exclusives, Book II, Rana	$18.95
4557	**Barbie**, The First 30 Years, Deutsch	$24.95
4657	**Barbie** Years, 1959–1995, Olds	$16.95
3310	**Black Dolls**, 1820–1991, Perkins	$17.95
3873	**Black Dolls**, Book II, Perkins	$17.95
1529	Collector's Encyclopedia of **Barbie** Dolls, DeWein	$19.95
4506	Collector's Guide to **Dolls in Uniform**, Bourgeois	$18.95
3727	Collector's Guide to **Ideal Dolls**, Izen	$18.95
3728	Collector's Guide to Miniature **Teddy Bears**, Powell	$17.95
3967	Collector's Guide to **Trolls**, Peterson	$19.95
4571	**Liddle Kiddles**, Identification & Value Guide, Langford	$18.95
4645	**Madame Alexander** Dolls Price Guide #21, Smith	$9.95
3733	**Modern Collector's** Dolls, Sixth Series, Smith	$24.95
3991	**Modern Collector's** Dolls, Seventh Series, Smith	$24.95
4647	**Modern Collector's** Dolls, Eighth Series, Smith	$24.95
4640	Patricia Smith's **Doll Values**, Antique to Modern, 12th Edition	$12.95
3826	Story of **Barbie**, Westenhouser	$19.95
1513	**Teddy Bears & Steiff** Animals, Mandel	$9.95
1817	**Teddy Bears & Steiff** Animals, 2nd Series, Mandel	$19.95
2084	**Teddy Bears, Annalee's & Steiff** Animals, 3rd Series, Mandel	$19.95
1808	Wonder of **Barbie**, Manos	$9.95
1430	World of **Barbie** Dolls, Manos	$9.95

FURNITURE

1457	American **Oak** Furniture, McNerney	$9.95
3716	American **Oak** Furniture, Book II, McNerney	$12.95
1118	Antique **Oak** Furniture, Hill	$7.95
2132	Collector's Encyclopedia of **American** Furniture, Vol. I, Swedberg	$24.95
2271	Collector's Encyclopedia of **American** Furniture, Vol. II, Swedberg	$24.95
3720	Collector's Encyclopedia of **American** Furniture, Vol. III, Swedberg	$24.95
3878	Collector's Guide to **Oak** Furniture, George	$12.95
1755	Furniture of the **Depression Era**, Swedberg	$19.95
3906	**Heywood-Wakefield** Modern Furniture, Rouland	$18.95
1885	**Victorian** Furniture, Our American Heritage, McNerney	$9.95
3829	**Victorian** Furniture, Our American Heritage, Book II, McNerney	$9.95
3869	**Victorian** Furniture books, 2 volume set, McNerney	$19.90

JEWELRY, HATPINS, WATCHES & PURSES

1712	Antique & Collector's **Thimbles** & Accessories, Mathis	$19.95
1748	Antique **Purses**, Revised Second Ed., Holiner	$19.95
1278	Art Nouveau & Art Deco **Jewelry**, Baker	$9.95
4558	**Christmas Pins**, Past and Present, Gallina	$18.95
3875	Collecting Antique **Stickpins**, Kerins	$16.95
3722	Collector's Ency. of **Compacts, Carryalls & Face Powder Boxes**, Mueller	$24.95
4655	Complete Price Guide to **Watches**, #16, Shugart	$26.95
1716	Fifty Years of Collectible **Fashion Jewelry**, 1925-1975, Baker	$19.95
1424	**Hatpins** & Hatpin Holders, Baker	$9.95
4570	Ladies' **Compacts**, Gerson	$24.95
1181	100 Years of Collectible **Jewelry**, 1850-1950, Baker	$9.95
2348	20th Century Fashionable Plastic **Jewelry**, Baker	$19.95
3830	Vintage **Vanity Bags & Purses**, Gerson	$24.95

TOYS, MARBLES & CHRISTMAS COLLECTIBLES

3427	**Advertising Character** Collectibles, Dotz	$17.95
2333	Antique & Collector's **Marbles**, 3rd Ed., Grist	$9.95
3827	Antique & Collector's **Toys**, 1870–1950, Longest	$24.95
3956	Baby Boomer **Games**, Identification & Value Guide, Polizzi	$24.95
3717	**Christmas** Collectibles, 2nd Edition, Whitmyer	$24.95
1752	**Christmas** Ornaments, Lights & Decorations, Johnson	$19.95
4649	Classic Plastic **Model Kits**, Polizzi	$24.95

4559	Collectible **Action Figures**, 2nd Ed., Manos	$17.95
3874	Collectible Coca-Cola Toy **Trucks**, deCourtivron	$24.95
2338	Collector's Encyclopedia of **Disneyana**, Longest, Stern	$24.95
4639	Collector's Guide to **Diecast Toys & Scale Models**, Johnson	$19.95
4651	Collector's Guide to **Tinker Toys**, Strange	$18.95
4566	Collector's Guide to **Tootsietoys**, 2nd Ed., Richter	$19.95
3436	Grist's Big Book of **Marbles**	$19.95
3970	Grist's Machine-Made & Contemporary **Marbles**, 2nd Ed.	$9.95
4569	**Howdy Doody**, Collector's Reference and Trivia Guide, Koch	$16.95
4723	**Matchbox®** Toys, 1948 to 1993, Johnson, 2nd Ed.	$18.95
3823	**Mego** Toys, An Illustrated Value Guide, Chrouch	15.95
1540	**Modern Toys** 1930–1980, Baker	$19.95
3888	**Motorcycle** Toys, Antique & Contemporary, Gentry/Downs	$18.95
4728	**Schroeder's Collectible Toys**, Antique to Modern Price Guide, 3rd Ed.	$17.95
1886	Stern's Guide to **Disney** Collectibles	$14.95
2139	Stern's Guide to **Disney** Collectibles, 2nd Series	$14.95
3975	Stern's Guide to **Disney** Collectibles, 3rd Series	$18.95
2028	**Toys**, Antique & Collectible, Longest	$14.95
3979	**Zany Characters** of the Ad World, Lamphier	$16.95

INDIANS, GUNS, KNIVES, TOOLS, PRIMITIVES

1868	Antique **Tools**, Our American Heritage, McNerney	$9.95
2015	Archaic **Indian** Points & Knives, Edler	$14.95
1426	**Arrowheads** & Projectile Points, Hothem	$7.95
4633	**Big Little Books**, Jacobs	$18.95
2279	**Indian** Artifacts of the Midwest, Hothem	$14.95
3885	**Indian** Artifacts of the Midwest, Book II, Hothem	$16.95
1964	**Indian** Axes & Related Stone Artifacts, Hothem	$14.95
2023	**Keen Kutter** Collectibles, Heuring	$14.95
4724	**Modern Guns**, Identification & Values, 11th Ed., Quertermous	$12.95
4505	Standard Guide to **Razors**, Ritchie & Stewart	$9.95
4730	Standard **Knife** Collector's Guide, 3rd Ed., Ritchie & Stewart	$12.95

PAPER COLLECTIBLES & BOOKS

4633	**Big Little Books**, Jacobs	$18.95
1441	Collector's Guide to **Post Cards**, Wood	$9.95
2081	Guide to Collecting **Cookbooks**, Allen	$14.95
4648	Huxford's **Old Book** Value Guide, 8th Ed.	$19.95
2080	Price Guide to **Cookbooks & Recipe Leaflets**, Dickinson	$9.95
2346	**Sheet Music** Reference & Price Guide, 2nd Ed., Pafik & Guiheen	$18.95
4654	**Victorian Trading Cards**, Historical Reference & Value Guide, Cheadle	$19.95

GLASSWARE

1006	**Cambridge Glass** Reprint 1930–1934	$14.95
1007	**Cambridge Glass** Reprint 1949–1953	$14.95
4561	Collectible **Drinking Glasses**, Chase & Kelly	$17.95
4642	Collectible **Glass Shoes**, Wheatley	$19.95
4553	Coll. **Glassware** from the 40's, 50's & 60's, 3rd Ed., Florence	$19.95
2352	Collector's Encyclopedia of **Akro Agate Glassware**, Florence	$14.95
1810	Collector's Encyclopedia of **American Art Glass**, Shuman	$29.95
3312	Collector's Encyclopedia of **Children's Dishes**, Whitmyer	$19.95
4552	Collector's Encyclopedia of **Depression Glass**, 12th Ed., Florence	$19.95
1664	Collector's Encyclopedia of **Heisey Glass**, 1925–1938, Bredehoft	$24.95
3905	Collector's Encyclopedia of **Milk Glass**, Newbound	$24.95
1523	Colors In **Cambridge Glass**, National Cambridge Society	$19.95
4564	**Crackle Glass**, Weitman	$19.95
2275	**Czechoslovakian Glass** and Collectibles, Barta/Rose	$16.95
4714	**Czechoslovakian Glass** and Collectibles, Book II, Barta/Rose	$16.95
4716	**Elegant Glassware** of the Depression Era, 7th Ed., Florence	$19.95
1380	Encyclopedia of **Pattern Glass**, McClain	$12.95
3981	Ever's Standard **Cut Glass** Value Guide	$12.95
4659	**Fenton** Art Glass, 1907–1939, Whitmyer	$24.95
3725	**Fostoria**, Pressed, Blown & Hand Molded Shapes, Kerr	$24.95
3883	**Fostoria Stemware**, The Crystal for America, Long & Seate	$24.95
3318	**Glass Animals** of the Depression Era, Garmon & Spencer	$19.95
4644	**Imperial Carnival Glass**, Burns	$18.95

COLLECTOR BOOKS
Informing Today's Collector

3886	**Kitchen Glassware** of the Depression Years, 5th Ed., Florence	$19.95
2394	**Oil Lamps II,** Glass Kerosene Lamps, Thuro	$24.95
4725	Pocket Guide to **Depression Glass,** 10th Ed., Florence	$9.95
4634	Standard Encyclopedia of **Carnival Glass,** 5th Ed., Edwards	$24.95
4635	Standard **Carnival Glass** Price Guide, 10th Ed.	$9.95
3974	Standard Encyclopedia of **Opalescent Glass,** Edwards	$19.95
4731	**Stemware Identification,** Featuring Cordials with Values, Florence	$24.95
3326	**Very Rare Glassware** of the Depression Years, 3rd Series, Florence	$24.95
3909	**Very Rare Glassware** of the Depression Years, 4th Series, Florence	$24.95
4732	**Very Rare Glassware** of the Depression Years, 5th Series, Florence	$24.95
4656	**Westmoreland Glass,** Wilson	$24.95
2224	World of **Salt Shakers,** 2nd Ed., Lechner	$24.95

POTTERY

4630	**American Limoges,** Limoges	$24.95
1312	**Blue & White Stoneware,** McNerney	$9.95
1958	So. Potteries **Blue Ridge Dinnerware,** 3rd Ed., Newbound	$14.95
1959	**Blue Willow,** 2nd Ed., Gaston	$14.95
3816	Collectible **Vernon Kilns,** Nelson	$24.95
3311	Collecting **Yellow Ware** – Id. & Value Guide, McAllister	$16.95
1373	Collector's Encyclopedia of **American Dinnerware,** Cunningham	$24.95
3815	Collector's Encyclopedia of **Blue Ridge Dinnerware,** Newbound	$19.95
4658	Collector's Encyclopedia of **Brush-McCoy Pottery,** Huxford	$24.95
2272	Collector's Encyclopedia of **California Pottery,** Chipman	$24.95
3811	Collector's Encyclopedia of **Colorado Pottery,** Carlton	$24.95
2133	Collector's Encyclopedia of **Cookie Jars,** Roerig	$24.95
3723	Collector's Encyclopedia of **Cookie Jars,** Volume II, Roerig	$24.95
3429	Collector's Encyclopedia of **Cowan Pottery,** Saloff	$24.95
4638	Collector's Encyclopedia of **Dakota Potteries,** Dommel	$24.95
2209	Collector's Encyclopedia of **Fiesta,** 7th Ed., Huxford	$19.95
4718	Collector's Encyclopedia of **Figural Planters & Vases,** Newbound	$19.95
3961	Collector's Encyclopedia of **Early Noritake,** Alden	$24.95
1439	Collector's Encyclopedia of **Flow Blue China,** Gaston	$19.95
3812	Collector's Encyclopedia of **Flow Blue China,** 2nd Ed., Gaston	$24.95
3813	Collector's Encyclopedia of **Hall China,** 2nd Ed., Whitmyer	$24.95
3431	Collector's Encyclopedia of **Homer Laughlin China,** Jasper	$24.95
1276	Collector's Encyclopedia of **Hull Pottery,** Roberts	$19.95
4573	Collector's Encyclopedia of **Knowles, Taylor & Knowles,** Gaston	$24.95
3962	Collector's Encyclopedia of **Lefton China,** DeLozier	$19.95
2210	Collector's Encyclopedia of **Limoges Porcelain,** 2nd Ed., Gaston	$24.95
2334	Collector's Encyclopedia of **Majolica Pottery,** Katz-Marks	$19.95
1358	Collector's Encyclopedia of **McCoy Pottery,** Huxford	$19.95
3963	Collector's Encyclopedia of **Metlox Potteries,** Gibbs Jr.	$24.95
3313	Collector's Encyclopedia of **Niloak,** Gifford	$19.95
3837	Collector's Encyclopedia of **Nippon Porcelain I,** Van Patten	$24.95
2089	Collector's Ency. of **Nippon Porcelain,** 2nd Series, Van Patten	$24.95
1665	Collector's Ency. of **Nippon Porcelain,** 3rd Series, Van Patten	$24.95
3836	**Nippon Porcelain** Price Guide, Van Patten	$9.95
1447	Collector's Encyclopedia of **Noritake,** Van Patten	$19.95
3432	Collector's Encyclopedia of **Noritake,** 2nd Series, Van Patten	$24.95
1037	Collector's Encyclopedia of **Occupied Japan,** Vol. I, Florence	$14.95
1038	Collector's Encyclopedia of **Occupied Japan,** Vol. II, Florence	$14.95
2088	Collector's Encyclopedia of **Occupied Japan,** Vol. III, Florence	$14.95
2019	Collector's Encyclopedia of **Occupied Japan,** Vol. IV, Florence	$14.95
2335	Collector's Encyclopedia of **Occupied Japan,** Vol. V, Florence	$14.95
3964	Collector's Encyclopedia of **Pickard China,** Reed	$24.95
1311	Collector's Encyclopedia of **R.S. Prussia,** 1st Series, Gaston	$24.95
1715	Collector's Encyclopedia of **R.S. Prussia,** 2nd Series, Gaston	$24.95
3726	Collector's Encyclopedia of **R.S. Prussia,** 3rd Series, Gaston	$24.95
3877	Collector's Encyclopedia of **R.S. Prussia,** 4th Series, Gaston	$24.95
1034	Collector's Encyclopedia of **Roseville Pottery,** Huxford	$19.95
1035	Collector's Encyclopedia of **Roseville Pottery,** 2nd Ed., Huxford	$19.95
3357	**Roseville** Price Guide No. 10	$9.95
3965	Collector's Encyclopedia of **Sascha Brastoff,** Conti, Bethany & Seay	$24.95
3314	Collector's Encyclopedia of **Van Briggle** Art Pottery, Sasicki	$24.95
4563	Collector's Encyclopedia of **Wall Pockets,** Newbound	$19.95
2111	Collector's Encyclopedia of **Weller Pottery,** Huxford	$29.95
3452	Coll. Guide to **Country Stoneware & Pottery,** Raycraft	$11.95
2077	Coll. Guide to **Country Stoneware & Pottery,** 2nd Series, Raycraft	$14.95
3434	Coll. Guide to **Hull Pottery,** The Dinnerware Line, Gick-Burke	$16.95

3876	Collector's Guide to **Lu-Ray Pastels,** Meehan	$18.95
3814	Collector's Guide to **Made in Japan** Ceramics, White	$18.95
4646	Collector's Guide to **Made in Japan** Ceramics, Book II, White	$18.95
4565	Collector's Guide to **Rockingham,** The Enduring Ware, Brewer	$14.95
2339	Collector's Guide to **Shawnee Pottery,** Vanderbilt	$19.95
1425	**Cookie Jars,** Westfall	$9.95
3440	**Cookie Jars,** Book II, Westfall	$19.95
3435	Debolt's Dictionary of **American Pottery Marks**	$17.95
2379	Lehner's Ency. of **U.S. Marks** on Pottery, Porcelain & China	$24.95
4722	**McCoy Pottery,** Collector's Reference & Value Guide, Hanson/Nissen	$19.95
3825	**Puritan Pottery,** Morris	$24.95
4726	**Red Wing Art Pottery,** 1920s–1960s, Dollen	$19.95
1670	**Red Wing Collectibles,** DePasquale	$9.95
1440	**Red Wing Stoneware,** DePasquale	$9.95
3738	**Shawnee Pottery,** Mangus	$24.95
4629	Turn of the Century **American Dinnerware,** 1880s–1920s, Jasper	$24.95
4572	**Wall Pockets** of the Past, Perkins	$17.95
3327	**Watt Pottery** – Identification & Value Guide, Morris	$19.95

OTHER COLLECTIBLES

4704	Antique & Collectible **Buttons,** Wisniewski	$19.95
2269	Antique **Brass & Copper** Collectibles, Gaston	$16.95
1880	Antique **Iron,** McNerney	$9.95
3872	Antique **Tins,** Dodge	$24.95
1714	**Black** Collectibles, Gibbs	$19.95
1128	**Bottle** Pricing Guide, 3rd Ed., Cleveland	$7.95
4636	**Celluloid Collectibles,** Dunn	$14.95
3959	**Cereal Box** Bonanza, The 1950's, Bruce	$19.95
3718	Collectible **Aluminum,** Grist	$16.95
3445	Collectible **Cats,** An Identification & Value Guide, Fyke	$18.95
4560	Collectible **Cats,** An Identification & Value Guide, Book II, Fyke	$19.95
1634	Collector's Ency. of Figural & Novelty **Salt & Pepper Shakers,** Davern	$19.95
2020	Collector's Ency. of Figural & Novelty **Salt & Pepper Shakers,** Vol. II, Davern	$19.95
2018	Collector's Encyclopedia of **Granite Ware,** Greguire	$24.95
3430	Collector's Encyclopedia of **Granite Ware,** Book II, Greguire	$24.95
4705	Collector's Guide to **Antique Radios,** 4th Ed., Bunis	$18.95
1916	Collector's Guide to **Art Deco,** Gaston	$14.95
3880	Collector's Guide to **Cigarette Lighters,** Flanagan	$17.95
4637	Collector's Guide to **Cigarette Lighters,** Book II, Flanagan	$17.95
1537	Collector's Guide to **Country Baskets,** Raycraft	$9.95
3966	Collector's Guide to **Inkwells,** Identification & Values, Badders	$18.95
3881	Collector's Guide to **Novelty Radios,** Bunis/Breed	$18.95
4652	Collector's Guide to **Transistor Radios,** 2nd Ed., Bunis	$16.95
4653	Collector's Guide to **TV Memorabilia,** 1960s–1970s, Davis/Morgan	$24.95
2276	**Decoys,** Kangas	$24.95
1629	**Doorstops,** Identification & Values, Bertoia	$9.95
4567	Figural **Napkin Rings,** Gottschalk & Whitson	$18.95
3968	**Fishing Lure** Collectibles, Murphy/Edmisten	$24.95
3817	**Flea Market Trader,** 10th Ed., Huxford	$12.95
3976	Foremost Guide to **Uncle Sam** Collectibles, Czulewicz	$24.95
4641	**Garage Sale & Flea Market Annual,** 4th Ed.	$19.95
3819	**General Store Collectibles,** Wilson	$24.95
4643	**Great American West** Collectibles, Wilson	$24.95
2215	Goldstein's **Coca-Cola** Collectibles	$16.95
3884	Huxford's Collectible **Advertising,** 2nd Ed.	$24.95
2216	**Kitchen Antiques,** 1790–1940, McNerney	$14.95
3321	Ornamental & Figural **Nutcrackers,** Rittenhouse	$16.95
2026	**Railroad** Collectibles, 4th Ed., Baker	$14.95
1632	**Salt & Pepper Shakers,** Guarnaccia	$9.95
1888	**Salt & Pepper Shakers** II, Identification & Value Guide, Book II, Guarnaccia	$14.95
2220	**Salt & Pepper Shakers** III, Guarnaccia	$14.95
3443	**Salt & Pepper Shakers** IV, Guarnaccia	$18.95
4555	**Schroeder's Antiques Price Guide,** 14th Ed., Huxford	$12.95
2096	**Silverplated Flatware,** Revised 4th Edition, Hagan	$14.95
1922	Standard **Old Bottle** Price Guide, Sellari	$14.95
4708	Summers' Guide to **Coca-Cola**	$19.95
3892	**Toy & Miniature Sewing Machines,** Thomas	$18.95
3828	Value Guide to **Advertising Memorabilia,** Summers	$18.95
3977	Value Guide to **Gas Station** Memorabilia, Summers & Priddy	$24.95
3444	**Wanted to Buy,** 5th Edition	$9.95

This is only a partial listing of the books on antiques that are available from Collector Books. All books are well illustrated and contain current values. Most of these books are available from your local bookseller, antique dealer, or public library. If you are unable to locate certain titles in your area, you may order by mail from COLLECTOR BOOKS, P.O. Box 3009, Paducah, KY 42002-3009. Customers with Visa or MasterCard may phone in orders from 7:00–5:00 CST, Monday–Friday, Toll Free 1-800-626-5420. Add $2.00 for postage for the first book ordered and $0.30 for each additional book. Include item number, title, and price when ordering. Allow 14 to 21 days for delivery.